EMPIRE & THE WORD
Prophetic Parallels Between The Exilic Experience & Central America's Crisis

by Philip Wheaton & Duane Shank
Introduction by Richard Shaull

Philip Wheaton first went to Latin America in 1952 as a pastor and missionary of the Episcopal Church in the Dominican Republic until 1964. He returned to serve as a pastor/priest in Brockport, New York for four years. Since 1968, he has been the Director of the Ecumenical Program for Interamerican Communication & Action in Washington, D.C. Well known, as a public speaker, historian and analyst of the Central American and Caribbean region, he is the author or co-author of six books and eight special reports on the Gran Caribe. Presently he is also coordinator of the D.C. Metro Sanctuary Committee & National Sanctuary Defense Fund Board and a member of the Christian Institute for North/South Dialogue.

Duane Shank has been active in the U.S. peace movement since 1969. He was a Mennonite draft resistor during the Vietnam war and has worked as staff for the National Inter-religious Service Board for Conscientious Objectors (NISB/CO), the Committee Against Registration and the Draft (CARD), the Vietnam Trial Support Committee and for SANE (now SANE/FREEZE) where he is currently acting as Executive Director. He was active in Christians for Socialism (CFS) and other religious and community organizations.

© Copyright 1988 EPICA Task Force
First Edition
ISBN 0-918346-08-8

Cover by Carlos Arrien, Centro de Arte, Washington, D.C.
Design and production by Rock Creek Publishing, Washington, D.C.

Table of Contents

INTRODUCTION

by Richard Shaull

With the publication of *Empire and the Word*, Philip Wheaton and Duane Shank provide an invaluable resource for those of us who, motivated by our religious faith, find ourselves compelled to carefully re-examine what our government is doing in Central America and elsewhere. Their book speaks directly to our needs and comes to us at precisely the right moment.

Future historians may conclude that the decade of the Eighties marked a turning point in U.S. relations with Third World peoples; a time when a significant number of U.S. citizens became aware of the bankruptcy and cruelty of the policies their country has pursued, began to envision an alternative future for the USA in solidarity with the struggles of emerging nations of Asia, Africa and Latin America, and developed the determination to struggle for major changes in our foreign policy.

I belive these historians will also conclude that President Reagan and the politicians, intellectuals and reporters who bought, articulated and marketed his policy, made a major contribution to this change, in spite of themselves: By their dogged pursuit of a policy so out of touch with reality that it was destined to fail; by their constant use of lies and deception in order to sustain it; by their persistence in blatant violation of the U.S. Constitution and of international law; and by their utter lack of concern about the suffering and destruction their policies were producing among the people especially of Central America.

In the end, they contributed decisively to the awakening of conscientious North Americans to a new awareness of what is happening in the Third World and what the USA is doing there, and also to the realization that our nation could follow an alternative policy which would encourage and support the struggle of these people and at the same time offer us a new future as well.

Thus far, this possible breakthrough to a new era has its primary popular base in religious communities, Catholic, Protestant and Jewish. The reason for this is not hard to find. For a century, the missionary movement has brought Western Christians into contact with other peoples and cultures. Many of those who have lived abroad for extended periods of time have returned to the USA with a special sensitivity to what is happening around the world. Every year, mission study programs have cultivated this awareness among small groups in local parishes all across the country. Visits to this country of Christians from the "younger churches" have made their impact. And many of those reached by these means not only come to a new and richer understanding of world affairs; they also find that their biblical and theological heritage re-orients their perception of it, sensitizes them to the suffering of poor and marginal victims of injustice and stirs their conscience. In fact, many have found that this encounter with the sufferings and hopes of Third World Christians has led them to a richer experience of faith and to a fuller life.

If this movement continues, what began as a protest against a few specific irrational and destructive actions of the Reagan Administration in Central America will provide a foundation for fundamental re-thinking of U.S. policy and sustain a long-term struggle for change. Whether that happens or not may well depend upon whether these new faith communities have at their disposal the resources they need for such a process of thought and action.

Empire and the Word makes an important contribution at this point. In it, Wheaton and Shank focus attention on Central America and what the USA has been doing there, while keeping in mind the wider global context. Their reflection combines social and historical analysis, the use of factual information gathered from years of experience and study, and a persistent effort to interpret what is happening in Central America from a biblical and theological perspective. They seek to understand, but their search for truth is motivated by their personal anguish in the face of what their government is doing. In their search for understanding their own world and that of the Bible, they have found themselves called to action for change and this book has been written in the midst of that struggle.

Because they speak out of an experience many of us have not had, with a passion we may not know, some may find their tone too harsh and their critique of the USA too radical. For those who react in this way, I would like to propose something I learned the hard way during my years in Latin America. I was often shocked by the harshness of what my students and colleagues had to say about what the USA was doing. But I eventually came to the conclusion that they were confronting me with realities I needed to face. The important thing was not whether I agreed with them but whether I would engage in serious dialogue with them, allow their witness to break open my limited world, lead me to further study and thought, and thus help me to move beyond where I was at that moment.

I would urge the reader to respond in a similar way to what Wheaton and Shank lay before us. They confront us with realities we should not ignore and their witness offers us an opportunity to move forward in our understanding and action. As one who has been shaped by experiences similar to theirs and has struggled with these issues for years, I find that their book has enriched my thinking at a number of points and has provided me with resources I need. I want to mention briefly three of these areas.

1. Wheaton and Shank use the word *empire* to speak of the United States and its pattern of relationships with the countries of Central and South America.

For years I tried to avoid using that word and have felt uneasy around others who do. Even when I have been most disturbed by the way my country has used its power to maintain its hegemony over Latin America and use the area economically for its own ends, I had the sense that there was something about our democratic vision and our achievements as a nation that made us somewhat different from the imperial powers of the past. But the Reagan Administration — and those who have bought and mouthed its slogans — have convinced me that the time has come when we have no choice but to use the word empire to name the reality and thus compel ourselves to analyze the structures of domination by which it functions.

For this reason, I appreciate what the authors of *Empire and the Word* have done. For they not only use the word but help us understand the special character of our imperial system: "empire as a way of life under the mantle of democracy." By exploring the meaning of this and illustrating it repeatedly, they help us not only to walk through our own history as an imperial power but also to perceive the drive toward empire in ourselves as well as in earlier generations. They enable us to see the devious rationales we and others have used over the years to justify it, as well as our own self-deception. They point out, again and again, how, in our policy, the pursuit of power and privilege takes precedence over principle or sensitivity to human life. And in the midst of all this, they lay before us the testimony of the people who are the victims of our actions, their perception of what we are doing, their awareness of the contradictions between our professed democratic and social ideals and our support of political tyranny, economic exploitation of the great majority by a small elite, and our continued exploitation of them.

2. In recent years, quite a number of books have been published which deal with the historical development and present reality of imperial America. What makes *Empire and the Word* unique is the fact that its authors discuss these issues from the perspective set for them by THE WORD. They dare to put together the story of our nation in dialogue with the biblical story, particularly the story of the People of

Israel as found in the Hebrew Scriptures. As members of a faith community, they analyze what is happening in U.S.-Central American relations as persons who find themselves addressed by a compelling Word, a Word that awakens conscience and lays an imperative upon them from which they cannot escape.

Moreover, as a consequence of their long contact with Third World Christians and the movements of spiritual renewal emerging among them, Wheaton and Shank experience this Word as a dynamic and disturbing Word which speaks of a God who hears the cry of the poor and calls people and nations to establish justice on the earth; a Word that exposes the lies and deception by which the wealthy and powerful try to hide what they are really about; and above all, a Word which awakens the poor, calls them to struggle for life and sustains them in the midst of their suffering. By thus juxtaposing the reality of the American Empire and this biblical message, the authors of this volume offer us an opportunity to reflect on First World-Third World relations in greater breath and depth than usually happens in academic discussions.

3. *Empire and the Word* not only sets up a dialogue between the experience of living in imperial America and the biblical word; it focuses that engagement sharply on the exilic experience of the Israelites and the prophetic interpretation of it. In the major central section (Parts 2 and 3), the authors draw parallels between what happened during the most critical period in the Kingdoms of Israel and Judah before their fall as well as during the exile of the Jewish people in Babylon and what is now happening in Guatemala, El Salvador and Nicaragua — and in the USA as it is involved in that region and its crises. They do this by drawing on the rich writings of the Hebrew prophets, who presented to their contemporaries a shocking message of judgement and hope. During the crisis leading up to the time of exile, they declare that the nation of Israel stands under God's judgement because it abandoned its vocation to establish a new order of justice, striving rather to be like other imperial powers around it. And during the time of exile, the prophets come up with a radically new reading of the situation: they perceive that the God of justice is moving, in strange ways, in the midst of their suffering, and opening the way for a future of promise.

This, I believe, is the most important part of this book, which can make a lasting contribution to the thought and action of individuals and groups working for a new foreign policy. By making this connection between the exilic experience of the Jewish people and the crisis in Central America, Wheaton and Shank demonstrate once again that the

Bible speaks a new and compelling word for new situations and thus interprets life and the world for those who are open to it in surprising ways:

• For the poor and those standing in solidarity with them in Latin America, the Exodus narratives and their message of liberation have been at the heart of this new engagement of the Biblical story. The authors of *Empire and the Word* are convinced that for us as North Americans the prophetic writings around the experience of exile can provide us with a similar experience as we look at what our nation is doing from their perspective of judgement, re-read our national history in light of God's passion for justice to the poor, and allow ourselves to dream once again of a *new* future that can come only as the present order of things is overcome. I believe they are right and I hope that what they offer us in these pages will lead many of us to enter more deeply into dialogue with these prophets of the pre-exilic and exilic periods.

• Through the Sanctuary Movement and other movements of solidarity, many North Americans have begun to build relationships with Central Americans in our midst. But with all our commitments to the support of their struggle and to them as persons, these relationships have often remained superficial. However, if we are willing to join with them in serious study of this biblical literature, we may well experience a breakthrough to a new quality of relationship. For Salvadorans and Guatemalans in our midst, the biblical story of exile is their story. It names their suffering as well as their hope; it expresses their spiritual anguish as well as their deep faith in God and trust in God's justice. As we read and reflect on the prophetic word with them, we can experience a new quality of sharing with them, and by the Word be transformed. Wheaton and Shank introduce us to this reality as they share with us the thoughts and stories of Central American Christians; those who are now neighbors to us can help us to continue the process.

Philip Wheaton and Duane Shank have been exposed, for years, to what the USA has been doing against the poor people of Central America and elsewhere. They are horrified by it and denounce the evil they see as did the prophets of Israel. They challenge us to understand and to act. But, at the same time, *Empire and the Word* looks with hope toward the future and offers us life. For in its faithfulness to the prophetic witness and to the witness of Central American Christians, it invites us to risk going beyond the dead ends in which we are caught and to expect a new and more promising future for ourselves as a nation and in our relations with Third World people. They tell the stories of Central Americans who have given their lives in struggles for liberation, knowing that these women and men, through their suffering, are offering us a gift, if only we dare to receive it. They speak of the destructive power of those who now rule and feel the pain of those who are now suffering; they also speak of the hope born among those who sacrifice their lives for the sake of others, confident that Good Friday will be followed by Easter. And as they lay before us the testimony of Archbishop Romero, Miguel D'Escoto and unnamed members of Christian Base Communities, they suggest to us that the crisis and decline of the North American empire offers us a new opportunity for our redemption as a nation.

Richard Shaull

Richard Shaull first went to Latin America in 1942 serving as a pastor and missionary in Colombia for ten years; then as professor of Church history at Capinas Presbyterian Seminary in Brazil for another decade. From 1962 to 1980 he was professor of Ecumenics at Princeton Theological Seminary, and since then a speaker and author of several books and articles, his latest *Naming the Idols: Biblical Alternatives for U.S. Foreign Policy*. He is presently serving as Academic Director of the Instituto Pastoral Hispano in New York City.

PREFACE

Many North Americans unconsciously assume that the poverty and oppression in Third World countries is due to those "benighted" peoples' economic underdevelopment and political backwardness, but a growing number of us have come to understand that Central America's agony is the tragic by-product of the United States' attempt since 1979 to suffocate any attempt at liberation from its imperial domination. Our growing awareness of this dark side of U.S. foreign policy has come about through direct contact with Central Americans, either as political refugees living in this country or through visits to the Isthmian region. This new awareness did not arise out of ideological premises or personal prejudices but from people-to-people relationships, producing a growing solidarity — religious and political — between U.S. citizens and the Empire's victims.

Reflecting on this phenomenon of suffering which led to a mass exodus of refugees in 1980 and following, we became increasingly struck by the similarities between today's imperial occupation of Central America by the United States and that of ancient Palestine by the Babylonian armies of Nebuchadnezzar in the 6th century B.C. Probing this parallel led us into an incredible matrix of comparable policies and attitudes between the empires of these two historically disparate times, not only in terms of human suffering and imperial strategies but also in relation to the respective prophetic pronouncements emerging from each tragedy. More importantly, we discovered that the pivotal moments in these two monumental dramas of death and rebirth — 587 B.C. and 1980 A.D. — represent in each case the beginning of a decisive drama: the rising creativity and determination of a dominated and exiled people and the decline of the dominating and repressive empire. Thus the *Exilic experience* becomes the key paradigm of our time, greatly clarifying theologically our understanding of today's Isthmian crisis while, in turn, this crisis illuminates the biblical experience making it far more relevant and historically clear.

The crisis in Central America today is what the Bible calls *kairos*, an historical moment of extreme disjuncture in history, one laden with both negative and positive potential: the fall of old orders and new openings for the poor and exiled. While this book has been written primarily for concerned North Americans, we must be clear that this *kairos* is the result of a confrontation between two opposing forces: the suffering and resistance of the Isthmian peoples and an imperial system of death imposed from outside. It implies, moreover, that their struggle

— pacific and armed, political and prophetic — is one between Life and Death, as we read in the document entitled *Kairos Centroamericano*: a) "Never as now has the Empire had to base itself so irrationally on the use of force;" and b) "This is the moment; the critical hour...God's move through our history, through Central America." The document describes the implications of this critical moment:

> *Central America has been converted into a **kairos** of unforeseen consequences: either we close this space of hope for the poor for many years, or we open ourselves prophetically to a New Day for humanity, for the Church.* (1)

What surprised us most about this struggle, however, was that Central America's efforts at liberation — reflected so poignantly in but not limited to the Nicaraguan people's overthrow of the Somozas' dynasty — has not led to a simple, direct process moving from captivity into liberation and thence to the building of new societies. Rather, it has produced a whole new episode of oppression and suffering, this time affecting the whole region. This new imperial intrusion into the Isthmus is precisely the kind of process experienced by the Jews in the fall of Jerusalem: the old Judaean kings like today's despotic leaders fell from power only to be replaced by a far more sophisticated Babylonian captivity. In both instances, history moves forward *dialectically*, producing a contradictory change which while struggling forward towards eventual liberation and a return to the land does so out of the context of an even worse repression, impoverishment and exile. This Exilic experience, unlike the Exodus event, also forces "the chosen" people to look critically at their faith, to a conversion from their old ways and steels their resolve to build new societies based on justice for all.

As in those ancient biblical times so once again today, it is the victims and exiles who best understand this disastrous process and its redemptive possibilities — something serious students of the Bible will recognize as a fundamental dynamic within the process of Scriptural judgement and redemption. Therefore, we North Americans — notwithstanding all our education, skills and sophistication — have had to learn these truths from our poor neighbors to the South, from the oppressed and outcast. These persecuted and exiled peoples of Central America have taught us incredible lessons in courage, faith and determination, while they have also inculcated in us a political consciousness and hopeful vision for the future. Their forgiveness and generosity towards us as citizens of the very imperial system which has for so long oppressed them, has produced in us a profound moral, theological and political conversion.

Our purpose in writing this critique on *Empire* and our reflection on *the Word* of God is to raise questions, discern realities and point directions for "the faithful remnant" here in the United States in terms of how we understand our calling and so as to clarify our solidarity. As the faithful remnant — by which we mean both secular and religious persons engaged in solidarity with the poor, who also recognize ourselves as "exiles in Babylon" — we know that we must choose between what the Deuteronomic historian calls "blessing and curse." That is, we are faced by a transcendental option: we can either side with the victims, the poor and oppressed, or remain wedded to imperialism, blinded by its idolatry. Many of us as American citizens who are genuinely committed to the best principles of this nation, believe that this imperial idolatry — that so often goes un-named — is rapidly seducing and corrupting the democratic and populist processes of our national life. Therefore, in making a choice to stand with the victims, we are actually serving as witnesses to an alternative way of life in a non-imperialist America by which this nation might be rescued from its present mad course. Or, at least, as voices to the truth and prophets of warning to prepare our fellow citizens for the decline and ultimately the downfall of America as Empire.

We wish to thank a number of people who have helped sharpen our insights and focus our thoughts on these matters. Especially, we thank Julia Esquivel and Rigoberta Menchú of Guatemala for opening up new dimensions in spirituality, both Mayan and biblical; to José Porfirio Miranda of Mexico and Jon Sobrino of El Salvador for their incisive theological clarification on the nature of human commitment; to William Appleman Williams and Tomás Borge for their insights into the structural nature of imperialism; to Erich Fromm and M. Scott Peck for their insights into the demonic; to Larry Kuenning and Ralph Klein for their ideological and historical analysis of the Exilic experience; and to Franz Hinkelammart and Victorio Araya of Costa Rica for their clarifications on the nature of sacrifice. All of these *compañeros* and *compañeras* are part of a growing process which Pablo Richard and Edmundo Desueza have defined as our North/South dialogue.(2) At a more pragmatic level, this manuscript might not have been written without the encouragement of Sara Nelson of the Christic Institute and clearly would not have been completed without the hard work and patience of our Colombian compañera Margarita Suárez.

Our determination to see this work through came, however, from the memory of those tens of thousands of "little" sisters and brothers in Central America who have given their lives in the struggle for justice and liberation over the past decade. Especially those unsung persons of courage who took their stand alongside the poor: the catequists and *campesinos*, delegates of the Word and workers, nuns and revolutionaries, priests and young people especially in Guatemala, El Salvador and Nicaragua...all those intentionally murdered by the Powers for standing with their oppressed Peoples.

Specifically, we dedicate this book to two persons who held high the vision of a new creation in the hemisphere and who died as a result of doing so. One of them is a tragic figure, reflecting the tragedy and death in the continent today, an Argentinian Baptist pastor-theologian Estéban Daniel Statello. Married to a North American woman, Daniel had high hopes of building through their marriage a new kind of life, reflecting the best from both North and South. That marriage failed because of his wife's fixation on values inculcated in her by the imperial way of life, leading to Daniel's despair at being separated from his children and to his committing suicide. But even in that despair, he did not lose sight of the dream, reflected by his writing a brilliant PhD thesis on this crisis and his attendance at the Theology in the Americas conference held in Detroit the very year he died; that ominous year 1980.

The other person is a hopeful figure, a symbol of new life in the Americas and a representative of the solidarity between North and South, a Jewish engineer, Benjamin Linder. While involved in helping build a new society within the context of the Sandinista revolutionary process, he was intentionally murdered by the *contras* in 1987. For his stand, his technical expertise, his humor (as a clown for Nica children) and thus his ability to laugh at the Devil with the people of El Cuá, Nicaragua...he represents an alternative to the "*rambo*" type of American symbolizing death and destruction, these North Americans who have chosen to resist the old order by building a new world with the poor.

The vision of Daniel and Benjamin, one a Christian the other a Jew, each operating out of biblical principles and traditions, point the way to our continuing search and struggle for a Promised Land in the Americas in behalf of people seeking Life in the face of Death and therefore necessarily rejecting that "abomination of desecration" known as U.S. imperialism.

En la buena lucha,
Philip Wheaton and Duane Shank
Washington, D.C., July 4, 1988

Ben Linder, 27 years old, shown above during the 1984 Nicaraguan cotton harvest, was the first North American *internacionalista* to be killed by the contra. He had been there since 1983—not 1985 as sometimes reported—building small power plants in Nicaraguan villages. At the time of his death, he was at work. Two Nicaraguan militiamen were killed with him.

---

1 *Kairos Centroamericano, Un Desafío a las Iglesias y al Mundo,* Managua, Nicaragua, 1988, Parte II, Sec. 3, p. 30.

2 "*North/South Dialogue*" is the name given to the whole process of analysis, development and conversation meant to counter the false conflict between East and West and used by a growing number of groups and publications in Latin America, Europe and the United States. Cf. "Christian Institute for North/South Dialogue," Newark, Delaware.

PART I
TOWARDS UNDERSTANDING AMERICA'S IMPERIALIST ENVIRONMENT & THE WORD OF GOD AS PROMISE TO THOSE IN CAPTIVITY

CHAPTER 1
EXILE

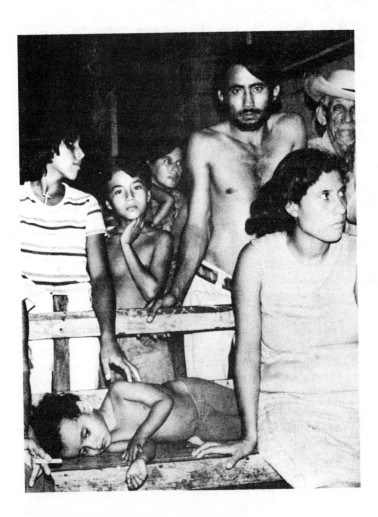

CHAPTER 1 EXILE

If a stranger lives with you in your land, do not molest him. You must count him as one of your own countrymen and love him as yourself— for you were once strangers yourselves in Egypt.
                                                              —Lev. 19:33-34

The present administration of Ronald Reagan has responded to the Central American refugees in our midst in a way that totally contradicts the mandate from the Torah (1) about the nature of our covenant with God, namely, that whether the "other" is a friend and citizen or a stranger and alien, they are to be treated justly. The Reagan administration, like others before it, has taken a negative view on these "strangers in our midst" by deporting and disemploying them as a way of preserving our nation against foreign and presumably adulterating influences. Moreover, as more and more Christians and Jews realized that these strangers had fled to this country not merely because of abhorrent practices by those in power in Central America *but in collusion with our leaders towards the end of maintaining U. S. domination over the hemisphere*, they gradually became witnesses against this imperialistic side of America. Whereas, the Empire views the stranger as an alien and enemy, the Torah perceives that same stranger as an object of love to be treated as a fellow citizen because we are all at times and places "strangers" in this world. Here we have the basic outlines of the fundamental conflict we have defined as "the Empire and the Word".

Modern Exile from Central America into America's Babylonian Captivity

Between the years 1980 and 1983, the long-standing reality of unjust exploitation and repression in Central America exploded into a mass exodus which overflowed our borders with Mexico and impacted the tranquil lives of many unpoliticized, middle-class religious American families. The visual realization of just how potentially explosive the situation in the Isthmian region had become first hit the American public through video reports and newspaper stories about the suffering of the Nicaraguan people under the Somoza dictatorship and their heroic struggle to liberate themselves from that tyranny in 1979. But it was the massive influx of hundreds of thousands of refugees from El Salvador and Guatemala during the years 1980-83 that made this suffering personal and their tragedy a matter demanding immediate response.

This mass exodus of the 1980s was quite different from the smaller ongoing flow of immigrants from Central America who had been drifting into this country over the previous two decades looking for jobs and hopefully a better life. The enormous influx of hundreds of thousands of desperate, terror-stricken refugees was the by-product of death squad killings, peasant massacres and intentional disappearances of loved ones meant to terrorize whole populations. They were **political refugees** who had not come to the United States because it was a "land of opportunity" but because of scorched-earth tactics that were so total and brutal their nations had been turned into wastelands. Nor did these refugees want to remain in this country, and even more disturbing, they were witnesses to the collaboration of our government with the military and para-military forces devastating their countrysides.

Under past administrations — whether Democrat or Republican — the U.S. government had been able to hide its involvement in such repressive enterprises overseas or justify them to the American people. Sometimes, they simply lied about what was really happening, but more often they justified such atrocities as heroic exploits of the U.S. Marines, or, regretfully, as necessary tactics required to save **their** "democracy" and preserve **our** "freedom". Media distancing and propaganda justification were aided, furthermore, by the ignorance of the American people about the issues and their isolation from the "field of battle". At times, such distancing broke down as in the case of the Vietnam war when occasional TV reports or newspaper articles would detail some horror of that conflict. But Vietnam was a long ways away, few Americans had ever been there and we had almost no contact with the victims, the Vietnamese civilian population. In the case of the refugees from El Salvador and Guatemala, however, the reports of torture, murder and disappearance were first-hand... and these shook America's religious composure.

> *The (Salvadoran) military went after unarmed members of the popular organizations. Death squads combed the cities for leaders and decapitated their bodies. They were less discriminating in the countryside; any peasant would do to intimidate the rest.(2)*

Americans had heard of such horrors going on "south of the border" whereas knowledge of U.S. linkages to extreme repression were largely unknown before 1980. Some knew that the United States had long maintained close ties with right-wing dictatorships, such as that of the Somozas in Nicaragua (1934-1979) and that the CIA had overthrown democracy in Guatemala in 1954. Most Americans assumed, however, that we were involved in such unsavory activities in order to prevent communism from penetrating the hemisphere and rationalized them on that account. After 1980, however, the connection between our policies and the terror going on in Central America could no longer be hidden, indeed, it took on a very personal face through contact between North Americans and the refugees from the region. **The growing gap between middle-class morality and U.S. imperial practices was becoming too great to be tolerated without a challenge**. An example of this rising contradiction is seen in the fact that the United States could contract with the state of Israel to arm, fund, and train the fascist military machine in Guatemala since the U.S. Congress had cut off funds to that government in 1978 because of its extreme abuse of human rights.(3) This was too great a contradiction for those faithful Americans who began to wonder whether both Israel and the United States had not lost their spiritual ways.

Such connections were a new experience for most American humanitarians who had long been accustomed to helping refugees fleeing to the United States from unjust, anti-democratic and totalitarian regimes into the "land of the free and the home of the brave." Many of these mass refugee movements (since WWII) had come from communist countries, such as from Hungary in 1956 (after the Soviet Union moved its tanks into Budapest), or the refugees from Cuba who fled to Miami after the 1959 revolution led by Fidel Castro. In such cases, the traditional cold war thesis: "refugees flee from communist regimes to come to free America" reinforced the simplistic understanding we had of ourselves, indeed, many Americans still believe that this is the only way to evaluate the United States. However, when refugees began pouring into this country from the totalitarian regimes of El Salvador and Guatemala which were allied to the United States by policy and funding, they contradicted the cold war thesis. More and more Americans began to realize that at times their own country operates in ways very similar to the Soviet Union, particularly in cases of rebellion among dominated peoples living in U.S.-controlled satellite regions.

This questioning was concretized after 1980 by other examples of collusion between the U.S. government and those responsible for the terror in Central America. For instance, many of the refugees who came into this country, did so by crossing the Rio Grande aided by guides who had been contracted in El Salvador, the so-called **coyotes**, who often preyed on their charges by robbing, raping or abandoning them in the desert.(4) These **coyotes** often collaborated with Mexican and U.S. Immigration agents, turning refugees back into the terror from which they had fled, thereby collaborating with the military regimes in both countries. The religious community along the border became particularly incensed at this practice of forced return. **Indeed without the INS practice of deportation the Sanctuary movement might never have materialized.** Gary MacEoin comments:

> *It was a traumatic awakening for many, and the trauma was intensified by the bureaucratic response of the Immigration and Naturalization Service (INS). The terrified survivors of the desert ordeal were arrested, and preparations began to ship them back to the tender mercies of the regimes of institutionalized injustice from which they had just fled. The instinctive response was the only one open to people of faith, a response that in addition resonated with the deepest traditions of the United States. This abomination could not be allowed.(5)*

The moral question for these concerned Americans was: Why doesn't our government allow these refugees to remain here as it has done with so many other refugees who have fled from similar situations of terror? Certainly other administrations have allowed political refugees from right-wing regimes to enter and remain in the United States, even at times in large numbers. For instance, in the case of the Constitutionalist rebels from Santo Domingo in 1965, tens of thousands of supporters of Juan Bosch fleeing the repressive government of Joaquin Balaguer were allowed to migrate to New York City and settle there without harassment.(6) Similarly, the U.S. Government was fairly lenient towards Chilean refugees who came here after the overthrow of Salvador Allende in 1973 because of their suffering under the repressive dictatorship of Augusto Pinochet.

The difference in the case of the Salvadoran and Guatemalan uprisings which led to scorched-earth tactics as part of the U.S. counterinsurgency philosophy, was the fact that the bloody repressions in Santo Domingo (3,000 dead) and in Chile (40,000 dead) fundamentally ended the resistance in those cases, whereas in El Salvador and Guatemala the struggles went on. Furthermore, the Sandinistas in nearby Nicaragua represented a successful revolution which gave encouragement to these other efforts to end their captivity. In all these examples, the pattern of collusion between the United States and repressive regimes was the same; the difference in Central America was the ongoing nature of the revolutionary struggle. These linkages proved that the U.S. government did not care about the suffering of the people nor the injustice visited upon them as exiles, but only about the maintenance of its control over the hemisphere, reinforcing the specter of the United States as an empire.

If the Reagan administration admitted that such repression was going on in El Salvador and Guatemala and that it was the primary motor force behind these mass exoduses, it could easily have led to a public outcry forcing Congress to cut off military funding thus undermining the whole imperial project. So the decision was made by Reagan's advisors that they had to "tough it out" and in effect **lie to the American people about the reason for this mass flight.** The State Department and the Immigration and Naturalization Service (INS) therefore claimed that these aliens were not political refugees but "economic immigrants" who therefore fell under Immigration law and not the 1980 Refugee Act, which allows refugees to apply for political asylum. Whenever these Central Americans did apply, they were systematically dismissed, that is, only 3% of all Salvadorans and only 1% of all Guatemalans were approved as legitimate asylee cases under its political refugee criteria.(7) Arbitrarily, the INS had virtually closed the door on such refugees being able to remain in the States legally.

In light of these circumstances, religious congregations which had begun to befriend these refugees by providing them social and legal assistance were faced by systematic opposition from the INS, something they had never encountered before. Refugee prisoners moved at night, lawyers prevented from seeing them, bonds arbitrarily increased, greatly straining the congregations' ability to assist the refugees. Increasingly during 1980 and 1981, the faithful asked themselves: Why are they deporting these poor people back into such situations of terror? Why won't the immigration judges accept these asylum cases as legitimately justified given the extreme circumstances from which the refugees had fled? Seeing their natural and traditional forms of humanitarian aid to these refugees rejected, the faithful assisting Salvadorans and Guatemalans became angry and desperate to know what else they do to stop the deportations. On March 24, 1982, congregations having covenanted together on an ecumenical and interfaith basis both in Tucson and Berkeley, declared themselves to be "public witness sanctuaries", and with those actions the Sanctuary movement was born. Without fully understanding the consequences or impact of their actions, they were in fact recovering the ancient biblical mandate of the Torah concerning the outcast.(8)

The low-level of knowledge about Central America on the part of most Sanctuary participants is proof that initially their challenge of immigration policies regarding Central Americans was not based on opposition to U.S.foreign policy in the region. *It was motivated by the mistreatment of the stranger in our midst.* As refugees testified and witnessed to what they had seen and heard, as more and more of the truth about what was going on in El Salvador and Guatemala came out, including the fact of U.S. complicity with those repressive regimes, they gradually became politicized. But it was the government's policy of deportation and deception that created the Sanctuary movement and led to this growing politicization of religious America.

Personal relationships between the faithful and the refugees have become the most decisive aspect in the process of consciousness-raising about U.S. government policies. It is this "marriage" between the Empire's victims and its citizens that has had the greatest impact on the Sanctuary movement which began initially as a somewhat desperate humanitarian gesture of "rescue". Sharing and dialogue between those from the "North" and those from the "South" would lead to serious questioning about how domestic democracy in America is related to U.S. repressive practices overseas. This search to understand the nature of imperial America was not based, therefore, on any "leftist" ideology but on this human inter-action and our need to better understand our common biblical calling as children of God. As the Rev. Marta Benavides said during the Sanctuary Convocation held in Tucson in January, 1985:

> It is very important that we see that God is in our company because God created us. For we are made in God's image. We are alike. So we are companeros with God and God's creation. It is important to be companeros with you.(9)

Parallels Between Ancient and Modern Exilic Experiences

This modern experience of forced exile from Central America to the United States closely parallels the biblical experience of exile by the Jews who were forced to leave their homeland in Judah in 587 B.C. to become resident aliens in Babylon, exiled into the so-called "Babylonian captivity." These parallels are far more than symbolic and psychological; they reflect amazing similarities with the political, cultural and theological problems faced by the Jewish exiles in the 6th century B.C. In order to assess the legitimacy of this assertion, we need to put aside our typical religious notions of the ancient exilic experience long enough to study its political implications, while we must also temper our political views about Central America today so we can see the theological implications of this modern exilic experience.

The fall of Jerusalem in 587 B.C. before the armies of Nebuchadnezzar, king of Babylon, represented a traumatic shock for the Judeans that was far more soul-searching than the fall of Samaria had been for the ancient Israelites in 722 B.C. The reason was that the fall of the northern kingdom of Israel led to a total dispersion of its citizens and their absorption into other societies and foreign cultures. In the case of the Judean exiles, however, *they remained together as a people* thereby forcing them to wrestle with the implications of their fall from God's grace, i.e., the destruction of Jerusalem. While most Jews in exile might never return again to Jerusalem themselves and while Jewish politics and worship would never be the same again, yet they would hold fast to their faith, indeed, struggle to regain the spirit of the covenant they had nearly lost. Thus **it was a radical event in history that forced upon them a profound re-examination of God's call and covenant**. In fact, many scholars hold that the year 587 B.C. represents a watershed event between the old and new Israel. As the theologian Walter Bruggemann has put it, that year became a *"pivotal point"* in Hebrew history...

> ...*the date and the events of 587 B.C. are decisive. The year 587 is the occasion when the temple in Jerusalem was burned, the holy city was destroyed, the Davidic dynasty was terminated, the leading citizens deported. Public life in Judah came to an end.(10)*

In this light, we hereby assert that the year 1980 A.D. is a similar *"pivotal year"* in the history of the people of Central America as a whole, especially for the suffering exiles. Whereas there was repression before that date and while it has continued since, that date marks a critical moment in this history of suffering for two major reasons. First, it was the year of the return of the U.S. Empire to direct control over the region and the beginning of the devastation of the lands of El Salvador, Nicaragua and Guatemala which has meant untold human suffering. Secondly, it marks the year of the exile of hundreds of thousands of refugees forced to flee to the USA, into what many of them feel is a modern "Babylonian captivity." Like the ancient Jews from Judah, these oppressed and exiled people from the Isthmian region are doing everything within their power to remain together as a people and from that context to understand their calling as a people of God in light of this present dialectic process of captivity/liberation.

Since *suffering* has always been — at least in Catholic circles — a fundamental criteria in the perception of God's truth and the meriting of God's grace, we believe it is legitimate to draw these parallels between the ancient and modern exile experiences. For instance, using 1980 as our starting point and focal example for the rest of the decade, we note that there have been over 150,000 persons killed in Central

America between 1978 and 1986.(11) This total includes 40,000 in Nicaragua (under Somoza); 60,000 to date in El Salvador (U.S. counterinsurgency); 50,000 in the Guatemalan holocaust in the highlands (in which Washington, D.C. was complicit); and at least 15,000 in Nicaragua by the **contras** (coordinated by the CIA) since 1979. This human slaughter is far higher than the number slaughtered in the fall of Jerusalem.

Similarly, the totals of those exiled from El Salvador and Guatemala since 1980 reach at least 1,000,000, while the numbers of those internally displaced stands at about 1,500,000 for these two countries alone (not counting Nicaragua).(12) About 35,000 Judeans were deported to Babylon in the combined exiles of 596 and 587 B.C.(13) making that exile about 1/30 the size of those forced into exile since 1980 from their homelands in Central America! In terms of suffering, therefore, there is no question that the present trauma is, quantitatively speaking, far more tragic and disruptive than the events surrounding the date 587 B.C.

The question remains whether the events of 1980 A.D. are as **politically traumatic and theologically decisive** as were those of the ancient exile. To answer this question, consider the following events which occurred during this decisive year:

> *1980 was the year the United States returned to Central America with its own military forces and mercenary forces operating out of Honduras;*

> *1980 was the year of the beginning of the scorched-earth project in El Salvador that claimed 30,000 lives;*

> *1980 was the year of the assassination of Oscar Romero (March 24), a man today recognized as the prophet of Central America and the voice of the voiceless;*

> *1980 was the year that the CIA began drawing up plans for supporting the **contras** and began dealing with Steadman Fagoth toward organizing Misquito **contras**;*

> *1980 was the year of the Spanish Embassy fire-bombing and killing of the Indians and all the embassy staff persons working there in Guatemala City and that this marked the beginning of the Indian decision to "go to war;"*

1980 was the year of the rape, torture and murder of the four Maryknoll sisters in El Salvador and the beginning of widespread consciousness-raising about Central Americans among North Americans; and finally

1980 was the year Ronald Reagan was elected president of the United States, a political action that would usher in nearly a decade of aggressive and sophisticated repression and deception for the whole region.

In evaluating these two exilic parallels, we must recall that just as the year 587 B.C. was a radical turning point for the Jews while it was not so for the Babylonians, so too, 1980 A.D. is a crucial date for the Central American people though not necessarily perceived as such by the American imperialists. These exilic events imply an "*endtime*" for Central America, not only in terms of all those visited by death, destruction or exile, but in terms of the end of any political, economic and social hope under the conditions established by the USA. This moment in time has to be viewed prophetically as their **kairos**, a time of absolute crisis, laden with disaster and pregnant with new possibility, just as the ancient exilic experience was for the Judean Jews.

Further examination reveals even more parallels between these two epochal moments in history. At the *cultural* level, it is clear that the original exile was a forced march into an alien environment since the Jews had no choice and were obliged to live for decades in a place that was totally foreign to them culturally. Yet one of the surprising similarities between these two exilic experiences is that when the Jews arrived in Babylon (their place of captivity), they found neither a devastated Palestine nor a Sinai wilderness, but rather, the wealthiest, most beautiful and technologically advanced society on earth: a place of affluence and "peace". Indeed, Babylon was the "center of the world":

As a place to live in, Babylonia was far better than Palestine. Instead of a mountainous country where only by incessant terracing and cultivating one might wrest a living from the soil, the Jews now possessed a rich alluvial plain where crops grew almost by themselves. A stable government under wise kings had created and preserved impressive irrigation works for the benefit of all. Great reservoirs like that near Sippar, huge navigable canals like the Kabaru (the river Chebar of Ezekiel) that ran southeast from Babylon to Nippor, and smaller inter-

secting canals that meshed the whole plain, were both life-
bringers to the soil and arteries of traffic.(13)

While it is true that the Jewish exiles had no political rights in
Babylon, they were relatively free to make a new life for themselves and
indeed, were commanded to do so by Jeremiah himself, for there was
frequent communication between Judah and Babylon. The prophet
urged the exiles to settle down to business and raise their families in
preparation for the future (Jer.29:5-6).

This is a close parallel to what the Salvadorans and Guatemalans
experienced in their forced march "**al norte**" across Mexico and the Rio
Grande into the Babylonian States of America. They too, had to pass
through extremely harsh conditions to get here, whereas once inside
the USA, although undocumented and without rights, they too, found
themselves in the most highly "developed" society on earth, technologically advanced and prosperous; the "center of the world". Obviously,
America was no "**el dorado**" for these aliens any more than Babylon
was for the Jews of old, but relatively speaking both exiled communities
were economically far better off than those back in ancient Judah or in
modern El Salvador and Guatemala!

The most difficult cultural problem was not the adjustment to their
immediate environment nor even economic survival, but the loss of the
land of their birth which they might never see again. Caught in limbo
between a poor fatherland with a rich cultural tradition and a wealthy
country with all kinds of things which at the same time is a cultural
wasteland...this was the real pain. In our American Babylon, there are
towers of Babel, incredible wealth, unlimited supermarkets, vacuous
TV programs, unlimited diversity, governmental lying. Is it any wonder
that these exiles in the United States cry out just as the Hebrews of old
did, saying, "How can we worship God in a foreign land?"

> *By the rivers of Babylon we sat down and wept*
> *when we remembered Zion.*
> *There on the willow-trees*
> *we hung our guitars,*
> *for there those who carried us off*
> *demanded music and singing,*
> *and our captors called us to be merry*
> *"Sing to us one of the songs of El Salvador."*
>
> *How could we sing the Lord's song*
> *in a foreign land?*

> *If I forget you, O Guatemala*
> *let my right hand wither away;*
> *let my tongue cling to the roof of my mouth*
> *if I do not remember you,*
> *If I do not set Nicaragua*
> *above my highest joy.*
> — *Ps.137:1-6 (adapted)*

The problem went deeper than merely feeling the loss of one's homeland; there was also bitterness: that they had to live in the Empire which had forced them to flee; that they had to be nice to those who had caused them so much pain and suffering. Unlike our being accustomed to refugees being grateful that they are finally "in America", in this case there were feelings of deep hatred towards those who had destroyed their past! The Jews in exile had similar feelings about ancient Babylon as reflected in the Psalms, even though our modern liturgies often omit the bitter lines so as not to offend our liberal sensitivities. They give us an insight into just how deep the feelings of these modern exiles from Central America towards the United States as empire must go:

> *Down with it! down with it!*
> *even to the ground!*
> *O Daughter of Babylon, doomed to destruction,*
> *happy the one who pays you back for what you have*
> *done to us!*
> *Happy shall he be who takes your little ones,*
> *and dashes them against the rock!*
> — *Ps.137:7-9 (Bk. of Common Prayer)*

Third, consider the **theological** parallels between these two exilic experiences. While the ancient Exile was grounded in the hard political reality of the fall of Jerusalem and Jews being forced to adapt to an entirely new culture in Babylon, still the hardest part was trying to understand what this disaster and dislocation meant in terms of their faith and covenant with God. Why would Yahweh have allowed such devastation to fall upon them, the "chosen" people? This anguishing cry of **Why?**, reflected so poignantly in the Psalms and Lamentations is not a question about the "ultimate" meaning of life nor about life after death as we so often interpret it, but about this death-in-life situation that doesn't seem to have any end:

We have watched and watched
for a nation powerless to save us
When we go out, we take to by-ways to avoid the public
streets
our days are all but finished
our end has come.

— *Lam.4:17-18*

Out of such unanswered questions and future uncertainties emerge the deeper theological questions: Why have we been made to suffer so? What does God have against us? This struggle to comprehend such a radical judgement comes from the inconsistency between personal deeds and the extremity of this collective societal exile. Since there is no individual justification for such political extremes, answers have to be found at the larger political level and societal levels: the totally unjust rule of the coffee and banana oligarchies; the extreme repression of the military; the obsession of the Empire to maintain its control at all costs...even when that cost over so many years resolves nothing. Yet even such "explanations" are not enough to provide a guide for the future or meaning for the present. In despair, the exiles cry out about the indifference and ignorance of their North American hosts:

Then, in tears, I prostrated myself
and cried out: "Lord, what can we do?"
If they have no time
to hear the truth
and even less to seek it for themselves?
They are a people too ignorant and too comfortable.
Come to me, Lord, I wish to die among my people! (14)

In all these ways, we find poignant parallels between that ancient exilic experience and this modern one. Far from the two exiles having just symbolic and psychological similarities, both peoples struggled with fundamental questions about connections between the past and the future in terms of history and land; in terms of people and faith. Therefore, **the key paradigm for Central America today is clearly the Exile Revisited**. That ancient prophecy about societal death and rebirth is being played out before our very eyes: a human/divine drama of judgement and redemption which will not be put off by America's cynicism and indifference. The American people must come to realize that time doesn't merely "march on", it moves forward towards moments of crisis and choices for the Empire as well as the people of

God. Significantly, modern Babylon doesn't realize any more than ancient Babylon did that this **kairos** time for the exiles ultimately implies an endtime for its own arrogant ways.

FOOTNOTES — CHAPTER 1

1   Hebrew law or instruction, but more specifically, the "Teaching" of the Pentateuch, the first five books of Hebrew Scriptures.

2   Philip Wheaton, *Agrarian Reform in El Salvador*, EPICA, Washington, D.C., 1980, p.10.

3   EPICA, *Indian Guatemala: Path to Liberation*, Wash., D.C., 1984, p.93: "A deal was struck between Washington and Guatemala for resuming U.S. military aid" through Israel. Indeed, Israel had been involved in counterinsurgency training of the Guatemalan military since 1978 when Congress first restricted military aid to that country. Israel thus became a U.S. surrogate; an instrument of North American imperialism.

4   **Coyotes** are paid guides usually requiring a payment of $1,500.00 per head to guide someone from El Salvador just across the Mexican-U.S. border. It was their abandoning such refugees in the desert in 1980 that triggered the "Underground Railroad" movement. From reports by Salvadoran refugees in Washington, D.C.

5   Gary MacEoin, *Sanctuary*, Harper & Row, San Francisco, 1985, p.16.

6   In order to reduce the militancy of Bosch adherents as members of the Dominican Revolutionary Party (PRD), thousands of Dominicans were given visas to the United States by the U.S.Consulate in Santo Domingo. By 1970, 600,000 Dominicans had moved to NYC. Reports of the Tenth Anniversary Conference of the U.S. Invasion of the Dominican Republic held in New York City in 1975.

7   The average approvals of all other nationalities applying for asylum is between 25-30%; for those from communist countries it often reaches as high as 60-70%.

8   See Numbers 35:11-15. The setting aside of "cities of refuge" by the ancient Hebrews again became commonplace during the Middle Ages when cathedrals became sanctuaries to protect those being pursued or persecuted by the State or King.

9   Rev. Marta Benavides, "Reflections on Being a Minister and a Refugee" Gary MacEoin, *Sanctuary*, ibid., p.160.

10   Walter Brueggemann, *Hopeful Imagination*, Fortress Press, Philadelphia, 1986, p.3.

11   These figures, compiled from the three solidarity networks: Nicaragua Network, CISPES and NISGUA are conservative estimates since many persons were disappeared and unaccounted for. In Nicaragua, the estimate of CRIES organization is that over 200,000 have been killed since 1980.

12   Catholic authorities in Guatemala claim over 1,000,000 displaced after the holocaust; in El Salvador, the Church estimates 500-750,000 internally displaced.

13   A.E. Bailey & C.F. Kent, *History of the Hebrew Commonwealth*, Chas.Scribner, New York, 1935, pp. 254-255.

14   Julia Esquivel, *Threatened with Resurrection*, The Brethren Press, Elgin, Ill.,1982, p.89.

CHAPTER 2
EMPIRE

U.S. Marines arrive for Operation Big Pine II, Puerto Castilla, Honduras, continuing the practice of U.S. interventions in the hemisphere since 1898.

CHAPTER 2 EMPIRE

Imperialism has penetrated the fabric of our culture, and infected our imagination, more deeply than we usually think.
— Martin Green (1)

...this is no longer "one nation under God." It is **two** *nations. Two very different Americas. One based on arrogance and a false sense of superiority. The other based on ethical, biblical principles— the principles on which this nation was founded.*
— CALC, Oct., 1986 (2)

America As Both A Democracy & An Empire...From the Outset

The only inaccuracy in this second evaluation of America comes in the last line, for this nation was *also* founded upon an imperial dream and it is our political schizophrenia of being, in fact, *two nations from the very outset* that creates this apparent contradiction and our confusion. The United States and its citizens are a product of both of these dreams and drives, as exemplified by "America the Beautiful" and the "Ugly American (Empire)." Unless we understand this duality in ourselves and our history, we shall never fully come to grips with why U.S. foreign policy is so horrendous and so contrary to the personal moral values we hold. Thanks to the Reagan administration — with its extreme aggressiveness overseas and its blatant lying at home — more and more Americans are beginning to seriously question U.S. policy abroad. But the deception certainly didn't begin with Reagan; it goes far back in our history and has been perpetuated by every administration. Nor is the problem merely one of misinformation or disinformation, but the fact that at a much deeper level than policy-deception, we try to hide from ourselves the fact that as a nation we are **both a democracy and an empire**.

The reason we have so much difficulty admitting this duality or being able to analyze it objectively is because "democracy" and "empire" have been part of the American dream from the very beginning of our history. Most Americans are not aware of this because no such dual reality is ever mentioned in our history books nor admitted in the media. Americans still believe that this is only "one nation under God" and that America is based solely on the ideals embodied in our Constitution. Since our earliest days, however, a number of our founding fathers dreamt of America as a mighty empire, as well that it should also be a democracy! This presumably contradictory vision came out of our espousal of the advantages of British imperialism while rejecting the onerous aspects of British colonialism. While many Americans wanted to be free of the British colonial yoke (not all by any means) (3), many others also wanted the power and prestige which Britain as an empire represented, but they wanted it for themselves as the American establishment. In other words, the American dream was born and bred within the British imperial/colonial context and our dual reaction to it.

The architect of this dual dream was James Madison, who in 1787 wrote to Thomas Jefferson: "This form of government (The Constitution), in order to effect its purposes, must operate not within a small but an extensive sphere." (4) Madison himself was a classic mercantilist and imperialist but he faced certain limitations: while Americans wanted more land and trade, they were also antagonistic towards a strong federal government; while they wanted more territorial rights and power granted by Washington, they also believed fiercely in personal freedom and States' rights. So "(Madison) had, in short, to change people's minds — their way of thinking — about the relationship between empire and freedom."(5) America's foremost expert on empire, William Appleman Williams, explains that Madison had to turn conventional wisdom about revolution on its head; had to convince people that empire was essential for freedom:

> *Extend the sphere, and you take in a greater variety of parties and interests; you make it less probable that a majority of the whole will have a common motive to invade the rights of other citizens; or if such a common motive exists, it will be more difficult for all to feel it...to act in unison with each other.(6)*

Behind this reasonable-sounding logic, Madison was in fact arguing for and indeed predicting that the United States would become the biggest "consolidated empire" in history, but he claimed it was for the purpose of guaranteeing freedom for all its citizens. Here we have, if you will, a manifesto for **empire as a way of life under the mantle of democracy**. This architect of the American dream convinced none other than the pro-democratic, anti-federalist Thomas Jefferson who wrote in 1809: "I am persuaded no constitution was ever before so well calculated as ours for extensive empire and self-government." (7) Madison had won the ideological battle. However, as Williams reminds us, the American people can hardly blame the architect.

> *Very simply, Americans of the 20th century like empire for the same reason their ancestors favored it in the 18th and 19th centuries. It provided them with renewable opportunities, wealth and other benefits and satisfactions including the psychological sense of well-being and power.(8)*

Our schizophrenia between democracy and empire lies deeply embedded in our collective psyche. We want to be Number 1 — the most powerful, wealthy and technologically advanced nation on earth — and, at the same time, we want to be loved and admired for our idealistic principles: democracy, freedom and the pursuit of happiness. The problem is that these two sets of goals are often in basic conflict with each other and historically they have often clashed even in our domestic sphere. America's role in Vietnam was an example of a war fought to defend our imperialist goals which in practice contradicted almost every moral value we hold as a democratic and religious community. However, to get the American people to admit that this conflict exists, much less to choose between the two, will be no small task, for we have a great deal at stake in maintaining the "pure" democracy mythology about ourselves, namely, *our self image.*

This marriage between empire and democracy obviously favored some Americans more than others, namely *the rich, whites and males.* During our nation's development and expansion Westward, from the original colonies to the territories and onward towards continental consolidation, many people suffered terribly, especially *the poor, blacks and women.* Indeed, the Constitution reflected such discrimination from the outset, explicitly excluding blacks from citizenship. As Supreme Court Justice Thurgood Marshall has written, "while the Union survived the Civil War, the Constitution did not..."

> *In 1857, Supreme Court Chief Justice Roger Brooke Taney...delivered the opinion of the Court in the awful Dred Scott decision (he wrote) "the framers of the Constitution never intended to include blacks in 'the whole human family.'" (9)*

While there have been some important rectifications in the status of blacks and women in our society since the 1960s — in terms of civil rights and feminist emancipation — none of us can overlook how partial these changes have been nor deny how deep racism and sexism still run. The slogan "life, liberty and the pursuit of happiness" has always been less than egalitarian within our domestic reality, whereas in our dealings with Central America and the Caribbean it is totally contradicted where the weakness of democracy and the goals of imperialism are magnified a hundred-fold. If domestically empire meant land, opportunity and the good life for many white Americans north of the border, it meant disaster for the poor, blacks, browns and women on the other side of the Rio Grande.

Our First Imperial Experiment: the Trans-Isthmian Passageway

The first clear experiment in U.S. imperialism occurred long before we technically became an empire, although it was part of that process we call "empire-building" and it directly affected Central America. Romantic stories and movies abound about covered wagons and the opening up of the West, but they omit the fact that those Americans with money did not go West **overland** to seek gold in California in 1849 or to claim land in the Oregon territories. They went by ship through the Caribbean, the only impediment to that tranquil maritime passage to the West Coast being the Central American isthmus which they had to cross over in order to reach the Pacific. They did so primarily through Panama and Nicaragua.

In the case of the Panamanian passage, William Aspinwall, a New York financier, obtained from Nueva Granada (Colombia), an exclusive 49-year long contract to build and operate a railroad across the Isthmus. In the process, Aspinwall disrupted life in Panama in three ways: he imported foreign laborers from Europe, India and China; he hired a Texas ranger to organize an Isthmian Guard which became "law and order" in the central strip across Panama; and, whenever there were problems the Guard couldn't handle, U.S. Marines were called in:

> On September 19, 1856, two warships were ordered to occupy the territory and 160 U.S. Marines landed, taking possession of the railroad at both terminals. Though the troops were recalled three days later, this marked the first of five U.S. military interventions in Panama between 1856 and 1865.(10)

As a result, a model for future U.S.-Central American relations was unconsciously being formed, with ominous implications for the rights of the Isthmian nations. Namely, the presumed right of North Americans to use the territory for their own ends, by authority of their money and power, regardless of how adversely it affected the rights of the people to self-determination and national integrity.   In the case of Nicaragua, Cornelius Vanderbilt also set up a transit system — by water and overland — and then, in order to provide what he called "a stable climate for his investment" (a term since used by almost every U.S. corporation overseas), brought into the country a filibuster named William Walker.(11) Backed by Vanderbilt money, Walker raised a small mercenary army, took sides in Nicaragua's internal politics, overthrew those in government, took power and claimed himself president in a tainted election in 1856. Seeking support for his cause back in the Sates, Walker re-instituted slavery into Nicaragua, making him "the darling of the southern slave expansionists." Racism was an inherent element in the southern dream of establishing a Caribbean empire and thus Walker was widely supported in the South, inspiring one newspaper to write in an editorial:

> *The miserable republics of Central America, peopled by a degraded half-race of humanity, will yet bow to the rule of the Anglo-American... (and Americans will carry) moral and material well-being to the disintegrating communities and decaying races of Spanish America.(12)*

Although Walker's flamboyant exploits were generally opposed by the U.S. government (the North) — because of the anger and fear he was creating among Central American governments — his timing, just before the Civil War, turned Walker's misadventures into a **cause-celebre**, over which Northerners and Southerners took sides. When he was taken prisoner by the U.S. Navy in 1858 and returned to the States, Walker received a hero's welcome in the South. Some accused him of "laying the basis for a Southern Slave Empire"(13) while most historians believe he was merely planning to set up an empire of his own. In either case, such expansionist dreams and imperialistic attitudes were held by many Americans at that time, though the moment for a full-scale U.S. expansion into the Caribbean had not yet arrived.

When we consider U.S. imperialism in light of international law or even our own stated policy in relation to foreign powers operating in *our* hemisphere — that is, the Monroe Doctrine — we note that **power and privilege take precedence over principle**. During the 19th century when the United States was relatively weaker than the European powers, it failed to act according to this principle of non-intervention. It did not stop Spain from taking over Santo Domingo in 1861; it did not stop the French from taking Mexico in 1864; nor did it challenge the French attempt to build a canal across Panama in the 1880s. The real principle was self-interest. When President Polk said,

> *We can never consent that European powers shall interfere to prevent such a union because it might disturb the 'balance of power' which they may desire to maintain upon this continent...(14)*

he was referring to such powers siding with the Confederacy. Thus challenging the French attempt in Panama, President Hayes said, "the policy of this country is a *canal under American control*" (15) Similarly, we challenged Great Britain's control over Venezuela's mouth of the Orinoco River in 1894 only when we were powerful enough to confront the British Navy in the Caribbean. As we approached the ominous year of U.S. imperial expansion (1898), Secretary of State Richard Olney, explaining President Cleveland's reaffirmation of the Monroe Doctrine, said, "The safety and welfare of the United States are so concerned with the maintenance of the independence of every American State as to justify and require the interposition of the United States whenever that independence is endangered "(16). This is why Jose Marti of Cuba was so concerned...that in the name of protecting the hemisphere from "foreigners," the United States would become the new foreign threat to Latin American sovereignty. The basis upon which the United States could say this, as Secretary Olney explained in 1895, was that it had become master of the situation, **not because of its principles but because of its power**:

> *Today the United States is practically sovereign on this continent, and its fiat is law upon the subjects to which it confines its interposition. Why? It is because, in addition to all other grounds, its infinite resources combined with its isolated position render it master of the situation and practically invulnerable against any and all other powers.(17)*

The actual impetus for U.S. expansion was sparked by the writings of Admiral Alfred Mahan in his famous book *Influence of Sea Power on History* written in 1890, which defined naval power as the key to "national supremacy" as he put it. Mahan, linking U.S. economic growth to overseas expansion wrote, "Whether they will or no, Americans must begin to look outward [outside continental USA]. The growing production of the country demands it..." (18) Mahan made it clear that this expansion depended on a strong U.S. Navy and control of the strategically-located territories of Cuba, Puerto Rico and Panama. His ideas made a major impact on such leaders as John Hay, Theodore Roosevelt and Henry Cabot Lodge, as well as on sectors of the religious community in the United States, thereby paving the way for the U.S. intervention into and subsequent domination over the **Gran Caribe** from 1898 and thereafter.

However, the ultimate goal of this expansionist strategy — in Mahan's mind — was not merely wresting control of the Caribbean from Britain and the Antillean islands from Spanish control, but a far more expansive dream: **control of the markets of the Orient!** For that purpose, a transisthmian waterway across Central America as well as control of the islands of the Pacific were crucial. In other words, the Spanish-American War was not aimed at eliminating a dying and enfeebled Spanish colonialism; its purpose was to launch the United States as a world imperial power.(19)

Certainly this was what the peoples of the Greater Antilles and Central America experienced over the next thirty years. In the decades following the war, the Gran Caribe would be dominated by "gunboat diplomacy" in which U.S. Marines would become *imperial gendarmes* who intervened 33 times into Cuba, Puerto Rico, the Dominican Republic, Panama, Honduras, Haiti and Nicaragua. In behalf of North American companies the Marines invaded, killed anyone who resisted and remained as long as was necessary, sometimes for months, sometimes for decades and in the case of Puerto Rico and Panama in perpetuity. In every case, some flimsy excuse or patriotic slogan was invoked to justify the adventure, such as "protecting American lives" or "saving the country for democracy" whereas the real goals were corporate expansion and geo-political consolidation.

There were also religious motivations behind our imperial conquest. The marriage of political expansionism and Protestant missionary zeal joined hands in this venture. Nor had this partnership of State and Church idealism only sprung up at the turn of the century. As early as the mid-19th century, John O'Sullivan had written in the **Democratic Review**:

> *Our mission is to smite unto death the tyranny of kings, hierarchs and oligarchs, and carry the glad tidings of peace and good will where myriads now endure an existence scarcely more enviable than the beasts of the field. (20)*

It was a holy crusade, a religious war of **noblesse oblige**, a divinely ordained call to save heathen societies so they might one day bask in the blessings of an enlightened society whose missionaries would then save their souls. This is why Protestant denominations so fully supported this imperial enterprise of the 20th century. For instance, shortly after the Marines had taken over Puerto Rico, secretaries of missionary boards from four denominations were standing over a map in New York City in 1899 dividing up the island into their exclusive missionary zones, one for each church body's evangelization. (21) The recipients of this aggressive beneficence often speak of this process as the invasion of the three Ms, "the Marines, the Merchants and the Missionaries!" (22)

Nationalists who resisted this American crusade, like Charlemagne Peralte in Haiti (1916-1919), the Eastern riders (**jinetes del Este**) in the

Dominican Republic, (1916-1922) or Augusto Cesar Sandino in Nicaragua (1927-1933), were always labeled by Washington as "bandits," "outlaws" or "bolsheviks." To the contrary, they were looked upon by their own people as national heros, patriots and revolutionaries resisting a foreign aggressor which was trying to rob the nation of its sovereignty. In the case of Sandino, he was neither a socialist or a Marxist, but a populist and nationalist, who resisted the Marines successfully for five years and who said of his cause:

> *This movement is national and anti-imperialist. We fly the flag of freedom for Nicaragua and for all Latin America. And on the social level, it's a people's movement; we stand for the advancement of social aspirations. People have come to try and influence us (to stop resisting the Yankees) from the International Labor Federation, from the League Against Imperialism, from the Quakers...We've always upheld to them our definite criterion that its essentially a national thing.(23)*

By the 1930s, the depression made it harder to sustain an active war overseas, especially when international opinion against the U.S. role in Central America was mounting. President Franklin D. Roosevelt, realizing that U.S. forces could not defeat Sandino, decided in 1934 to recall all the Marines from the Gran Caribe, but not before they had carefully trained, armed and left behind National Guard forces which were loyal to the United States, such as those in Haiti, Nicaragua and the Dominican Republic. These forces were not created as independent armies to protect their national interests, but as "praetorian guards" of the Empire guaranteeing U.S. interests. Future dictators like Rafael Trujillo and Anastasio Somoza — were hand-picked by the Marines to manage this new strategy. It was presented to the American people, however, as Roosevelt's "good neighbor" policy which had supposedly ended the long night of gunboat diplomacy, a benevolent act on the part of a well-intentioned and democratically based society. In effect, we were attempting to cover our imperial reality with a democratic face: using surrogate troops to replace the direct and more onerous presence of U.S. Marines.

U.S. Imperialism: Our Idolatry and Self-Deception

When any State becomes an empire, a world power, the temptation to self-glorification and the tendency to self-deception increase by geometric proportions. As with all big powers in the past, we Americans were also convinced that our experiment in greatness would be different because we were breaking away from the old, static and conservative ways of Europe. We believed that our dream could be carried on in isolation from the rest of the world, and that we only had to concern ourselves with the rights of American citizens, not those benighted souls whom we conquered. It was precisely because this brave new world became a nightmare for anyone who stood in the path of our ongoing rush towards greatness that it is now becoming our Achilles heel. The flaw in our self-image is that we assumed that mere size, power, wealth, technology and newness made our imperial project legitimate in itself. Since we were a democracy and a place of law and justice, we could intervene and occupy their lands without applying these same principles there for presumably we had come to save them from something worse.

The basis of this contradictory policy was that the **right of a democracy at home justifies the might of imperialism overseas**. Most Americans believed that this land had been given to us (by God) as white Anglo-Saxon settlers with no restrictions except those imposed on ourselves. This meant that we Anglos had the right to slaughter Indians and drive out the Mexicans until we controlled all of continental United States "from sea to shining sea." Indeed, we whites had the right to enslave and keep Blacks in their place while we men had the right to keep our women as household servants and second class citizens. Between us white American males there was a certain "gentlemen's agreement" that you play by the rules, **but that only applied to us and it only applied here in the States**! Thus even our continental empire-building contained deep-seated elitist, racist and sexist assumptions... which were then applied to our black and brown sisters and brothers overseas with a vengeance.

At both the ideological level (i.e., "this Empire is not an empire because it's a democracy") and at the power level (i.e.,"white males play by special rules"), our blindness went unchecked because there was no critical examination of these premises. Since we assumed God was behind this project — a theological assumption affirmed by almost all denominations — religion could not challenge these idolatries. Most preachers not only accepted these premises — being white males — they were also "court prophets" who reinforced the prevailing attitudes of Anglo-Saxon superiority while preaching moralistic piety. Here and there, a prophetic voice would speak out — a lawyer, parson, newspaper reporter, song writer, humorist, trade unionist, a black, and occasionally even a woman! When they did so, they became, ironically, our popular heros and heroines: Frederick Douglas, John Brown, Sojourner Truth, Joe Hill, Marcus Garvey, Rosa Parks, Martin Luther

King, etc. They gave us a vision of the better side of our personalities and of what our society should be, **but we didn't alter our policies and prejudices to accord with their vision, we simply honored their words and their names**, as in Martin Luther King's "I Have a Dream" speech. This is reflective of our myopic dichotomy wherein we only want to see one side of our schizophrenic nature.

When we expanded overseas, almost none of our Constitutional principles or Bill of Rights were applied. Indeed, in Central America and the Caribbean, we belied in practice the very values we said we believed in. We coerced weaker nations through our superior power; we bribed nations (and their leaders) through our enormous wealth; and we expected from those we dominated subservient obedience or grateful acknowledgement. Contrary to the Word of God, we exalted the proud and humbled the poor; we sat the rich on thrones and despised the blacks and browns; thereby contradicting the formula of Mary's *Magnificat*:

> *God has put to rout the arrogant of heart and mind. God has brought down monarchs from their thrones, but the humble have been lifted high. The hungry God has satisfied with good things, but the rich have been sent empty away.*
> —*Lk. 1:51-53*

The most serious aspect of this our American idolatry is that we continue to pretend the Empire doesn't exist. Because we have always refused to look at the two sides of our contradictory coin — democracy and imperialism — we had to sublimate who we were; **we had to deceive ourselves**! This self-deception is now returning to haunt us and the problem is that we don't know how to eradicate from our souls an idol which we have always believed didn't exist. The problem is that this illicit marriage between Empire and "we the people" is inside of us. As Appleman Williams says,

> *We have transformed our imperial way of life from a culture that we built and benefited from into an abstract self-evident Law of Nature that we must now re-examine in light of its costs and consequences. (24)*

FOOTNOTES - CHAPTER 2

1   Martin Green, *Dreams of Adventure, Deeds of Empire*, 1979, cited in William Appleman Williams, *Empire as a Way of Life*, Oxford Univ.Press, N.Y., 1980, Introduction, p.3.

2   Clergy & Laity Concerned, letter from staff, New York, Oct.,1986,p.1.

3   Historians generally estimate that one-third of all American colonists were Tories or pro-British.

4   W.A.Williams, *Empire as a Way of Life*, ibid, p.35

5   Ibid., p.45.

6   Ibid.

7   Ibid., p.55.

8   Ibid., p.13.

9   *Washington Post*, July 28, 1987, op-ed, "Honoring the 14th Amendment" by Courtland Milloy.

10 EPICA, *Panama: Sovereignty for a Land Divided*, Washington, D.C., 1976, p.11.

11 A freebooter or adventurer, engaging in unauthorized warfare against a foreign country with which his own country is at peace.

12 Robert May, *The Southern Dream of a Caribbean Empire*, Louisiana State University Press, Baton Rouge, La., 1973, pp.134.

13 Robert May, *The Southern Dream...*, ibid., p. 5.

14 J. Lloyd Mecham, *United States-Latin American Relations*, H. Mifflin Co., N.Y.,1965, p.65

15 Ibid., p. 63.

16 Ibid., p. 64.

17 J. Lloyd Mecham, *U.S.-L.A. Relations*, ibid., p 64.

18 Alfred T. Mahan, "The U.S. Looking Outward," *Atlantic Monthly*, LXVI (1890), p. 816.

19 Catherine Sunshine, *The Caribbean: Survival, Struggle & Sovereignty*, EPICA, Wash., D.C.,1985. See "Roots of U.S. Imperialism in the Greater Antilles," pp. 28-34.

20 Williams, *Empire as a Way of Life*, op. cit., p. 88.

21 Emilio Pantojas Garcia, *The Protestant Church And The Process Of Americanization of Puerto Rico*, reproduced by PRISA, Bayamon, Puerto Rico, 1979, p. 10, "...during the second half of 1899 that the secretaries of the mission boards of the Presbyterian, American Baptist, Congregational and Methodist Episcopal Churches met to define and divide the territories, using maps to do so." Major George G. Groff wrote "Puerto Rico is destined to become a State of the American Union. The kind of state it will make will in a measure depend upon the work done by the religious societies of the United States."

22 Interview of a young Dominican by Philip Wheaton during the U.S. Marine occupation of Santo Domingo in August 1965.

23 Gregorio Selser, *Sandino*, Monthly Review Press, New York, 1981, p.97.

24 Williams, *Empire As A Way of Life*, op.cit., p.14.

CHAPTER 3
CAPTIVITY

Nicaraguan Miskito Indians kidnapped by the **Misura** counterrevolutionaries on the Atlantic coast by Puerto Cabezas and taken to the **Mocorón** refugee camp in Honduras where they live in captivity.

CHAPTER 3 CAPTIVITY

*The Egyptians forced the sons of Israel into slavery, and made
their lives unbearable with hard labor, work with clay and
brick, all kinds of work in the fields; they forced on them every
kind of labor...In this way they built the store-cities of Pithom
and Rameses for Pharaoh...But the more they were crushed,
the more they increased and spread, and (the Egyptians)
came to dread the sons of Israel.*

— Ex. 1:12.14

*They twist the truth calling their intervention into Central
America and the Caribbean "peace and development" in
order to silence the outcry of the thousands being crucified in
El Salvador and Guatemala. (1)*

— Julia Esquivel

Latin America and the Caribbean operate within the overall
parameters of a system of domination known as imperialism in which
the United States is the Empire and the peoples of the southern half of
the continent are its captives. Any attempt by any nation in the
hemisphere to break out of this captivity, whatever its ideological
position or political alternative has been brutally attacked and systematically subverted: Guatemala (1954), Cuba (1959), Guyana (1963),
Brazil (1964), the Dominican Republic (1965), Chile (1973), Nicaragua
(1979), El Salvador (1980) Guatemala (1982) and Grenada (1983).
When one considers the wide variety of political goals and ideological
premises represented by these numerous experiments in self-determination, it is clear that the United States' simplistic categorization of all
of them as "communist-led" is a gross distortion. The real reason for the
Empire's consistent fury against all these attempts at liberation is
because its goal is *total hemispheric subservience*. Political variations
are tolerated only after there is a basic capitulation to the North
American imperial system.

Within this overarching reality of foreign domination, the **Gran
Caribe**, which includes Central America, functions under far greater
restrictions and more direct control than in the case of the South
American countries. Because of its proximity to continental USA, it is
geo-politically accurate to compare the Gran Caribe — called the
"Caribbean Basin" by the Empire — to the **Mar Mediterraneo** of the
ancient Roman empire, because of its comparable location and
importance to U.S. hegemony. While, in one sense U. S. policy is
equally concerned about the attempt by any nation in the hemisphere
to free itself from U.S. control, Washington becomes particularly

anxious when such revolts occur in her "back yard" and normally only directly invades this arena, not South America. While the United States has been quite successful in isolating those *islands* where revolutions have occurred — Cuba, the Dominican Republic and Grenada — the present struggle in Central America is particularly worrisome to the White House because of the inter-connecting land mass and the fact that a series of revolutions all came about at the same time. This created a fear of what has been called "the domino theory", that is, the idea that Marxist revolution might envelop one country after another, marching northward, until the "communist hordes stand at our very borders."(2)

By contrast, the majority feeling and growing preoccupation of the peoples of the hemisphere revolves around how to free themselves from our imperial domination, which in many countries also implies extreme poverty and political tyranny. At the end of WW II this kind of anti-Americanism was rare, especially since the United States had been fighting fascism in Europe and challenging the feudal Japanese empire in the Far East. But with the eruption of each of the aforementioned struggles for self-determination followed by the United States' brutal destruction or destabilization of these revolts, popular awareness grew and grew until Big Brother in the north was seen as a far more serious threat than either local despotism or European communism. If one considers Sandino's revolt in the 1930s, Guatemala's nationalism in the 1940s, Panama's rebellion in the 1960s, Salvador's democratization in the 1970s and the Indian uprising in Guatemala in the 1980s, none of these had Marxist ideology as their political agenda. While there have been Marxist advocates in leadership positions in the Cuban, Nicaraguan and Salvadoran revolutionary processes, the motor force which triggered them was military dictatorships (i.e. those of Batista, Somoza and Humberto Romero, respectively), not communism. Thus in today's dialectics of captivity/liberation in Central America, the primary causal agent behind these rebellions has been **national despotism supported and reinforced by U.S. imperialism**.

At first glance, the oppression and exploitation in Central America and the Caribbean suggests a biblical parallel to the Exodus history of the captivity of the Hebrews under a foreign empire like ancient Egypt, within which the mass of the impoverished function virtually as slaves to that system. So it seemed to many Latin American Christian revolutionaries during the 1950s and 1960s, when the focus was on a Somoza dictatorship or a Salvadoran oligarchy. Thus it is understandable that biblical comparisons should have been drawn from the Exodus in the minds of many religious folk concerned about this exploitation and repression, that is, between these *national despotic rulers* and the role of Pharaoh, his soldiers and slave drivers. However, as awareness grew about the role of the United States as empire, ideological analysis among students and progressive groups, and then among trade unionists and peasants, shifted the focus from national despotism to hemispheric imperialism. However, within the religious community, the typical paradigm used to illustrate **this crisis of modern captivity remained the Exodus event** and the call of liberation from national tyranny.

While the Exodus obviously holds within its dynamic a number of important and pertinent metaphors that are still useful, the "invasion" of North American agents and forces, policies and funding in an imperial effort to replace the old despots and reform them, coupled with the mass migration of refugees to the United States, made it clear that the more pertinent model from which to draw biblical parallels about what has been going on since 1980 in Central America is the **Exilic experience**. Since the goal of the peoples of the Isthmus is not to flee from local despots like Somoza but to redeem their own land from such oppression and build new societies; since the dynamic is not to leave Egypt (i.e., Central America) for a promised land somewhere to the north; since the dream is to be freed from their present Babylonian captivity and return to their own Promised Land; and since the vision is how to create new men and new women who in turn will build these new societies, clearly, the most apt metaphor for all these dynamics is **the Exilic experience not the Exodus event**.

In attempting to apply this Exilic paradigm to Central America, however, we are faced by a number of unanswered questions that don't seem to fit the model. The role of the United States towards the region did not follow a colonial model but rather a *neo-colonial strategy*. Furthermore, the United States has since WW II claimed that its concern is with "*development*" *and* "*reform*", which, once again, does not appear to fit the traditional imperial/colonial model. The Central American countries have responded to the role and influence of the United States in two contradictory ways: one *revolutionary*, seeking liberation from imperial domination; the other *reformist*, apparently content with a collaborative relationship with the Empire. Therefore, before we can assert that liberation is the only viable political solution to the crisis in the Isthmus and that the exilic experience is the primary paradigm for the people of God, we must first examine these other forms of relationship and programs which at least suggest a possible *via media* between dictatorial repression and popular revolution.

Neo-colonialism & The Failure of Reform & Development

While today's captivity reflects certain objective conditions of oppression and exploitation in some countries of Central America, the question is often asked: why is there such a lack of consciousness about these conditions and the U.S. role in the others? While large percentages of the populations in Nicaragua, El Salvador and Guatemala have developed a singular clarity about U.S. captivity which has thrust them into a life-and-death struggle with the Empire, why is such clarity far less evident among the peoples of Honduras, Costa Rica and Panama? If, for instance, one can say that both Costa Rica and Nicaragua are held captive by the same imperial system, why are most **Costarricenses** unaware of their entrapment or have accepted it as a way of life while for most **Nicaraguenses** this captivity became an obsession which led to their liberation? Obviously, there are cultural and racial differences between the two societies, such as those which cause Costa Ricans to call Nicaraguans "hard-headed indians"(3) while considering themselves superior citizens of a country often called "little Switzerland." The real basis for these differences lies not in their culture, however, but in the contrast between Costa Rica's experience with neo-colonialism and Nicaragua's with neo-fascism.

Neo-colonialism — that great liberal stratagem employed by the USA since WW II as more acceptable (especially in the Third World) than colonialism(4) — produces, nonetheless, a colonized mentality which is even more dangerous for its subtlety and because it assumes itself to be free, even though it too is trapped by the imperial system. One important reason for people's willingness to tolerate neo-colonialism is that domination is more moderate and special advantages are offered to those who "go along." Consider the fact that Honduras is the poorest country in the region though dominated by U.S. banana companies; that there is an extreme economic crisis in Costa Rica today related to control by U.S. banks and the I.M.F.; and, that Panama has lived under the direct colonial yoke of of U.S. militarism since 1904. Yet up to 1980, none of these conditions had led to a critical consciousness among the people of these societies because of the relative social and economic advantages of neo-colonialism.

In the case of Panama, in exchange for accepting U.S. presence and control over the Canal Zone, Panamanians were freed from an arbitrary and indifferent Colombian rule, and later worked for the Canal Company which paid better wages than most workers in other parts of Central America received. However, they were paid under a "gold and silver" standard in which Panamanians received much less than Americans for the same work. The cost of these neo-colonial advantages was high: the presence of 14 U.S. military bases on their land; extreme distortion of the development patterns of the country with almost all activity concentrated in the port cities of Colón and Panama City(5); and for years, an unwritten rule of deference which *had to be shown* to all white North Americans. These negative by-products of neo-colonialism have produced a profound love/hate relationship between Panamanians and the Yankees which finally exploded into open rebellion in the 1964 flag riots.

In the case of Honduras, its domination by the U.S. banana companies (United Fruit and Standard Fruit, plus Chase Manhattan Bank) produced a dependency relationship wherein in order to make money, the country's elites had to link themselves to the U.S. companies, since these three corporations controlled 80% of the country's GNP between 1906 and 1945. Honduras to this day is still a "Company Country" — as in "company town" — where seven foreign corporations still control 80% of the GNP, making the "ruling class" *a dependent oligarchy*, quite unlike the independent coffee barons in El Salvador.(6) This pattern of dependency also produced a neo-colonial labor alternative in Honduras: during the same year that the United Fruit Company was destroying trade unionism in Guatemala (1954) it was offering Honduran workers certain rights, but *only* if they rejected their own unions and joined U.S.-controlled labor unions related to the AF of L!(7) Furthermore, one of the primary functions of the Honduran military was to settle labor disputes for the banana companies, i.e., keep its citizen workers from striking gringo firms. These advantages in turn produced a neo-colonial mentality of acquiescence to the Americans over the years, which is precisely what led the Honduran military to agree to "the plan" of 1980 which allowed the Pentagon to march into Honduras and set up its present regional counterinsurgency operation without objection.(8)

In the case of Costa Rica, the neo-colonial process is more complex but just as real. To compete competitively in the world market during the 19th century, the Costa Rican coffee oligarchy had to get their beans to the Atlantic Coast, requiring a railroad be built between the highlands and the port city of Limon. So they entered into a contract with a North American banana producer named Minor Keith, granting vast tracts of land alongside the railroad for banana plantings. In time, Keith married into Costa Rican aristocracy and became a key player in the national economy. Near bankruptcy in 1896 because of over-investment, he sold out to the Boston Fruit Company which became the famous United Fruit Company, with Keith as its general manager. From that time on, United Fruit and the railroad played a key role in the economy and Costa Rica was on its way to becoming another "banana/ coffee republic". The script was altered, however, by its Civil War of 1948, which produced significant social changes: progressive laws, reforms, and the nationalization of all utilities.(9) This required a huge state bureaucracy which could only survive as long as coffee and banana prices were high. When they fell in the mid-1970s just as petroleum prices were skyrocketing, Costa Rica fell into extreme indebtedness through heavily borrowing from U.S. banks. This led in 1980 to economic collapse and in 1982 to a takeover of its national economy by the IMF. Today, rising penetration by U.S. capital is making Costa Rica the most indebted nation *per capita* in all Latin America.(10) As a result, its traditional "neutral" political position has come under increasing pressure from the Reagan administration to cooperate with the United States in its war — both covert and overt — against Nicaragua.(11)

Thus in all three countries, neo-colonial dependency caused them to acquiesce to the Empire, making them politically subservient to Washington. Such subservience in turn produced a dependency mentality in each society which dulled political consciousness and weakened national resolve. This explains some of the differences between these three societies and the other countries in the region. However, the crisis of 1980ff in Central America began to moderate these differences as all three found themselves being gradually sucked into the regional conflict represented by the **contra** war against Nicaragua. The Reagan administration has been using them to advance its imperial policies in the process disregarding their national autonomy. For instance, he has violated Costa Rica's Neutrality Act of 1984 and has done everything to undermine the Arias Peace Plan. Similarly, the United States has invaded Honduran soil and forced the military in that country to put up with **contra** and **gringo** troops against rising popular opposition.(12) In the case of Panama, pressure to reclaim the U.S. military bases in the Canal Zone has led the Reagan administration to systematically default on the conditions of the Carter-Torrijos Canal Treaty of 1977(13) and recently the attempt to depose Gen.Manuel Noriega by starving the country into submission. Yet, while the 1980 crisis has deepened these neo-colonial societies' political and popular consciousness, the degree of such collective awareness and national determination remains at a much lower level than in Nicaragua, El Salvador and Guatemala.

Reforms of The Alliance for Progress and Why They Failed

The question remains in the minds of many North Americans, why not pacific reforms rather than the more "violent" approach suggested by liberation struggles? Many ask: "Isn't reform a more creative way to bring about social change?" Americans assume incorrectly that Latin American and Caribbean peoples haven't seriously tried moderate alternatives or are hopelessly dominated by "tin horn" dictators or are not politically "advanced" enough to make democracy work. Such North American prejudices reflect an ignorance perpetuated by media mythologies. In fact, over the years the hemisphere has tried every possible reformist measure: peaceful protests, union organizing, electoral politics... only to find their efforts consistently opposed or systematically crushed by reactionary elites and repressive military.

Another typical objection to the thesis of U.S. imperialism/captivity comes from those North Americans who mistakenly assume that the United States has been encouraging development and reform in the hemisphere since WW II. While it is true that many projects have been advanced and programs funded by certain U.S. agencies, it has always been with two fundamental provisos: a) U.S. business interests come first, and b) such experiments are not to basically alter the dominant structure favoring the ruling elites... who are tied into U.S. economic interests. This has produced what some economic experts call a developmentalist model, in which specific development projects do create some new jobs and limited economic activity, but they do *not* lead to *independent national development of the country;* rather they reinforce dependency on foreign capital and specifically U.S. corporations.

There were genuine efforts at regional *development* in the 1950s when four countries came up with the idea of a Central American Common Market (CACM) which would remove tariffs on all goods produced in the region in order to stimulate inter-country trade, while they would place a common tariff on all goods imported from outside the region, thus reducing dependence on foreign trade. The U.S. government adamantly opposed the plan because it saw any regional bloc development project as discriminatory to North American traders. However, when these tariff restrictions were eliminated and the CACM began to operate as an investment and loan resource for U.S. corporations, Central America in the 1960s became a new frontier for North American investment.(14) Import substitution (that is, producing needed goods locally instead of importing them) initially stimulated the economies of the region as CACM received loans and grants from both the U.S. government and the private sector. But foreign capital quickly bought out nationally-owned plants and banks while it frustrated indigenous development and expansion. Furthermore, greedy oligarchs — especially those in El Salvador and Guatemala (who were more closely tied to U.S. corporations — distorted and changed the plan of equitable inter-country trade in their favor, angering Honduran and Nicaraguan businessmen in particular. The new wealth was simply redistributed among the corporations and ruling class elites so that by the end of the 1960s, the CACM had failed.

In the case of **reform**, the Alliance for Progress represented the last serious U.S. effort at finding alternatives to the old class structures in Latin America, but it was a crash program with a reactionary political motivation: to prevent another Cuban revolution from breaking out elsewhere in the hemisphere. The Alliance's reform measures initiated by the Kennedy administration between 1961-64, did represent a sharp departure from previous decades of absolute inflexibility towards social change by the traditional oligarchies. But by the middle of the decade, the Alliance alternatives — land tenure projects, cooperatives, infusion of capital, controlled liberal elections — had failed. The problem was not that U.S. aid was too little or too late nor that such reforms were not welcomed by the poor wherever they were temporarily allowed, but rather, because *they were withdrawn under pressure from the elites.*(15) The fact that the reforms and resources had come from the United States and were then removed, leaving the poor worse off than before, helped many people see more clearly the **linkages between their local oppressors and the supposedly more benign and paternalistic Empire**.

Indeed, the Alliance strategy which from the outset had been conceived of as a policy involving "reform *and* repression" *became nothing but repression* (especially in El Salvador, Guatemala and Nicaragua) during the second half of the decade. Because social inequities and political injustice were so extreme in these three countries, from the very beginning the Alliance, oligarchic and military leaders had warned Washington that reformist openings might spark uncontrollable popular demands, thus requiring the back-up of the repressive side of the formula. Behind the scenes of Alliance reforms, therefore, U.S. agencies were busy training men and shipping sophisticated instruments of control to the police and military throughout Latin America and the Caribbean.(16) Especially ominous was the appearance in three countries of new programs aimed at extreme control: ORDEN (a peasant spy organization) in El Salvador (1961); CONDECA (a regional military organization headed by Somoza) in Nicaragua (1964ff) and PACIFICACION (a counter-insurgency, scorched-earth strategy in Guatemala (1967-68). None of these programs were created by local elites or their national military but by the Empire in Washington, D.C.!

With the failure of the Alliance and the end of the modest pressure which had been exerted by the Kennedys for reform, the repressive governments in the regions took the U.S. retreat as a go-ahead signal for unleashing the repressive side of the Alliance strategy in all its brutal fury. In El Salvador, labor and peasant leaders were murdered in cold blood; in Nicaragua, Tachito Somoza expanded his repression and torture of political prisoners; in Guatemala, the sadistic killings of the mid-1960s escalated into a slaughter of the entire male population in the Zacapa region under Col. Arana at the urging of the CIA.(17) As a result, traditional class antagonisms and anti-dictatorial hatred were now increasingly linked in people's minds to U.S. imperialism.

The Dark Side of Imperial Captivity: The National Security State

While this rising repression revealed the "dark side" of the Empire's operations, it also disillusioned liberal hopes held by both middle class Latin Americans and North American social reformers (missionaries and Peace Corps volunteers). Seeing the new anti-riot gear — bullet-proof jackets, plastic face protectors, walkie-talkies, high-powered weapons, jeeps ("made-in-the USA") — the "brave new world" envisioned by the Kennedy administration died a quiet but troubling death.(18) These more aggressive responses not only tore away the reformist mask exposing the United States' blatantly militaristic face, but they created a moral vacuum which liberal and pro-democratic advocates could no longer fill. **The idealistic liberal vision of the 1960s was gone**.

The Empire's militaristic side was further exposed by two external acts of aggression which bracketed the post-Alliance period historically: the U.S. Marine invasion of the Dominican Republic in 1965 and the U.S. coordinated destabilization of the democratic government of Salvador Allende in 1973. As a result of these anti-popular interventions, one overt against Santo Domingo and the other covert against Santiago, everyone in the hemisphere now knew that the United States would not hesitate to destabilize any government where people engaged in a serious attempt to overthrow tyranny, even when such movements were led primarily by pro-democratic and non-Marxist-led forces, as in these two reformist revolutions.

While Washington used the excuse of a "communist threat" to justify both interventions, (President Johnson in the case of the Dominican Republic and President Nixon in the case of Chile), tens of thousands of non-Marxists, populists, pro-democratic and middle-class

Christians were now becoming aware that not only was U.S. equipment being employed to throttle their legitimate demands for justice, but that the North American system, after the dust had settled, fully backed the dictatorial regimes that replaced their non-extreme political alternatives; namely the neo-fascist governments of Joaquin Balaguer and Augusto Pinochet. Seeing this, they realized that their enemy was no longer the Trujillos, Batistas, Somozas and Pinochets *but the Empire itself!* As a result, thousands of middle-class Christians crossed the line from being liberal reformers to become advocates of national revolution.

Mounting repression and foreign intervention could not stop the rising popular demands for change as more and more labor, peasant, democratic and religious groups developed during this period (1965-1973). This forced Washington to re-evaluate its previous strategy of hemispheric control through sheer repression. A trip made by Nelson Rockefeller to Latin America in 1968 and his Report which followed became the basis for this reassessment including his stern warnings about liberation theology.(19) More importantly, the United States began pressing upon the military leaders of every country in Latin America (only the Spanish-speaking Caribbean was included in this process) a philosophy first developed in the United States in 1947 called "*the national security state*". What was unique about this philosophy of absolute and systemic control of society was that it was not directed against external enemies but against *internal foes, namely its own people*:

> *...thanks to its supposed imperative of national survival, geopolitics justifies and stimulates the foundation of absolute power. In actual practice, the absolute power of the Latin American states, is not intended to face other states, but rather, the people, the citizens who are to submit to and be involved in government programs.(20)*

In addition to the fascist potential of such a doctrine, this State Security philosophy was based upon the questionable analysis that any challenge to the old order (feudal oligarchies) or to the new state (military dictatorship) would be interpreted as a direct threat to the Empire. It was a blueprint for maintaining the imperial *status quo* throughout the hemisphere.

With the downfall of the Allende government in Chile — during which time liberation theology had taken a great leap forward in the continent, especially in the Southern Cone(21) — Christian analysts and theologians in South America were faced by a profound crisis: "What should they do when liberation is simultaneously necessary and impossible?", i.e, given the fascist repression of the Pinochet government and its absolute control over Chile after 1973. (22) As the Belgian theologian Jose Complin reflected, "The theology of liberation had entered a crisis because its subject matter — the Chilean experiment — had disappeared from the historical perspective, at least for the moment."(23) In light of this historical dead end (like the crucifixion), it is not surprising that prophetic voices from the progressive Catholic community in South America should begin to formulate **a biblical perspective of liberation based on captivity**. In 1975, Leonardo Boff wrote this from Brazil:

> *With the establishment of the military regimes in our countries of Latin America and in the face of totalitarianism and the ideology of national security, the tasks of liberation theology have changed. We now have to think and live from **within a situation of captivity**; we have to develop a true theology of captivity. This is not an alternative to the theology of liberation; it is a new phase of it from within and out of these oppressive regimes. Captivity constitutes the primary context within which we have to work and think liberationally.(24)*

This perspective was the product of their *experience with captivity*, it was not a theological formulation drawn from foreign ideology, such as Marxism. In fact, more than anything it reflected their realization that "development" and "reform" were merely sophisticated instruments and arguments employed by the U.S. to maintain and cloak the old domination.

Boff's words reflected the profound sobriety which had fallen upon South America after 1973, not only from the pain at the loss of thousands of their loved ones but from the realization that "liberation" would not be the kind of "cake-walk" the Hebrews had experienced in crossing the Red Sea in the case of the Exodus. Rather, it would require long years of Exile as refugees within America's Babylonian captivity. It would mean following a path which goes past the cross of Calvary. Yet, notwithstanding the hopelessness that permeated the Latin American religious community during the second half of the 1970s, God was already at work preparing for a new breakthrough in the ongoing divine-human liberating process. This time, greatly to their surprise, in "backward" Central America!

FOOTNOTES — CHAPTER 3

1   Julia Esquivel, *Threatened with Resurrection*, op.cita, p.89.

2   This theory was graphically depicted in a video "documentary" entitled "Attack on the Americas" prepared by Reagan supporters widely circulated in 1981, under the auspices of the American Security Council Foundation, Boston, Virginia.

3   Statement published in a San Jose, Costa Rica newspaper, made by an upper-class, light-skinned Costa Rican university student, op-ed, March, 1985.

4   In 1941, Franklin D. Roosevelt urged Winston Churchill to take England out of its colonial relations and into a more benign and less explosive neo-colonial model. cf EPICA, *Grenada: The Peaceful Revolution*, 1982, Washington, D.C., pp.31-32. Samuel Bemis *A Diplomatic History of the United States*, N.Y., Henry Holt & Co., pp. 863-864.

5   Xabier Gorostiaga, "Financial Analysis of the Canal Zone," *Panama: Sovereignty for a Land Divided*, EPICA, Washington, D.C., 1985, pp.187-89.

6   *NACLA*, "On the Border of War," Nov-Dec, 1981, New York, Steve Volk, p.5.

7   Philip Wheaton, *Inside Honduras*, EPICA, Washington, D.C., 1982, p.5.

8   Ibid., pp. 7-8.

9   Catherine Sunshine, *The Caribbean: Survival, Struggle & Sovereignty*, EPICA, 1986, pp.187-188.

10   *North/South Dialogue*, "An Analysis on Costa Rican Economy" by DEI, San Jose, Costa Rica, April, 1987, presented by Franz Hinkelammert, calculates the debt as approximately $4,000 per citizen, compared to approximately $1,500 per capita in Mexico.

11   Christic Institute, "The Secret Team" and its relations with the attempt against the life of Eden Pastora from the Hull ranch in Costa Rica, 1987, Washington, D.C.

12 ANN, *Central American Information Bulletin*, Mar.25, 1987, William Robinson,"Growing Anti-Contra Movement in Honduras," pp.6-7.

13 Luis Restrepo, "50 Violations of Treaty with Panama," *Frontera News*, Berkeley, CA, Feb.-Mar., 1988. See also: Philip Wheaton, "Perspectives on Panama: Reagan's Attacks on Noriega Cloak U.S. Goals for the Region," CISPES, *ALERT!*, May, 1988; plus, *The Militant*, July 17, 1987, "Behind Anti-Government Protests in Panama", by Ernest Herch.

14 Walter LaFeber, *Inevitable Revolutions*, WW Norton, New York, 1984, pp. 190-191.

15 The Alliance poured $20 billion into Latin America, no small sum for those days. While the economic incentives were welcomed by the elites, they vigorously opposed the social reform projects for the poor, creating great disillusionment. See: Frank & Wheaton, *Indian Guatemala: Path to Liberation*, EPICA, Washington, D.C., 1984, pp.38-39ff.

16 Hemispheric-wide police training began in the early 1960s under the auspices of the International Police Academy (IPA) based in the old car barns just beneath Georgetown University in Washington, D.C.

17 That the scorched-earth strategy of the Zacapa region was directed by the CIA was confirmed directly to Philip Wheaton by Luigi Eunaudi, a high-level State Department executive at a reception held in Berkeley, California in 1981.

18 Both the IPA police training and the "riot control" equipment of the 1960s was rationalized by Congress as not representing "military aid" but in fact both so escalated the power and efficiency of the police forces that they now became co-partners with the military in repressing the legitimate protests of the people.

19 U.S. Presidential Mission, *The Rockefeller Report on The Americas*, Quadrangle Books, Chicago, 1969, p.31.

20 Jose Complin, *The Church and the National Security State*, Orbis, Maryknoll, N.Y., 1979, p.70.

21 A continent-wide "Encounter of Christians for Socialism" was held in Santiago, Chile, in 1972.

22 The Pinochet regime murdered between 30,000 and 40,000 Chileans during its first two years in power.

23 Jose Complin, *The Church and the National Security State*, <u>ibid</u>, p.37.

24 Leonardo Boff, *Teologia Desde el Cautiverio*, Indo-American Press Services, Bogota, Colombia, 1975, p.23.

CHAPTER 4
THE WORD

Guatemalan mother and children worshipping in a church as part of the
Christian communities who worship under military repression or as part of the
Church in Exile, keeping the faith alive.

CHAPTER 4 THE WORD

I, the Lord, have spoken: the time is coming. I will act. I will not refrain nor pity nor relent. I will judge you for your conduct and for all that you have done. This is the very Word of the Lord God.

— Ez. 24:14

Moses went back to the Lord, and said, "Why, O Lord, hast thou brought misfortune on this people? And why didst thou ever send me? Since I first went to Pharaoh to speak in thy name he has heaped misfortune on thy people, and thou hast done nothing to rescue them." The Lord answered, "Now you shall see what I will do to Pharaoh. In the end, Pharaoh will let them go...

— Ex. 5:22-6:1

I summon heaven and earth to witness against you this day: I offer you the choice of life or death, blessing or curse. Choose life then and you and your descendents will live.

— Deut. 30:20

What does the Word of God say about these unjust realities which we have been considering: **exile, empire** and **captivity**? This is not a theoretical question. We ask it in response to the cry of the people in Central America today; in terms of their suffering unto death and search for new life; in terms of the continuing tragedy of the Nicaraguan, Salvadoran and Guatemalan peoples in their occupied homelands. This means we also have to ask what the Word of God says to the Empire and its leaders since the United States is responsible for much of the exploitation and repression in Central America today. When we apply the Word of God to these three realities, we are not seeking merely political answers, however, but an understanding about our call as a people of faith who are also citizens of the Empire.

To answer this question about the Word of God faithfully in terms of its biblical meaning, we have to affirm something often taken for granted or easily glossed over in the West...**that the Word of God is One Word**. Just as there is only one God, so there is only one Word of God. Not one Word for North America and another for Central America; (1) not a Jewish Word versus a Christian Word; not one Word for biblical times and another for our times...but the same Word, which we have had from the beginning:

Dear friends, I give you no new command. It is the old command which you have had from the beginning; this old

*command is the word which you have heard. And yet again,
I am giving you a new command— which is made true in him
and in you— because the darkness is passing and the true light
already shines.*

— *1 Jn. 2:7-8*

So, we must beware of impostors who speak dozens of different religious "truths" according to their own interpretations. We must beware of false prophets who, like the electronic evangelists, warn of an apocalypse while they are fleecing the people of their money. We must beware of sectarian, denominational, even "catholic" truths which won't allow themselves to be judged by the Word but use it for their own ends, as when the Pope makes pronouncements on Central America out of a strictly political agenda. The Word is not ours but it does have authority over us. Beware the Word then, for it speaks with power about the present Central American/United States crisis, judging both them and us.

But there is a discriminatory aspect to this one Word of God that is very disconcerting for many of us Christians & Jews in the West: it is above all **"Good News" for the Poor**, that is, it uniquely speaks in behalf of these impoverished, enslaved, imprisoned, captive and exiled peoples in the Third World. The relatively new Catholic concept about mission in Latin America — that the Church must make a "preferential option for the poor" — is not merely a sociological strategy because the great majority of the people are poor, but a theological recognition that the Word by its very nature is directed primarily to those suffering and oppressed, just as the Word first came to Hebrew slaves in Egyptian captivity and to Jesus' disciples as poor fishermen and to despised women marginalized from society. While it is theologically correct to include in this privileged poor majority those who are "poor in spirit" as part of its primary audience (as the Vatican argues), their inclusion must not be used to rationalize the fact that when the Bible says "poor and oppressed" it is speaking primarily in economic and class terms.

If the Word is one, then presumably it wouldn't make any difference where we plug into it, that is, which segment of Jewish or Christian scripture we might choose. Stated this way, however, many Christians would object, saying that the New Testament supercedes the "Old" Testament or Hebrew covenant because it announces the "Good News" that the Kingdom of God has come in the person of Jesus the Christ. Yet while we Christians talk about **incarnation** — that in Jesus God became flesh — in the West, this living Word has been very spiritualized, God's unity divided into two kingdoms, one of this earth and the other in heaven. While Jesus' Good News was clearly grounded in humanity and history, the Western Church split this one Word into a Greek dualism.(2) The end result is that its primary focus today has become **to save us from this world not to redeem this world**. Our focus in this reflection on the Hebrew prophets and Exilic experience is not only to understand the nature of the original covenant but to help us reincarnate the Gospel into the humanity and history of Central America today.

The question to be asked is why Western Christendom has so dichotomized and disincarnated the Word of God; what is the purpose behind this Hellenistic dualism, this spiritualizing of the Gospel? Very simply, because the Word represented a threat to the Powers challenging their dominion over the Peoples. The Word stands against the Western practice of rulers exploiting, states enslaving, the powerful holding captive and the empires exiling the poor, the people of God. By dividing the Word into a spiritualized and disincarnated promise, the marginalized and enslaved could have their Bible but its message wouldn't challenge the injustices of this world, only promise a kingdom which was "in heaven." The only difficulty with such an emasculation of the Word is that it then becomes **no longer "Good News" for this world**, but leaves human history hopeless, thereby denying the very liberating potential implied by the incarnation.

However, we cannot merely criticize those Western rulers and prelates who accommodated themselves to the State, nor can we only condemn those false prophets and cunning theologians who deceived and confused us theologically, for we ordinary Christians and Jews (at least here in America) went along with this dualistic message because the terrible command of God threatened our comfortable existence; it demanded that we change our "good life." More specifically, this wonderful Word has challenged today's American status quo which rationalizes the injustice in Central America. So we are, even as part of the faithful remnant, complicit with this justification of repression and continued captivity.

The question remains, how have we been able to both affirm the Word of God and justify what it opposes? How have we been able to both affirm the revelation and reject it at the same time? How does one both believe and deny the Word in the same breath? We do so by accepting the words while avoiding their prophetic intent; we love biblical ideas but hide from the divine encounter. As Jesus himself said:

Why do you not understand my language (lalia)? Because you cannot hear my Word (logos)!

— Jn. 8:43

Thus we talk about Jesus and use his words all the time, but when he comes, when the Word becomes incarnate in any time or place, we refuse to listen and reject its demand upon us.

The trick involves a kind of philosophical sleight-of-hand which has extremely important implications for us in relation to the crisis in Central America today. This philosophical manipulation is regularly referred to in the gospel and epistles of John...playing around with religious concepts while rejecting God's presence in our neighbor. The way this works, according to the Mexican theologian Jose Miranda, is that we use **concepts** to avoid encounter with the **"other"** and with the demand which that "other" makes upon us, i.e., the poor, oppressed and captives in Central America. We reduce our neighbor-in-need to an object-of-charity or turn his crisis into a category, calling him "exile," "undocumented" or "street person"...where as such we can deal with him. Jose Miranda explains:

> *Reduction to a concept is our most useful device for suppressing the otherness of the one who speaks to us, for enclosing ourselves in ourselves by use of categories that are not "other" but merely different beads from the same string of ourselves. The only time, according to John, that the Jews asked Jesus, "Who are you?" he answered, not with a predicate or an attribute, but "That I am speaking to you." He is the word as word.(3)*

Jesus as a category or attribute — called "prophet" or "good man" — was perfectly acceptable to his Jewish critics for that was a way of avoiding what he was saying. When the Word of God is spoken, it is not merely religious words or spiritual ideas, *but the other making demands upon us.* When the Pharisees realized that, they attacked him as a blasphemer (i.e., one who presumes to speak for God) because they could not face the truth he spoke nor the change he demanded. This is why the crisis in Central America is so important to us Americans today, because it is the truth about ourselves as North Americans; it is that "other" which we wish to avoid, namely, **that the crisis down there is caused by the status quo up here**! This is the truth, the incarnate Word, which we don't want to face.

Whenever this Word is actually spoken by a person who lives it clearly and publicly — a messenger of God like Mons. Oscar Romero to the oligarchic powers in El Salvador and the imperial powers in the United States — the system turns vicious. As the philosopher Frederick Nietzche once wrote: "In the presence of the hero everything turns into tragedy."(4) Why? Because he speaks the truth to a world which loves falsehood and deceives the people. As John said of Jesus, so we can say the same of Oscar Romero and of many other heros and heroines in Central America today who have given their lives:

> *The light has come into the world but men loved darkness more than the light, because their works are evil. For anyone who does evil hates the light and avoids it so that his works might not be denounced.*
>
> — *Jn. 3:19-20*

Yet in killing the hero and murdering the Word of life, the Powers necessarily reveal their own corrupt nature and through that revelation, we — as the faithful in these United States — are liberated from America's idolatry. In Jesus and through his Word, we have seen the truth and the truth has set us free.

The Word as Promise of Life To Those in Captivity

The Word of God is always a message of hope especially to those in captivity, to whom it offers the promise of liberation. The Word is *never* merely a word of comfort and consolation, as we see in the biblical history from which we all stem: the Hebrews' captivity in Egypt. If Yahweh had not acted in that oppressive situation to liberate but had only consoled and pastored the people, the Judeo-Christian tradition would have been little more today than a totem found in little Western shrines offering us vague promises about life after death, something any earthly deity could offer. But for the hopeless ones in Egypt, the fundamental question was a very pragmatic one: "Are you, God, going to act in history to liberate us?" God's answer is found in one of the quotes with which we opened this section:

> *I, the Lord, have spoken; the time is coming. I will act. I will not refrain nor pity nor relent. I will judge you for your conduct and for all that you have done. This is the very Word of the Lord your God.*
>
> — *Ez.24:14*

Remember that this prophetic word was spoken to the Jews while they were waiting in captivity, and it promises two things: that God will act in time; and that liberation and judgement are inextricably intertwined.

Many people think the idea of liberation came out of Latin America around 1968 A.D. whereas in reality it came out of Egypt around the year 1290 B.C., when Yahweh responded to the cry of the Hebrew people saying to Pharaoh "let my people go!"(5) Liberation is neither a concept nor a theology, but a promise and a process in history. The people in Latin America are not interested in the idea of liberation nor even in liberation theology per se, but **in being liberated from their captivity**. Nor is the word "captivity" a concept for it refers precisely to those economic, political and imperial structures which hold the peoples of Nicaragua, El Salvador and Guatemala captive today. Liberation means to free oneself from those structures in order to create new and better societies. Our redundancy here is because those of us in the North often play word games with these concepts whereas in Central America they stand very simply for the difference between life and death.

At the same time, God is not a magician nor are we puppets, so that the Holy Spirit has to work through us and in our historical processes, and because it takes time for the Word's promise of liberation to become effective, to be revealed. Many Americans have little appreciation for such historical unfolding: we want to make things happen, to force history, to get results. We have taken the biblical mandate "to order nature" to an absurd extreme; for us Americans *doing* is stewardship gone amok. Like Jesus' mother who wanted him to change water into wine with no sense of the socio-political implications that act would set into motion; indeed, an act that would lead to his death. Life and history cannot be speeded up or slowed down to satisfy our immediate needs. The Hebrews wanted action on God's part.. "When are you going to deal with Pharaoh?" It reminds us of those who say with the same urgency: "We must CHANGE CONGRESS!" What we find in this prophetic word, however, is something more powerful: the promise of the inexorable workings of God in history: "The time is coming; I will act."

This symbolizes the kind of hope that many Third World peoples have today, something we Americans lack; a sense of historical process which often is not in our hands. They believe that the time of their liberation is at hand because the present is so impossible and because they are willing to accept *how* that liberation comes, even if that means with negative implications. We in the States don't want any fundamental change and if there is to be "some" change, we want to direct it, yet we resist any change for we assume it will be negative. Therefore, we in the North see the Word of God differently from those faithful in the South: they want the new to come with power while we don't want it to disturb our comfort. **So we are skeptical about the future whereas for them the future is laden with hope**.

The Word as Judgement & Confrontation of The Powers

The Word as promise in history, anticipated by so many millions in the Third World today, implies at the same time judgement of the old Orders and confrontation with the Empire. History is rife with this kind of challenge of the old by the new. We have seen this both coming and fulfilled in our own day. We have seen dictatorships like those of Marcos in the Philippines and Duvalier in Haiti fall; we have watched Blacks openly confront the evil apartheid system in South Africa and the people of South Korea rising up against their neo-fascist military elites. Everywhere we look in the world today, we witness the power of the people against old structures. As we watch on our TV screens, however, the form of these confrontations is very harsh, often violent... and yet it is filled with power and life. We Americans would prefer there could be peaceful transitions towards democracy and justice, but as the Bible shows us, the process of change seldom goes like that because the old Orders and those in power do not give up easily.

In the case of the Exodus, the Hebrew people wanted to be free from Pharaoh but the king of Egypt would not let them go. Indeed, when the demands first came from Moses to free the people of Israel, Pharaoh became so angry he increased their burdens and expanded their punishment — no straw for making bricks, increased lashings, higher production schedules, no time off for worship. So Moses returns to his dialogue with Yahweh complaining that since the Word of liberation was spoken things had gotten worse for the people. Moses apparently hoped for some kind of divine miracle outside the context of history, without any resistance; some easy word that would convince Pharaoh he was wrong, and then, an easy departure from Egypt.

> *Moses went back to the Lord, and said, 'Why, O Lord, hast thou brought misfortune on this people? And why didst thou ever send me? Since I first went to Pharaoh to speak in thy name he has heaped misfortune on thy people, and thou hast done nothing to rescue them.' The Lord answered, 'Now you shall see what I will do to Pharaoh. In the end, Pharaoh will let them go...'*
>
> — *Ex. 5:22 — 6:1*

Consider what has happened in Central America since 1980 when the liberating Word was spoken in Nicaragua, followed by that of the poor in El Salvador and the indians in Guatemala. Their suffering and punishment dramatically escalated thereafter, increasing a hundred-fold, nay, six-hundred fold! **The Treasury Police** in El Salvador have disappeared thousands; the **kaibiles** in Guatemala have sadistically dismembered thousands of Indians; the **contras** have invaded Nicaragua, raping, killing and kidnapping thousands. **Suffering before the liberating Word was spoken was nothing compared to what has happened since!** Between 1980 and 1988, the American Empire has escalated by astronomical proportions its funding, shipment of arms and military presence in the region. The United States has refused every request, dismissed every protest, multiplied every burden, justified every form of war against the peoples of Central America... all because they dared to speak the liberating Word. Yet today, God is saying to America as Yahweh said to the Egyptians: "Now you will see what I will do."

While the question about the proper form any confrontation with the Powers should take is the subject of endless debate here in the States, we must remember that the people in Central America are fighting for their very lives. For many liberals and pacifists, the answer to the question "how?" evokes many equivocal responses, whereas the Scriptures are absolutely clear that captivity is illegitimate and oppression intolerable in God's eyes. We see this during Jesus' ministry in the example of his rejection of those evil powers dominating a powerless victim, the Garazene demoniac. (6) Jesus and his disciples found this poor man tormented and screaming out, chained and throwing himself against the rocks and Jesus confronts the demons (for there were many of them) and demanded that they come out of him. The **liberator** would not tolerate for one moment a possession that was destroying that man's body and life. When we translate this example into societal terms in Central America as *land, people, work* and *hope*, it is clear that the present oligarchic exploitation and imperial domination of these people is just as intolerable to the Holy One of Israel today as that demonic possession of the Garazene was for Jesus. Just as Yahweh demanded of Pharaoh and Christ of the demons, so God is saying to the Somozas and Imperialists of our day, "Let my people go!"

The Word as our Choice between Blessing & Curse

The choice laid out to the Hebrew people of old in the Book of Deuteronomy — between life and death, blessing and curse — is the same one we are facing in the Americas today. We could define this choice as between two opposing ideologies: between the mandate of the Word of God and the siren songs of the Empire reflecting how our nation has become an idol.(7) It is very difficult for most Americans to see this alternative clearly, much less choose between them, because the Empire's propaganda is so sophisticated. Consider that in Central

America today an absolutely legitimate struggle by the people is going on to liberate themselves from national despots, yet the Empire labels this worthy effort a "communist threat." In order to justify its continued imperial domination over the region, the United States says that what it is doing is in "defense of democracy!" Such distortion of reality and sophisticated propaganda coupled with America's fear of communism, blinds and confuses us citizens as to the nature of our choice. This is why only by focusing on the victims of that oppression — the poor, captive and exiled — can we see what is really happening and thereby begin to challenge the idolatry; **only by focusing on people not on concepts and slogans can we see the Empire**.

To clarify this point — of the human versus the ideological — we refer to an experience some of us Christians had during the 1970s when we participated in a movement called Christians for Socialism (CFS). That movement arose out of a similar one by the same name which had flourished in South America between 1970 and 1973, especially in Chile during the Allende years.(8) Although individually most of us were involved in other solidarity movements or socially-progressive causes during those years, CFS as an organization was not.(9) CFS was based on the idea of socialism as a viable alternative to capitalism as described in the New Testament:

> *They had all things in common, and sold their possessions and goods and distributed them to all, as any had need.*
> — *Acts 2:44-45*

Yet it was difficult for us to convince many Americans at the time that CFS was a viable option for them. The authors of this book as former members of CFS now perceive our problem as arising from the fact that we were not collectively unified around any specific social project or any common struggle in solidarity with people for justice and liberation. Because we were mainly defending socialism **as a concept**, CFS died a quiet death around 1980.(10)

By contrast, the crisis which emerged during the 1980s in relation to Central America has clarified the choice facing us North Americans as between **the victims and the Empire**. We believe that the option laid out in Deuteronomy between life and death is precisely what is facing the people in the Isthmus today. The difference for us is that unlike the CFS experience, our choice now is not seen as an ideological question but as a historical-human option which is biblically-based, ultimately representing a political-theological decision: a choice between blessing and curse for this nation.

This tension between ideology and sociology in relation to our faith was constantly confronting Jesus in his debates with the rabbis and pharisees of his day. The classic example of such encounters involved the parable of the Good Samaritan in which an astute lawyer asked him, "What must I do to inherit eternal life?" The ultimate question! Jesus answered by telling this parable in which he challenges the lawyer to choose between the victim and the system. Jesus laid out the story of a man fallen among thieves, beaten and left half-dead along the road. The two most respected members of that Judaean society—a priest and a levite — passed by on the other side because they were too busy or "above" messing around with such tragic individuals. Then a Samaritan comes by, picks up the wounded man, anoints him with oil, takes him to an inn and pays the bill. To the lawyer's theoretical question "Who is my neighbor?" Jesus answers...the one you happen upon along your way...such as the Central American refugees who entered the United States during the early 1980s.

This parable doesn't clarify, however, something which every Jew in Jesus' day understood perfectly: that Samaritans were the most hated, despised and politically rejected caste of persons in all Palestine. For the Jews, the term "Samaritan" represented exactly what the label "Communist" means for us today, with all the same religious, political and social antipathies which this epithet carries for us. What Jesus was saying, in effect, is that God doesn't care about such labels but rather about what one does about those in trouble whom we find along our way. If we apply this metaphor to Palestine today, God would clearly be pleased with today's "Good Palestinian" who helps his Arab neighbor but not with those Jews who walk by on the other side. If we apply the metaphor to the United States, God would be pleased with the "Good Communist" who lays down his life for his neighbor who is suffering in Central America. Just as Jesus' parable was anathema to the pharisees in his day, so its application is anathema to the Israeli government today or to the high priests of the Institute on Religion & Democracy in our country.

Yet our problem is more complex and our choice more difficult today in relation to Central America. Our moral dilemma is that while we are prepared to respond to our fallen neighbor in terms of personal charity, the problem is a systemic one. Today, whole societies and indeed the whole region is strewn with the bodies of those who have been beaten by the system's thieves and left half-dead alongside the highways of El Salvador, Guatemala and Nicaragua. So we must respond not only to the specific and individual human tragedies facing us but to the causes behind them; we must question the systems, classes and empires which systematically create thieves and perpetuate injustice against the poor majorities. One American prophet who struggled with this very question was Martin Luther King. Jr. who, using this same Good Samaritan parable spoke at Riverside Church in New York City in 1968, saying:

> *A true revolution of values will soon cause us to question the fairness and justice of our past and present policies. On the one hand we are called to play the Good Samaritan on life's roadside; but that will only be an initial act. One day we must come to see that the whole Jericho Road must be transformed so that men and women will not be constantly beaten and robbed as they make their journey on life's highway.*
>
> *True compassion is more than to fling a coin at a beggar; it is not haphazard and superficial. It comes to see that an edifice which produces beggars needs restructuring.*
>
> *These are revolutionary times. All over the globe men are revolting against old systems of exploitation and oppression, and out of the wombs of a frail world new systems of justice and equality are being born... We in the West must support these revolutions.(11)*

The Word of God thus not only speaks to the issues of exile, empire and captivity but to us as complicit with these problems; we who often prefer to pass by on the other side. Many of us faithful would like to know "What must I do to inherit eternal life?" This Word which we thought we understood so well is challenging us today, not intellectually but pragmatically in terms of those who are refugees held captive and oppressed in Central America. That crisis represents an ultimate question for us and depending on how we choose may hang both our own salvation and the very destiny of America.

FOOTNOTES — CHAPTER 4

1   *North/South Dialogue*, EPICA, Washington, D.C., Summer, 1987, "Samaritan Servanthood" by Victorio Araya Guillen, from a talk to the World Council of Churches. Third World theologians and social analysts frequently speak of the "logic of the poor majorities" who live in the "South" or southern half of each continent in contrast to the affluent minorities. In one sense, the one Word of God is perceived differently by the rich as over against the poor; on the other hand for all poor and oppressed in the world, the singular message of the Word of God is perceived in almost precisely the same way regardless of continental, cultural and linguistic differences.

2   Greek dualism holds that there are two mutually antagonistic principles in the universe, one good and one evil; the doctrine that man has two natures, physical and spiritual.

3   Jose Miranda, *Being and the Messiah*, Orbis, Maryknoll, N.Y.. 1977, p.116.

4   Ibid., p.109.

5   "Moses probably lived during the XIX Dynasty of the Pharaohs in the Late Bronze Age (1353-1205 B.C.), during the rule of Rameses II," *The Holy Bible*, Westminster Press, Philadelphia, 1948, Concordance, p.18. The date 1968 is used to mark the beginning of liberation theology in the sense that the book *Theology of Liberation* was written by Gustavo Gutierrez in 1967 and published in 1968 by Orbis Press in English, Maryknoll, N.Y.

6   Mt.8:28-34; Mk.5:1-20; Lk.8:26-39

7   We usually call these "**ideological**" choices except that the philosophy of the United States has been so deified by civil religionists and religious advocates of the capitalist system (Institute on Religion & Democracy) that the term "opposing theologies" is more apt.

8   Some leaders of the Encounter of Christians for Socialism held in Santiago, Chile, in 1972, were instrumental in encouraging CFS to work on the "Theologies in the Americas" conferences held in Detroit in 1975 and 1980.

9   Many CFS members took their commitment to socialism very seriously, however, living austere lifestyles, receiving very small incomes, living in collective households and sharing their goods with the poor. In this sense, our criticism is not about the moral-personal integrity of CFS members, but in terms of the limitation of our socio-political approach to change, i.e., it was too ideological.

10 The most important aspect of CFS was its disciplined study of socialism and some of these study groups continued long after its institutional demise in 1980.

11 "A Time to Break Silence", *A Testimony of Hope: The Essential Writings of Martin Luther King, Jr.*, San Francisco, Harper & Row, 1986, pp.240-241.

PART 2
PRE-EXILIC EXPERIENCE:
GOD'S JUDGEMENT ON SELL-OUT OF
THE NATION TO THE EMPIRE

CHAPTER 5
POWER

Paolo Bosio

Capt. Michael Sheehan, a Green Beret officer walking in La Virtud, Honduras near the Salvadoran border in August, 1981, symbolizes the linkage between imperial and national military power.

CHAPTER 5 POWER

Of all the ingredients in the (American) policy mix... the element that gave body to it all was an awesome sense of power. By every index available, save that of men in arms, the United States was the strongest nation in the world.

— Stephen Ambrose

If you reverence and serve Yahweh and obey his voice and do not rebel against his order, and if both you and the king who rules over you follow Yahweh your God, all will be well. But if you do not obey the voice of Yahweh, if you rebel against his order, his hand will be against you and against your king.

— I Sam. 12:14-15

Concentration of power in the kings of Israel and abuse of that authority constitute both the "glory" and "sin" of ancient Israel and explain why the monarchy divided and the kingdoms eventually fell. In the process of creating the nation of Israel out of the twelve tribes (which took about two hundred years; from 1225 to 1025 B.C.), the Hebrews increasingly turned to conquest and war as the solution to their problems. This mode of creating a new nation of Israel necessarily required military leaders and from that the notion they had to have kings "like the other nations." Perhaps the legitimate symbol of nation formation — little David courageously standing up to the giant Goliath — was overshadowed by the idea that power was more important than faith. Thus the monarchy and the kingdoms came to be based far more on might than on the precepts of the original covenant with God coming out of Egyptian slavery.

In a similar way, the expansion of America westward and its consolidation of the northern continent into the nation we call the United States was increasingly dominated by notions of power and war, often contradicting the precepts of the Constitution. Our wars against the Indians and the slaughter and decimation of their tribes plus our wars against Mexico and the usurpation of approximately one-half of its territory are proof that aggrandizement through military might often dominated the thinking of America's leaders, not justice or the territorial integrity of other societies. While historians may question the motives of the minority parties in these disputes, their fundamental claim of right to the land — defended by both the Indians and the Mexicans, (predating by centuries the claims of the Gringos) — made no difference. Might made right in those early years of continental expansion and empire-building.

In allowing ends to justify the means, by operating out of fear and prejudice, by handing more and more power over to kings and presidents, the original ideals upon which Israel and the United States are supposedly based were compromised to power motivations. While the Jewish Covenant and America's Constitution were preserved and employed internally (domestically) in running the new Republics, an undermining of those visions and moral precepts also went on, **especially when it came to dealing with foreign peoples and lands — and especially in moments of crisis**. Indeed, military exploits and foreign wars were perceived of as reinforcing covenantal and constitutional principles whereas, in fact, they increasingly compromised those original ideals.

Consolidation & Corruption Of Power In The Jewish Monarchy

Pressure on the Hebrews to consolidate under a single leader in order to become a single nation arose out of the fear that the Philistines would conquer a disunited Israel. There was no threat from the "world" powers at that time, either from Assyria to the north or Egypt to the south. An imperial vacuum had developed because of divisions within the Egyptian empire and threats to Assyria from the Hittites, Phoenicians and Aramaeans...

> *the rise and establishment of the Davidic State, the first really Israelite constitution with independent power, took place in the shadow of this remarkable change in history of the Near East about 1000 B.C. (1)*

Pressure to unify the Hebrew tribes was not motivated, therefore, out of a search to create a nation based on the Exodus covenant or the principles of the Decalogue, but out of the fear of losing their newly-gained control over Caanan. Similarly, Saul's rise to power from a local warrior from the tribe of Benjamin to become the first king of Israel did not result from popular acclaim but from expediency bred of fear. They needed a military leader, anyone who could help them defeat the Philistines and fend off Israel's other numerous enemies.

The mode of kingly leadership which endured for the next 400 years, flowed directly from this external threat forcing them to adopt the model of government employed by other nations: **warrior kings who could fight their battles**. The fact that Yahweh opposed the adoption of kingly rule as contrary to the covenant made no difference. Even the warning of their prophets would not dissuade the Hebrews:

He will take the best of your fields, of your vineyards and olive
groves and give them to his officials. He will tithe your crops and
vineyards to provide for his eunuches and his officials. He will
take the best of your menservants and maidservants, of your
cattle and your donkeys, and make them work for him. He will
tithe your flocks, and you yourselves will become his slaves.
— *I Sam.8:14*

God's acquiescence to the people's insistence on having a warrior
king is curious. In spite of the warning by Samuel about the potential
abuse of power by such monarchs, — Yahweh accepts their demand
and the kingship model quickly becomes the standard. As far as we
know, no other form of government was tested by Israel until after the
fall of the kingdoms. It was as if once the decision was made, God
decided to allow the drift towards abuse of power to run its course even
though it might lead to disastrous consequences. God's only counter-
balancing was to raise up the prophets, who constantly warned the
people and challenged the kings about the consequences that would
befall Israel if they disobeyed the covenant:

If you reverence and serve Yahweh and obey his voice and do
not rebel against his order, and if both you and the king who
rules over you follow Yahweh your God, all will be well. But if
you do not obey the voice of Yahweh, if you rebel against his
order, his hand will be against you and against your king.
— *I Sam.12:14-15*

The terrible misunderstanding in all this was that the people of
Israel thought that the implications of disobedience and faithlessness
would be merely personal chastisement. While the moral character of
any leader of Israel was always an important factor for the prophets, it
was the nature of the kingship itself— the concentration of power in
one man and one office— that worried God and the prophets. In Saul's
case, for instance, he was basically an honest man who did not take
personal advantage of his office. When the Hebrews grumbled about
his leadership, Saul responded:

Whose ox have I taken, whose ass have I taken? Whom have I
wronged, whom have I oppressed? From whom have I taken a
bribe, to turn a blind eye? Tell me, and I will make restitution.
— *I Sam.12:3-4*

Personal morality wasn't the issue...power was! Under the threat of defeat and the corruption of power, Saul revealed his true weakness and insecurity. His main sin, in the eyes of the prophet Samuel, was his lack of trust in God's command. Faced by a possible Philistine victory, the king committed a small error which had tremendous theological implications for the future: he presented God a "burnt offering" — a living sacrifice — so Yahweh would deliver the Israelites out of the hands of their enemies (I Sam.13:9). That is, God's word was not sufficient for Saul, he attempted to compromise the covenant through a bribe in order to win a short-term victory. Not only was Saul defeated but he ultimately lost his throne to David. Too much power had been given to one man and it was that earthly power that would blind the eyes of many of Israel's leaders to the precepts of the Covenant.

Centralization of Power Under David in the Metropolis

David's great accomplishment as king of Israel was his unification of the monarchy: his ability to forge the Israelite tribes into a single people for the first time in their history. However, David had to proceed carefully given Hebrew tribal resistance to centralized authority and the antagonisms which had already begun to emerge. For this reason, David did not use troops from either the northern and southern regions — which would later become the kingdoms of Israel and Judah — but rather, he employed mercenaries.

> *Transference of rule over the northern tribes to David brought about a personal union; it did not establish a completely united state. Judah and Israel retained their independence, and also their own group consciousness. They merely accepted the sovereignty of David. (2)*

Because of these tensions, David used Jerusalem as a kind of symbolic capital of the union, located as it was geographically "between" Israel and Judah. It was a place where Hebrews from both north and south could come together as one people. Through Jerusalem, David was thus able to take this tentative tribal relationship and transform it into a united territorial entity with definite boundaries, something Saul had been unable to accomplish. In the process, the City of David became a kind of "international" city which belonged to neither Israel or Judah and indeed which was somewhat alien to the new state. (3)

This meant, of course, that Jerusalem became a center of power and wealth in contrast to the rest of the monarchy. In addition to state offices which were part of the king's entourage, ministries of government were created which had nothing to do with ordering or coordinating the operation of the tribes. David also made Jerusalem the center of Jewish religion, not only as the place for the Ark of the Covenant (2 Sam.6:5) but as the place where he reigned as priest-king. Within this ambience, David gradually developed an imperial ideology with talk of "dynastic promise" and "divine succession."(4) Such royal presumption was obviously anathema to God.

Even more serious, in time, was the fact that wealth and power were increasingly concentrated in Jerusalem by contrast to the impoverishment of the countryside and the weakening of the tribes, thus creating a metropolitan power center. As time went on, this gradually turned Israel into a *class society* marked by metropolitan affluence versus rural poverty, contradicting the vision of social equality and neighbor-justice projected on Mount Horeb. Even where rules of justice were set up to counter human abuse, such as in the Levitical *jubilee* — which called for wiping out debts and returning lands every fifty years (Lev.25:8:17) — such visionary ethics were seldom put into practice. The class structures created out of the demands of the court and David's ego would not admit to correction nor allow any fundamental change. Thus the glory of the royal House of David, which has inspired poets and historians, implied increasing impoverishment and ignominy for the poor.

Slavery & Sin Under Solomon

We find in King Solomon yet another example of the abuse of power in the monarchy, in this case the attempt to glorify and preserve a kingdom that had begun to crumble from within. History has so romanticized Solomon's building of the Temple that it glosses his primary goal of maintaining power, an attribute that led directly to the break-up of the monarchy. Unquestionably, Solomon's greatest feat was building the Temple, but though it was dedicated to the glory of God its real intent was to enhance the majesty of his reign and increase the ostentatiousness of Jerusalem as a royal city. The enormous cost of its construction not only drained the treasury and forced the king to impose crippling taxes upon the people of Israel, it also necessitated the enlistment of forced labor. We read: "King Solomon raised a forced levy from the whole of Israel amounting to thirty thousand men" (1 Kings 5:13). In another part, it says that the laborers were prisoners from Israel's spoils of war against the Amorites, Hittites, Perizzites and Jebusites,

*that is their descendants who survived in the land, wherever the
Israelites had been unable to annihilate — were employed by
Solomon as perpetual forced labor, as they still are. But Solo-
mon put none of the Israelites to forced labor.*
— *I Kings 9:20-22*

This suggests that the Jewish leaders assumed it was all right to enslave
others while it was an abomination to the Jews themselves. Some
authors, think, however, that the first citation (I Kgs.5:13) and its word
"*the whole of Israel*" refers to the "inhabitants of the northern state,
excluding Judah",(5) i.e., *that Israelites were also enslaved.* This would
explain Israel's deep antagonism for Judah which led in time to their
separation from the monarchy under Jeroboam (I Kgs.12:3-4).

Furthermore, Solomon did not maintain the monarchy intact
through military exploits as David had done, but through the acquisi-
tion of foreign wives. In order to keep peace with his neighbors, the
king married the daughters of neighboring non-Jewish kings, making
them queens of Israel, paying a hefty dowry in each case, a practice
called "harem diplomacy!" Such peace was bought at a very high moral
price since each queen brought with her to Jerusalem her own deity and
then pressured Solomon to build an altar or "high place" to her god. This
pantheon of divinities, located on the Mount of Olives, not only
introduced idol-worship into the life of Israel but may have led to the
practice of human sacrifice.(6) Clearly, there is a close relationship
between *using forced labor* to build the Temple and *offering human
sacrifice within it!*

In spite of trying to glorify God and maintain the monarchy united,
Solomon's methods flew in the face of God's law and justly merited the
judgement which followed: the division of the House of David soon
after his death. The drift towards power and glory led to a rejection of
the very Covenant which the Temple was supposed to exalt.

As a result of these sins by the three great kings of the Monarchy
— Saul, David and Solomon — their example of the abuse of power
was passed on to the subsequent kings of Israel and Judah and was
practiced by most of them. While space does not allow us to trace all
these connections, a classic story of the abuse of kingly authority serves
as an example. The famous story of Naboth's vineyard is useful for our
purpose since it parallels precisely the thousands of examples of the
expropriation of lands from their rightful owners by the oligarchs,
dictators and even the Church in Latin America. We review the history
of Naboth's injustice in terms of the key phrases which point to final
judgement:

Greed vs.	**King Abab** :	*Give me your vineyard for silver.*
Tribal Law	**Naboth** :	*I cannot, it is my family's ancestral land.*
Indulgence & Deceit	**Jezebel** :	*Take heart, I will give you Naboth's vineyard as a gift.*
	to Elders :	*At the feast, have two scoundrels charge Naboth with cursing God and the king, and so, kill him.*
Murder & Possession	**Elders** :	*Tell Jezebel that Naboth has been stoned to death.*
	Jezebel :	*Get up, Ahab. Take possession of the vineyard; rejoice!*
Judgement	**Elijah** :	*Because you two have done evil in God's sight, I will destroy the house of Ahab.* — I Kgs.21

Consolidation of Power in the Imperial Presidency

The issues which dominated the formation of the Israelite monarchy — fear, expediency and the corruption of power — find their counterparts in the expanding power of the U.S. presidency between 1945 and 1948 A.D. While the circumstances of ancient Israel were vastly different, the substance of these issues, leading to the consolidation of power in the executive branch of the United States are frighteningly similar:

> *Of all the ingredients in the (American) policy mix...the element that gave body to it all was an awesome sense of power. By every index available, save that of men in arms, the United States was the strongest nation in the world... The West saw Poland in reverse, as the outpost of European civilization holding back the hordes of Asians ready to overrun the Continent. This great fear, a constant in European history, was heightened in 1945 because of the vacuum in Germany and because of the Red Army, by then incomparably the strongest power in all Europe. (7)*

We mark this shift in the power of the American presidency as beginning in 1944, not because of the death of Roosevelt that year but through the tremendous escalation in the power and prominence of the

United States at that point in time. As we have noted, America became an imperial power in 1898 in terms of its expansion into the Caribbean and Pacific, but domestic reality did not match up to this bold international thrust for many years to come. Between the two World Wars, America's economic power was still trying to catch up to that of Europe; politically, the American people remained isolationist until 1941; and the presidency still operated under clear checks and balances. While it is true that Franklin D. Roosevelt strained these limits — by reason of the crisis of the depression — both his perspective of the office and that of the American people remained predominantly circumscribed by Congress and the Courts.

A dramatic change in this perspective occurred when Harry Truman assumed the presidency, reflecting the rapidly escalating power of the United States relative to both its allies and enemies. Objectively, this change flowed from the shift in the balance of power worldwide as a result of three factors: the rapid growth of U. S. industry during the war years, the absence of any infrastructural damage to continental USA, and the total devastation and impoverishment of Europe, Russia and Japan. This meant that by 1944, the United States was the #1 power in the world as well as in the West.

America's leaders, especially its financial decision-makers, recognized this change in power dynamics at least a year before the war was over, reflected by the Bretton Woods economic conference held in 1944, establishing the dollar as the world's standard by which all other currency would be measured, including gold. They also set up there the World Bank which would help develop (reconstruct) the Western world and the International Monetary Fund (IMF), which would regulate (control) all Western economies thereafter, according to our criteria and on our terms. To be sure, the United States sought allied support in this project, but basically *our allies had to go along* because of the devastation to their countries. Structurally, the United States was emerging as a superpower — before most Americans realized it and, more importantly, months before the atomic bomb was exploded!

It must be emphasized that Russia was not a superpower at the time: it did not have the atom bomb; its cities and industries had been devastated; and it was economically demolished. Nonetheless, Russia was seen by Truman as the great enemy, partly due to Soviet moves into Eastern Europe and equally because it was a communist state... **but certainly not because Russia was a threat to the United States**. Nonetheless, the new president made an ideological shift overnight in terms of how America perceived this new enemy. Notwithstanding the absolute ruthlessness of Nazi Germany, Truman began to focus on the Soviet Union as America's principal foe.

> *Roosevelt felt that post-war collaboration (with the Soviet Union) was possible and that it could be achieved through the United Nations. To get Stalin's cooperation, Roosevelt was willing to overlook much...Truman brushed that aside..."from the eminence of eleven days in power Harry Truman made his decision to lay down the law to an ally which had contributed more in blood and agony to the common cause than we had... the basis for the Cold War was laid on 23 April (1945) in the scourging which Truman administered to Molotov, giving notice that in areas of the most crucial concern to Russia our wishes must be obeyed."(8)*

Arrogance In The Imperial Presidency: Truman, Johnson & Reagan

Like the relatively unknown Saul, "little" Harry Truman was suddenly thrust into the limelight in 1944 after the death of his "giant" predecessor Franklin D. Roosevelt. Known as a scrapper from Missouri as Saul had been a fighter from the tribe of Benjamin, Truman suddenly had to deal with enormous power and make monumental decisions. He became president at that moment during WW II when the United States had become the king-pin of the allied war effort. This meant Truman was sitting down with such notables as Winston Churchill and Joseph Stalin to decide the fate of the world. While like King Saul, Truman was personally an honest man, when he had to deal with powerful enemies and fearful issues, he tended like Saul to be guided by impetuousness and prejudice, fear and insecurity. In his first major decision — how to end the war against Japan — Truman responded out of his new sense of power and his prejudice against the "yellow hordes". Expediency played a large role in his decisions to press the Soviet Union to declare war on Japan and to order the U.S. Air Force to drop the atom bomb on the island in order to hasten the defeat of Hirohito's empire.

The atom bomb as a military weapon was conveniently perfected at the very moment the United States was emerging as a superpower, and thereafter it became our symbol of power, America's awesome "tower of Babel".(9) The incredible potency of the bomb represented almost unlimited technological and political possibilities, creating a corresponding escalation in our national ego. In spite of the warnings of caution which he received from his scientific and military advisers, Truman acted precipitously, deciding to drop the bombs not on some depopulated section of Japanese countryside but on the very heart of the huge industrial cities of Hiroshima and Nagasaki, so that Tokyo would "get the message". With almost complete indifference to the human suffering his decision would cause, the president quickly — in the space of a few moments — justified the death by burning of 100,000 Japanese, arguing that it would protect the lives of many American boys and shorten the war. The bomb represented Truman's "burnt offering" to the god of war in which the Japanese people would be the sacrificial victim.

After the war and because of the bomb, the American people and the U.S. Congress almost unconsciously conceded more and more power to the presidency, just as the Israelites had conceded more and more power to Saul and David out of their fear of the Philistines and exigencies of the moment. As a result, there developed a new phenomenon in the United States ... **the imperial presidency**. From that point on the power of the U.S. presidency escalated rapidly with few restraints. Though civics classes would go on for decades teaching (as before) that there was in America a perfect balance between the executive, legislative and judicial branches of government, in fact the White House quickly outdistanced the others in resources and power. Furthermore, this escalation of executive power was aided and abetted by the secrecy and fear which surrounded the atom bomb and communism:

> *The ideology of anti-Communism and the technology of nuclear weapons have promoted the further development of a system of secrecy in the area of foreign affairs. Foreign policy elites believe it important to conceal lots of information about weaponry and foreign affairs from Soviet spies, which leads to concealing much of the information and more, from Congress and the public.(10)*

The imperial presidency would be expressed by two monumental policy decisions, both of which would have an enormous impact on U.S. foreign policy thereafter, and in our day create Central America's post-war crisis. The first evolved from our rapid escalation of antipathy towards the Soviet Union, a shift from being our ally in war to becoming our primary enemy in peacetime. From 1945 on, every attack on the *status quo* anywhere in the world, or any uprising by people against despotic leadership would be seen by the White House as a master-plot by the Kremlin to conquer the world.

> *Truman had made an incredible mental leap. Hitler was*
> *hardly in his grave; already Truman had substituted Stalin for*
> *Hitler as the madman who had to be stopped. The tone of the*
> *Cold War had been established.(11)*

This extreme interpretation became the centerpiece of the Truman Doctrine enunciated in his speech to a joint session of Congress on March 12, 1947, in which he justified sending aid to the Greek military to oppose their own people:

> *I believe that it must be the policy of the United States to support*
> *free peoples who are resisting attempted subjugation by armed*
> *minorities or by outside pressures.(12)*

In that single sentence, Truman outlined American foreign policy for the next twenty years, a policy which would have devastating effects upon the peoples of Central America and indeed upon the whole world.

The second decision, a corollary to the first, called for the United States to develop a national security system and corresponding philosophy. Without objection, the U.S. Congress concurred with the president (July, 1947) on creating a National Security Council (NSC) to handle "domestic security" and a Central Intelligence Agency (CIA) to handle overseas security threats, euphemistically described as "intelligence gathering." In fact, the activities of both agencies became aggressive in nature: they engaged in acts of sabotage, counterinsurgency, destabilization and even the assassination of foreign presidents whom they deemed a threat to U.S. interests. In this process, the United States began to replace Britain, France and other European allies as the nation with primary responsibility for the security of the Western world.(13) Thus the imperial presidency which had emerged out of America's expanded war power in 1944-45, now produced in turn structures which would long outlast Truman, **a self-conscious, aggressive and popularly supported imperial state**. Clearly, presidential power in the United States like monarchical power in ancient Israel had deeply corrupted the democratic goals of this society.

Johnson and the Idolatry of Anti-Communism

If in President Truman we saw the creation of an imperial presidency, in President Lyndon Johnson we see a warrior-type leader who takes America into its greatest imperial fiasco beneath the banner of anti-communism. Like King David, Johnson believed in the power of America's armed forces; he was convinced that if enough troops were sent to Vietnam, the United States could easily defeat the Empire's chief enemy, communism. Blinded by this ideology, he attempted to prevent the indigenous people and popular forces in Indochina from over-throwing the last vestiges of French colonialism. Mighty Goliath from America was attempting to defeat little David from Vietnam, Ho Chi Minh, countering a war of liberation on foreign soil. With the example of Korea behind us — stopping the communist hordes at a given geographic line — we sought to repeat that feat in Vietnam. It would end in disaster.

There are fascinating parallels between King David and President Johnson, such as the fact that Johnson like David had just succeeded in "uniting" the nation — north/south, black/white — around his Civil Rights legislation and yet at that very moment of domestic success he sets off on an imperial war that would tear the nation apart, dividing the country between the "hawks and the doves;" between those who believe in imperial power and those who don't. Resistance to this overseas enterprise, — both in verbal debates and street protests — marked the beginning of a process whereby the American people would challenge the myth that foreign policy was the exclusive terrain and responsibility of an imperial presidency. Increasingly, the American people forced a reluctant Congress to become involved in this Great Debate. The issue was not only the question of foreign policy in Vietnam but who would control the soul of the nation, a process called the battle for the "hearts and minds" of America.

The price which the imperial presidency was willing to pay to prove that its ideology of anti-communism was a legitimate cause was very high. In the first place, the government had to deceive the American public by claiming that we had been attacked in the Bay of Tonkin, that we were the victims instead of the aggressors; a lie which justified the sending of a half-million American troops to Vietnam. Second, it cost this society the lives of over 57,000 service personnel, plus an additional 100,000 Vietnam veterans who have committed suicide since returning to the States! (14) The price America had to pay for this imperial adventure almost never includes mention of the 1,500,000 Vietnamese, Laotians and Cambodians who lost their lives from our imperial aggression, because their deaths hardly affected American public opinion. Thirdly, America became deeply divided over this war, and the pain, confusion and alienation which ensued from it still rests heavily upon our collective consciousness. Just as the prophet Samuel had warned the Hebrews about the high price they would have to pay for following warrior kings so too the American people had to pay dearly for following an imperial presidency.

The same anti-communist policy and propaganda was exercised by this same imperial president in the case of the Dominican Republic. In April 1965, the legitimate representatives of the Dominican people — the followers of the democratically-elected Juan Bosch government — rose up to reclaim what had been stolen from them in the 1963 *coup d'etat*. In response, President Johnson ordered 22,000 U.S. Marines to invade the island and occupy the capital city of Santo Domingo. (15) He claimed he did so because of the threat of "communism" whereas that charge came directly to the U.S. ambassador from General Wessin y Wessin of the Dominican Air Force, claiming that the "communists" were taking over the country and that the situation was "lost." Knowing the Yankees would come running, the general's true goal was to maintain the military's long-standing control over the country as the old guard of the assassinated dictator, Rafael Trujillo. When President Johnson was pressed to prove that the April uprising was communist-led, the U.S. embassy admitted it could only find 57 Marxists in the whole country — like Heinz' 57 tomato varieties — representing a broad spectrum of reformist and progressive ideological positions. The same anti-communist rhetoric used in Vietnam was employed once again by the United States to crush a legitimate popular uprising in this continent because it might threaten our imperial hegemony.

Reagan's Assertion of America's Glorious Past

With a style totally different from that of Lyndon Johnson and King David, — both of whom were "warrior" types — Ronald Reagan's personality resembles much more that of King Solomon, in that he also sought to glorify and reassert the greatness of the American empire. Just as Solomon had faced small rebellions in Edom and Syria, so Reagan had his "little problems" in Grenada and Nicaragua, but in neither circumstance did they represent any real threat to their respective metropolises. In order to maintain the peace, Reagan used his own form of "harem diplomacy" by sending massive contributions to Ferdinand and Imelda Marcos, to Jean-Claude and Michel Duvalier, to Augusto and Maria Luisa Pinochet. Like Solomon, Ronald Reagan dreamed of rebuilding the glory of America with military prowess, corporate wealth and star wars. The wealthy wouldn't pay taxes, the nation's wealth would be poured into the Pentagon's budget and the United States would control the heavens — our Tower of Babel. As in the case of Solomon's reign, however, the price which the poor, workers, farmers and trade unionists would have to pay for all this grandeur and power would be enormous in terms of loss of jobs, homes, farms, and social services. This was no problem for Reagan, who, like Solomon, was willing to sacrifice people to the goals of ostentation and appearance.

This contradiction between appearance and reality required an all-important "fix" to make it work for the American people...executive deception and political lying. If America was going to be strong and counter communism while appearing to be "at peace", sophisticated cover-ups and misrepresentations would be required. Reagan's deception went on for seven years before the bubble burst with the Iran-Contragate scandal (1986-87). In order to fund the **contra** rebels in Honduras when the U.S. Congress had ordered the cut-off of such funding, the administration entered into a complex subterfuge directed by the National Security Council (NSC) to sell arms to Iran and divert its profits for covert activities in Central America. When the plan was exposed and the threat of Congressional hearings developed, a second sophisticated deception was organized to protect the imperial presidency from yet another scandal and possibly impeachment. In the process, high-level servants of the White House violated the law, lied to Congress, deceived the American people and pretended the president knew nothing about it. The justification for all this deceit was precisely the same arguments used by the imperial presidency under Harry Truman: **the ideology of evil communism** taking over the world; **the fear for the national security** of the United States.

In the debate which has arisen out of this Reagan scandal, the main question addressed by the media is whether the presidency was justified in doing what was clearly illegal or whether the Congress is able to reassert its authority to regain the traditional balance of powers. Some analysts claim that it is "pointless to argue about the separation of powers in *"foreign affairs"* on the basis of the Constitution or the Federalist Papers because the issue of foreign affairs "is a very undefined, collective process involving a whole milieu of factors like government structures, national life, international exigencies and diplomatic practices."(16) The substance of this argument is that foreign affairs which has heretofore been handled by the executive branch/imperial presidency continues to wield enormous power:

> *By and large, of course, these factors have favored an expansive role for the presidency. By virtue of his ability to act decisively and definitively as chief of the executive branch, the president has **unquestioned authority** to undertake a host of measures associated with the day-to-day conduct of diplomacy...(17)*

Such logic about pragmatic power begs the larger question about what really guides this nation: **power or principle**? According to the above analysts, the error of the Reagan White House is that he didn't go through channels. Following this line of reasoning, if the U.S. Congress and the American people agree with the Executive's unjust imperial policies, there would be no contradiction. If Ronald Reagan has Congressional permission to invade Grenada, destabilize Nicaragua, occupy Honduras, fund the **contras** and in the process murder thousands of Central Americans, then presumably, it is all right. Such logic may satisfy pro-imperialist lawyers but God is not mocked. While democracy remains structurally intact in America, the question remains: who really runs this country? Just as King Solomon glorified the covenant in the great Temple while he ran his affairs of state according to power politics, so too in the United States today. No one talks more glowingly about the Constitution than the president of the United States, but he runs the government on the basis of hard-nosed politics and blatant imperial policies which consistently disregard those very principles. Power has profoundly corrupted not only the imperial presidency but the American society as well, precisely because the people refuse to see how the Empire uses our hallowed laws to cover up its malevolent practices.

FOOTNOTES — CHAPTER 5

1   Siegfried Herrmann, *A History of Israel in Old Testament Times*, Fortress Press, Philadelphia, PA., p.159.

2   Ibid., p.153.

3   Ibid., p.160.

4   Ibid., pp.162-163.

5   Ibid., p.177.

6   Cf. 1 Kings 11:7-11.

7   Stephen E. Ambrose, *Rise to Globalism*, Penguin Books, Baltimore, MD, 1971.

8   Stephen Ambrose, op. cit., pp.111 and 113, plus on p.115 a quote from D.F. Fleming, *The Cold War And Its Origins, 1917-1960*, Doubleday, N.Y., 1961.

9   A symbol both **is** and to a degree **effectuates** that which it symbolizes.

10 Mark Tushnet, "The Constitution, Civil Liberties and the Courts," *Domestic Roots*, PACCA, Washington, D.C., 1987, p.18.

11 Stephen E. Ambrose, op. cit., p.126.

12 Ibid., p.150.

13 Ibid., p.148.

14 "Post-service Mortality Among Vietnam Veterans," Center for Disease Control, Vietnam Experience Study, *Journal of the American Medical Association*, February 13, 1987.
    Report on the Status of Vietnam *Veterans*, Veterans Administration, Washington, D.C., 1979.
    John Wilson, *Forgotten Warrior Project*, (Cleveland: Cleveland State University Press, 1978).

15 Juan Bosch won the election in December, 1982, by an overwhelming margin and then was overthrown in a coup in September, 1983, by reactionary forces including U.S. business interests.

16 Seymour Melman, "Swords into Plowshares," *Technology Review*, January, 1986, p.64.

17 *Washington Post*, August 11, 1987, Jonathan Hecht and Alex Papachristou, "Foreign Policy and the 'Imperial' Congress," p.A-15.

CHAPTER 6
CLASS

Struggle by the Base Christian Communities (CEBs) to hold communities together against class pressures of exploitation, injustice, idolatry of property and materialism.

CHAPTER 6 CLASS

*Shame on you who live at ease in Zion, and you, untroubled
on the hill of Samaria...you who thrust the evil day aside and
make haste to establish violence.*

—*Amos 6:1 and 3*

*... out of love of Christ and of the Honduran poor. Just as Jesus
declassed himself and freely chose to become a man to incarnate himself as one of the class of poor and humble men.*

—*Guadalupe Carney*

Anyone who has ever visited Central America — with its extremes
of rich minorities and impoverished majorities — knows that the
fundamental threat to peace and stability in the region **is not communism but class injustice**. Indeed, one of the main motivations behind
anti-communist propaganda is to divert our attention away from this
fundamental societal sin. Similarly, the longer one studies Isthmian
history, the clearer it becomes that these endemic class injustices are
intimately linked to the influence of imperialism. While in some places
the two entities — Class and Empire — were initially separate forces,
one domestic and the other foreign, as time went on they became more
and more inter-linked by imperial pressure, national collaboration and
the common motivation of profit. Because of the human suffering
which such class injustice creates, the biblical promise of a just
Kingdom represents a direct "ideological" challenge to both of these
structures and the illicit marriage between oligarchs and imperialists.

Our reflection on class is not based, however, on any particular
political ideology, including Marxism. While we openly acknowledge
our indebtedness to Marx's analysis of class and recognize that it
provides important (though not definitive) insight into Central American class reality, still we do not base our analysis on Marx. While it is
true that some of the leaders of today's liberation movement in the
region are Marxists, it is also true that their philosophy of revolution is
also home-grown and based on personal experience with class
conditions in their own countries. In our case, however, we base our
thoughts of class on the pre-Exilic prophets whose analyses pre-date
Marx by 2,500 years. In this light, we challenge those American
Christians and Jews who may have heretofore rejected the importance
of class relations and conflict for being unfaithful to Holy Scripture.

In the following parallels between Judah & Israel on the one hand
and Honduras & El Salvador on the other, we have chosen two prophets
to help us clarify the social, political and theological implications of
class found in antiquity and today. The first is Amos, that prophet most

intimately associated with the poor in Hebrew scriptures who challenged the king of Israel on their behalf. The second is Guadalupe Carney, a priest-prophet from the United States who became a Honduran citizen and over the years became the most respected and beloved missioner of the poor peasantry in that impoverished country. Both are unique in the same way: though working with the poor as their servants, each had an absolutely clear understanding of class while remaining deeply religious men of God.

Israel's Prosperity & Amos' Condemnation of Class Injustice

During the period from 785 to 745 B.C., relations between the kingdoms of Israel and Judah improved somewhat leading to temporary prosperity which biblical historians have called an "Indian Summer" of good times before the harsh winter of Assyrian domination would once again descend upon Palestine. (1) While both kingdoms were still under obligation to pay tribute to Assyria, their relative freedom from direct pressures allowed them to develop their own resources, expand trade and modernize their chief cities. Israel was by far the wealthier of the two nations and its capital city of Samaria grew in splendor with houses of hewn stone in the hill-country overlooking the capital which symbolized their affluence. This new wealth — experienced by an upcoming business class as well as the traditional elites — was a pipe dream for the poor masses. In spite of this burst of prosperity, the urban poor were crushed by taxes and rising prices at the marketplace while peasants and sheepherders had their land, crops and livestock stolen from them or purchased at a price which threatened their very survival:

> *Under Jeraboam II, the northern kingdom of Israel had won a great victory over the forces of Damascus (2 Kgs.14:28) and had extended their borders both north and east. As a result, Israel now controlled the caravan routes of Damascus and Arabia. A class of wealthy traders had grown up and gained increasing mastery over the country's life. While commerce had brought with it material advantage, it also fostered many of the evils attendant upon such prosperity. **The sharpening distinctions between the rich and the poor**, unscrupulous business practices on the part of merchants and idolatry of all kinds became common in the social life of Israel.(2)*

Two primary aspects of these class relations in ancient Palestine had to do with *land* and the *market*, that is, the powerful taking control of the land — buying or stealing it from its legitimate owners — and, unscrupulous merchants cheating the poor through unjust transactions, false weights and sleazy merchandise. These injustices were the primary concerns of the prophet Amos just as they are the fundamental issues facing most of the poor in Central America today.

For the Hebrews, land had traditionally been seen as belonging to God and was viewed as a gift from Yahweh to be faithfully worked by a given family but never sold because it is not "private" property but part of God's patrimony (the whole earth)! This theological premise began to change with the monarchy when new lands acquired through conquest were automatically claimed by the king and designated "royal domains."(3) These state lands, administered by court officials and maintained by hired laborers, were often located alongside of inherited land held by free Israelites. When the kingdoms divided and the kings became more and more unscrupulous — as in the case of Naboth's vineyard — they pressured the owners to sell their land or simply took it from them by force:

> it was only natural that there should be resentment among those who still held to the early Israelite beliefs, which were largely stamped by the development of tribal order. The prophets also became spokesmen of these groups. They took the side of the small people who had lost their defenses, who were at the mercy of the "apparatus" of the state and who could not cope with it. Thus the upper classes, including the state priesthood and, at least in the northern state, even the monarchy, became the butt of prophetic criticism. (4)

We can therefore draw a close parallel between those ancient elites — kings, nobles and priests — who obtained land from the small landowners or poor squatters in Israel through coercion, and, the dictators, oligarchs and Catholic hierarchy who have obtained land through coercion in Latin America for centuries. This is why Amos condemned the "whole house of Israel" because he knew that to rob a man of his land was to condemn him to servitude (slavery) and his family to poverty and often death. Elitist class relations represent more than personal injustice, and thus explain why the prophets warned of God's judgement against the whole system:

> Assemble on the hills of Samaria,
> look at the tumult seething among the people
> and at the oppression in her midst;

what do they care for honesty
who hoard in their palaces the gains of crime and violence?

Therefore these are the words of the Lord God...
An enemy shall surround the land;
your stronghold shall be thrown down
and your palaces sacked.

— *Amos.3:9-11*

Amos' other focus dealt with the class category we call the "middle class" — that is, "middle" in Third World terms (i.e., the 5-15% minority that is closely linked to the ruling class in Latin America), those who take advantage of the poor majorities through deceptive deals, legalistic contracts and shoddy merchandise. Most businessmen in Latin America as in ancient Israel, own little land nor were they in positions of political power, but they used the market system to make a nice life for themselves by exploiting the poor. Together with the rich and powerful, they dominated society and keep the poor down and marginalized. For them, like the modern businessmen in Central America and the United States, **profit is the purpose of everything** and its negative effects upon the poor are not their concern:

Listen to this, you who grind the destitute and plunder the humble,
> *you who say, "When will the new moon be over so that we can sell corn?*
When will the sabbath be past so we may open our wheat again,
> *giving short measure in the bushel and overweight in the silver,*
tilting the scales fraudulently, and selling the dust of the wheat,
> *that we may buy the poor for silver and the destitute for a pair of shoes?"*
The Lord has sworn by the pride of Jacob: I will never forget any of their doings.

— *Amos 8:4-7*

Into this situation of class injustice, the prophet Amos suddenly appeared in Israel around 750 B.C., having been called by God to leave his homeland in the village of Tekoa south of Jerusalem to go prophesy against the kingdom in the north. The prophet's strong critique of social injustice and religious hypocrisy went further and deeper than specific personal sins; it probed the whole societal system and ultimately the illegitimacy of the king himself. Understandably, Jeroboam II was not pleased with this "nobody" from Judah who was ordered back to where he came from:

> *Be off, you seer! Off with you to Judah! You can earn your living*
> *and do your prophesying there. But never prophesy again in*
> *Bethel, for this is the king's sanctuary, a royal place...*
> — *Amos 7:12-13*

Amos' importance to our study of today's Central American crisis cannot be underestimated precisely because he was **a poor peasant with a class analysis**. The first in a long line of prophets, Amos saw clearly the same fundamental class issues which plague most of Latin America and the Caribbean today: the rich and powerful robbing the peasants and Indians of their land; middle-class merchants aligning themselves with the power structure to make a better profit; and, puppet governments taxing and oppressing the people because of their sell-out to the demands of the Empire. Amos' condemnation of these abuses of the poor was not defined as a generic social malady, as in the New Testament gloss "you always have the poor with you" but as a *class problem.* Indeed, an injustice which begins with the kings at the apex of society and filters down through the nobles and priests, negatively impacting the struggling worker and peasant majorities.

Amos' unique criterion for measuring such class injustice serves us admirably today as a biblical evaluation of the antagonistic positions between the rich and poor: between Israel and Judah, between a poor dependent nation in Central America and the Empire: **the plumb-line of God**! Every individual, every government, every system is to be measured — according to Amos — by the same awesome criteria, whether or not they are *"straight"* in terms of honesty, justice and freedom. No religious excuses, no political justifications, no personal expediency were acceptable to him in avoiding this divine measuring stick. Nor was his only an *objective* evaluation of sin; it also measured the *subjective* motivation behind the deed, what the Bible calls "hardness of heart"...

> *This was what the Lord showed me: there was a man standing*
> *by a wall with a plumb-line in his hand. The Lord said to me,*
> *"What do you see, Amos?" "A plumb-line," I replied, and the*
> *Lord said, "I am setting a plumb-line **to the heart of my**
> ***people Israel**; (never again will I pass by) the hill-shrines of*

Isaac shall be desolated and the sanctuaries of Israel laid waste."

> — *Amos 7:7-9*
> *(emphasis added)*

This use of a divine criteria by which to judge the nations also means that God vigorously rejected the Jewish custom of scapegoating other nations and condemning one's enemies as a means of justifying one's own misdeeds. Thus the U.S. practice of rationalizing its military strategy in Central America and justifying the deaths of thousands of people because of the threat of "communism" is unacceptable to Amos. For him, all nations fall under the same criterion, the plumb-line of Yahweh:

> *Are you not like the Ethiopians to Me,*
> *O people of Israel? says the Lord.*
> *Did I not bring you up Israel from the land of Egypt,*
> *And the Philistines from Caphtor and the Syrians from Kir?*
> *Behold I, the Lord God*
> *have my eyes on **this sinful kingdom**,*
> *And I will wipe it off the face of the earth.*
> — *Amos 9:7-9*

It is obvious that such an extreme condemnation of a society because of its class injustices is both similar to aspects of Marxist analysis and yet goes far beyond it. This prophetic plumb-line can be held up to communist Russia as well as to capitalist America in behalf of truth and the people, and against any system and its elites. Thus we have in this criterion a basis for common agreement between Christians, Jews and other humanitarian advocates which moves us beyond the traditional polarization of communist/non-communist so that we can be faithful to our biblical calling while also being politically relevant and socially objective.

Guadalupe Carney's Condemnation of Class Injustice in Honduras

Honduras is a perfect example of the class issue in Central America, not only because it is the poorest country in the region but as a by-product of its complete dependence upon the North American banana companies. Here, we can see how the capitalist system uses the land and workers in Central America to make its profit and supply the

American people with a product (bananas) without any concern about how its presence reinforces class injustice locally.

Between 1906 and 1945, the banana complex — United Fruit, Standard Fruit and Chase Manhattan (Banco Atlantida) — represented 80% of the total GNP of the country.(5) After WW II and until 1980, four other companies joined the big three — Texaco, Mitsubishi, Cargill and Alberty Foods — which seven transnationals combined continued to represent 80% of Honduras' GNP. This massive foreign economic presence means that the upper classes there are a *dependent oligarchy*(6), that is, they depend on and serve the needs of those foreign corporations as their primary function. The Honduran military's acquiescence to the Pentagon's demand to move into that nation militarily in 1980 stems directly from this economic dependence.

In the late 1950's and for about a decade, a period of economic development and expansion occurred in Central America which affected the relations between Honduras and El Salvador. This involved new foreign corporate investment, middle class entrepreneurs who invested in cotton raising and cattle production, and a growing urban middle class sector which demanded modern improvements in major cities. As in Samaria, this also produced elegant housing projects on the hillsides overlooking the capital city but these elites could not avoid the sight of the poor masses living in squalid slums nearby. This period of temporary prosperity is thus comparable to the "Indian Summer" which occurred in ancient Israel and Judah, and like it, would be followed by the harsh winter of internecine warfare and direct incursion of U.S. troops which penetrated Honduras in the 1980's.

In Honduras, this temporary prosperity of the late 1950's under President Villeda Morales occurred even before the Alliance for Progress. His reform projects, including a new labor code, social security and proposals for a modest agrarian reform, led to the creation of the National Agrarian Institute (INA). In San Pedro Sula, Honduras' industrial center, both national and foreign entrepreneurs were busy expanding, building new plants, producing new jobs and creating a growing middle class in that region of the northern coast, near but separate from the banana companies. Out of the profits earned there, this new merchant industrial class began to expand into agriculture, particularly into production of cotton and cattle-raising.(7)

In El Salvador, the coffee oligarchy — initially cool to foreign investors — gradually opened up to the pressures of the Alliance and allowed new U.S. firms into the country. By the mid-1960's, this investment had produced some spectacular growth-rates in the Salvadoran economy, reaching a 12% expansion of the GNP during the years

1964 and 1965.(8) Accompanying this growth, an expanding middle-class demanded improvements in the capital city of San Salvador. Led by its new mayor, Jose Napoleon Duarte, many modernizing projects were introduced: street lighting, garbage pick-up, sewage disposal, new schools, shopping centers, etc... all to satisfy the demands of his middle class constituency.(9) This, in turn, resulted in the building of elegant houses in the hill country overlooking the capital city which again were unable to avoid the sight of the poor slums nearby.

Similar to the "Indian Summer" in ancient Israel and Judah, this prosperity of the 1960's in Honduras and El Salvador only intensified class injustices for the workers and peasants. The new industries exploited the workers paying extremely low wages (the primary reason the foreign companies investing there in the first place), while the cost of food, rents and taxes increased beyond the increased wages. In the countryside, it was even worse, with peasants driven off of squatter lands, repression of any organizing to demand their rights and better pay, and the buying up of fallow lands previously owned by the banana companies or oligarchic families who sold portions to these **nouveau riche** entrepreneurs.

In the impoverished Third World, the most important theological issue of the dialectic of oppression/liberation is land. Land which the rich use to make their profit (from export crops) means suffering and death for poor peasant families because that same soil is not producing basic grains for their survival. **Land is thus a symbol of either life or death; alienation or hope**. With land, the poor have their daily bread; without it, they face daily death.

Poor peasants in both countries suffered the most during this period of prosperity. While there was plenty of unused land in Honduras, the domination of the banana companies made the elites there even more jealous and aggressive about getting control of "undeveloped" land, so they began pushing the peasants off and vigorously opposed all popular organizing. In El Salvador, things were even worse for the peasants because of its huge population and limited land area. Following WW II and expanding rapidly in the 1960's because of the incursion of middle-sized landowners into rural El Salvador, thousands of **campesinos** were forced to cross the border into Honduras where there was relatively more land and into San Pedro Sula where the Salvadorans who had more skills often got jobs before their poorer Honduran counterparts. By the middle of the decade of the 60's, it is estimated that some 300,000 Salvadorans had migrated without papers into Honduras, of which some 220,000 were peasant farmers, many of them marrying Honduran women.(10) This only increased the pressures on the Honduran peasantry:

> *The peasants were trapped on four sides: their own lands disappeared... (because of) illegal expansion of large haciendas over peasant-tilled lands, the U.S. owned fruit companies controlled most of the remaining soil, few jobs existed in the towns, and the Salvadorans — squeezed out of their little country— streamed across into Honduras to compete for the little decent land that remained.(11)*

Into this situation, a modern prophet appeared in Honduras to work among the poor in the department of Progreso; a Jesuit priest by the name of James Carney, affectionately known as padre Guadalupe, or more simply, Lupe. Although a North American by birth, he identified so closely with the peasants of his parish in Yoro that he renounced his birthright and became a Honduran citizen. He had difficulty convincing officials at the American embassy in Tegucigalpa that he would voluntarily give up his American citizenship to become a Honduran! Lupe explained his reasons for doing so along class lines as he wrote in a letter to his Jesuit superiors:

> *...out of love of Christ and of the Honduran poor. Just as Jesus declassed himself and freely chose to become a man, to incarnate himself as **one of the class of poor and humble men**.(12)*

Like Amos, it was through his commitment to the poor that he became gradually politicized (*concientizado*) (13) and out of this awareness began to challenge first the landowners, then the fruit companies and finally the system as a whole.

During the 1960's, profound changes were taking place in Lupe's consciousness as he watched the brutal reaction of landowners and the fruit companies to peasant organizing. It was as if the moment they sought empowerment they became an "enemy" whereas if they were passive and conforming, they were "good Christians"; organized they became "communists". This awareness was reinforced by the North American banana companies as well. Regularly, padre Carney had to resist tempting offers from United Fruit: initially they offered free transportation which he sometimes accepted; later, the offer of religious centers and parochial lands was vigorously rejected. He warned his superiors not to compromise on the basis of the old church rationalization that ultimately such "religious space" could benefit the poor. Lupe told them.. "No Honduran will understand this and the masses of the poor will never forgive (us)."(14)

An explosive situation developed in the area of Progreso in 1966 in a place where padre Lupe was working called Guanchías, a section of land abandoned by the Tela Railroad years before when UFCO had closed part of its operation because of the Panama banana disease. By the mid-1960's, some 12,000 **campesinos** were living on idle Guanchias land, growing corn on subsistence plots. When the Tela RR stopped paying rent to the owners, they sold the land to a family named Echeverry which immediately began throwing the peasants squatting there off their property. Padre Guadalupe wrote a letter of protest to INA while also seeking church funds to set up a cooperative so that with their meager profits, peasant families could slowly save enough to buy up their small plots. Rejecting these alternatives, Echeverry...

> *ordered his men to take down the fences and plow up more than 85 acres of small pasture fields, not belonging to rich cattlemen, but to poor campesinos of the Village La 6 "... I personally saw, along with other witnesses, that many crops had been completely destroyed."(15)*

Lupe protested these actions to the Honduran military officer in charge of that area, Col. Melgar, who subsequently ordered padre Carney to stop meddling in agrarian matters because he was a foreigner and a priest (Lupe's request and papers to become a Honduran citizen were not yet approved), neither of whom were allowed "to take part in politics" according to the Honduran constitution. Like the reaction of the king of Israel to Amos, so Lupe as a prophet from a foreign land was warned not to challenge the system in Honduras and to return home. In 1968, he was physically removed from Honduras by the military for such meddling. After his fellow Jesuits in Yoro closed down their mission in protest over his expulsion, warning they wouldn't celebrate mass until padre Carney was allowed to return, the military acceded. The Jesuits' message read...

> *We are thousands of Christians who back up Padre Guadalupe in his tireless work as an apostle of Christ. We ask ourselves: Where are we going? Isn't this a Christian, democratic country? Why do they treat a minister of God with such barbarity, as if this were a communist country where they despise those who preach the doctrine of Christ?(16)*

In spite of such protests and this singular victory, ongoing class injustices continued and the indifference of the Honduran elites made reform virtually impossible. The rural class crises in both El Salvador and Honduras was reaching a critical stage that would soon erupt into open war between the two countries. The Empire, desperately searching for moderate solutions to these endemic problems, approved a $7.7 million grant from the Inter-American Development Bank for an agrarian reform project in Honduras to be administered by INA. But the lack of suitable land on which to carry out the reform — since neither the banana companies nor the Honduran elites were willing to give up any of their vast holdings — created a desperate situation. The Honduran government decided that the only solution was to expel all undocumented Salvadoran peasants from their minuscule plots and place Honduran peasants on them, calling that "reform"!

This forced expulsion began in early June, 1969 and the form of its execution was brutal. Thousands of Salvadoran men were beaten and driven out of their homes, husbands and wives forcibly separated, and many homes burned. The exodus of some 150,000 peasants back to El Salvador occurred during the first two weeks of June, coinciding with the regional soccer championship between Honduras and El Salvador created violence during those games over the expulsions which led to the conflict subsequently being called "the soccer war".(17) In understandable outrage at the manner of this forced emigration, the Salvadoran people condemned the Honduran government, while the ruling class there saw it as a chance to whip up patriotic feelings thus distracting the Salvadoran society from its own internal problems, principle among them the mounting peasant unrest and organizing. In retaliation, the Honduran government did the same thing on the other side of the border, condemning Salvadorans for their mistreatment of Hondurans at the soccer matches, and similarly whipping up patriotic emotions to cover over their class injustices.

With mounting antagonism on both sides, insults and threats flew back and forth across the border in the newspapers of each capital, finally culminating in a mutual declaration of war. As a result of the eight-day conflict in July, 3,000 persons died and 6,000 were wounded creating animosities that linger to this day: the war destroyed the Central American Common Market; it exacerbated the class contradictions in each country; it ruined many of the peasant coops which Lupe and other priests had so carefully nurtured over the years. In light of this tragedy, padre Lupe reflected,

The real causes of the war were, first of all, that both the Honduran and Salvadoran governments were corrupt military dictatorships that repressed the people and illicitly enriched themselves, and second, both peoples were rebelling against their governments with strikes and public demonstrations. The war solved this problem for both governments, because both peoples now had to back up their armed forces (i.e. in patriotic defense of the nation).(18)

Out of this war, Padre Lupe's understanding of class deepened during the 1970's. He saw it not merely as a problem of poverty in the countryside but as one of exploitation by the middle class in the cities through their control of the marketing system. In addition, he saw the complicity of power in the role of the military siding with the banana companies and the refusal of the Church to take sides...

The great majority of the bishops and priests still want to be on good terms with everyone, with the rich and with the poor, with the oppressed and with the oppressors. They want to avoid conflict, or class struggle; they do not want to choose one class against the other. That means that their option is for the status quo.(19)

The passion of Amos and Lupe for the poor arose out of their personal love for and commitment to the people, not out of some leftist ideology. Their messages and vision became radicalized because of the depth of their passion for the people whose lives were on the line. Justice/injustice wasn't a political thesis for either of them, but a social crisis... a matter of "life and death". Guadalupe Carney realized that the issue was not merely a matter of class injustice requiring reform but that it reflected a larger, more systemic evil that would — as it did in 1980 — erupt into open war or revolution. It was systemic sin which was provoking divine judgement upon an intolerable reality:

What does God think of class struggle, of having rich and poor classes, of some families eating better than others? Do you think God wants his children to live like that? Is that the way God made the world to be? Because some persons are more capable of earning money than others, does God therefore want them to have more than others? Well, I know that God doesn't want that, because that is unjust, it's sinful. The system of life in Honduras is very unjust, is very contrary to the will of God.(20)

Those in power in both ancient Israel and modern Honduras could not tolerate the words of Amos and Lupe because they enjoyed their privileges too much and had no intention of changing the system. At a particular moment in time, both of these prophets disappeared from sight, never to be seen again.(21) We know just enough about their lives and the forces and threats against them to be sure that they were murdered by those who could not tolerate the truth. Although they both "disappeared," their words and witness live on: the sheepherders in Palestine like the peasants in Honduras will never forget that in those years they were visited by true prophets, servants of God who preached the truth and lived according to the plumb line of justice.

FOOTNOTES — CHAPTER 6

1   Bailey & Kent, op.cita, p.184.

2   The Westminster Study Edition of *The Holy Bible* (King James Version), Westminster Press, Philadelphia, 1948, p.1292, emphasis added.

3   Siegfried Herrmann, op.cita, p.236.

4   Ibid, p.236.

5   NACLA, *Honduras: On the Border of War*, Nov.-Dec. 1981 by Steven Volk, pp. 3-5.

6   Ibid.

7   Walter LeFeber, *Inevitable Revolutions*, W.W.Norton & Co., New York, pp.177-180 and p. 182.

8   Ibid., p.174.

9   Armstrong & Shenk, *El Salvador: The Face of Revolution*, South End Press, Boston, p.51.

10   *EPICA Reports*, Washington, D. C., Sept. 1969, p.1.

11   Walter LeFeber, *Inevitable Revolutions,* ibid., p.182.

12   Padre Guadalupe Carney, *To be A Revolutionary*, Harper & Row, New York, 1985, p.318, emphasis added.

13   The word *concientizado* cannot be easily translated into English: it means coming to a social, political and collective consciousness of peoples' rights and self-empowerment.

14   Padre G. Carney, *To Be A Revolutionary*, ibid., p.176.

15   Ibid., p.226.

16   Ibid., p.249.

17   *EPICA Reports*, Washington, D.C., Sept. 1969.

18   P.G.Carney, ibid., p.261.

19   Ibid., pp.289-290.

20   Ibid., p. 308.

21   Padre James Carney disappeared in the Honduran jungle in September, 1983, at age 53. His family continues to actively search for him. Through a Honduran soldier who participated in his capture who has left the country, Padre Carney's family now knows that the Honduran military and U.S. officials interrogated him before he disappeared.

CHAPTER 7
HARLOTING

Photo of Brig. General Gustavo Alvarez, then head of the Honduran Armed Forces (1982-1984), taking orders from a U.S. Marine officer and thereafter from U.S. Ambassador John Negroponte as part of his sell-out to imperialism.

> *Go again and love a woman*
> *loved by another man, an adulteress*
> *and love her as I, the Lord, love the Israelites*
> *although they resort to other gods*
> *and love the raisin-cakes offered to their idols.*
> *—Hosea 3:1*

> *Right-wing repressive regimes' view their relationship to nation*
> *in a very macho, sexist, and male-dominating manner... By*
> *contrast, the vision of nationhood held by the Sandinistas*
> *implies looking for a real companion, a true wife, in their*
> *relationship with Nicaragua.*
> *—Philip Wheaton*

In the pre-Exilic prophets, the most serious national sin, after the abuse of kingly power and the exploitation of the poor by elites, is **harloting** — the selling of the nation as a whore to the empires. Traditionally in the West, we condemn dictatorship as the most extreme example of the abuse of nationhood while we fail to see imperialism as the most serious cause of systemic injustice for the nations of the Third World. The prophets emphasize the linkage between these two as fundamentally stemming from the sell-out on national patrimony by the elites because of their greed, their search for quicker and more abundant benefits through servicing the imperial powers beyond just exploiting their own people. Harloting also symbolizes the exploitative and coercive role of imperialism forcing the weaker powers to capitulate, selling themselves and prostituting their nations.

Harloting is thus the key link between domestic sin (adultery) and foreign sin (idolatry), the worship of foreign deities like the Baals versus the true worship of Yahweh. In this chapter, we will trace the parallels between Hosea with his prophecy against ancient Israel (Ephraim) for its sell-out to the Assyrian empire, and, the diatribes of a modern prophet, Pedro Joaquin Chamorro, against the sell-out of Nicaragua by the Somozas to the American empire. In both instances, these prophets were searching for a true nation (a *patria*) to be their loved one in contrast to the elites and kings who sell their nations to rich and powerful strangers as a harlot, compromising their patrimony for their own power and pleasure.

Israel's Harloting with Assyria & Hosea's Search for a True Lover

Unlike his **campesino** counterpart Amos, Hosea was a *middle-class prophet*, a family man from the city, a true patriot of the northern kingdom of Israel. He prophesied during the last two decades of Israel's existence (745 - 721 B.C.) during which time he painfully and angrily watched her disintegrate, her national integrity sold down the river by the greed of the rich and the self-interest of her kings. This sell-out involved financial dependence on and political subservience to the Assyrian empire by Israel's leaders, which would lead directly to her demise as a Jewish kingdom. Because Israel harloted with the empires, she would perish forever.

> *At Israel's sanctuary I have seen a horrible thing:*
> *there Ephraim played the harlot*
> >*and Israel defiled himself,*
> *And for you, too, Judah, comes a harvest of reckoning.*
> >>*— Hosea 6:10-11*

In the connubial imagery of Hosea, the prophet was ordered by God to take a harlot as his wife, to have children by a prostitute to symbolize Israel's unfaithfulness to Yahweh. In this living metaphor, Hosea is to remain faithful to his wife Gomer just as God would remain faithful to Israel despite her sin, indeed, both are to try and win back their lovers from their adulterous ways. The moral of this historical story is that if Israel will not be faithful to Yahweh she will fall as a nation; through unfaithfulness — national adultery & foreign idolatry — the covenant will be broken and she will be abandoned and lost forever.

According to some scholars, Gomer may have been a whore when Hosea married her, but the majority opinion is that she became a prostitute after bearing him children, reflecting the original purity of the marriage between the Hebrews and Yahweh in Egypt which broke down in Palestine when the Israelites went a-whoring after false gods.(1) Unique for that time in the history of male/female relations, the metaphor is not presented as pietistic moral judgement against female unchastity. Rather, in the prophecy, male chauvinism is condemned for this tragic state of affairs as the primary blame is placed upon *the men of Israel*:

> *Therefore your daughters play the wanton*
> >*and your sons' brides commit adultery.*
> *I will not punish your daughters for playing the wanton*
> >*nor your sons' brides for their adultery*
> *because **your men** resort to wanton women*
> >*and sacrifice with temple prostitutes.*
> >>*—Hosea 4:13-14*
> >>*(emphasis added)*

The real guilt lay not, however, with promiscuous men in general but with **the elite males** — the nobles, aristocrats, government officials and kings — who used Israel for their own avarice by pimping for her, selling her to Assyria for tribute. The final rape of Israel — the selling of her wealth to the empire — began in the year 745 B.C. when Menahem became king of Israel and Tiglath-pileser III reigned as king over Assyria.(2) In order to guarantee his throne for a decade (745-736 B.C.), Menahem agreed to pay an enormous tribute to the Assyrians, estimated at a thousand talents of silver, equivalent in our day to $30,000,000. In turn, the king taxed the 60,000 landowners in Israel fifty shekels each, who in turn squeezed an equivalent amount in taxes, wages and labor out of Israel's poor, leading to the further impoverishment of the whole society.(3) Thus the landed aristocracy collaborated with the king in the exploitation of Israelite society, in order to maintain their privileged status.

> *They may have included old-established Israelites as well as royal officials and administrators. The upper classes, once so autocratic, now began to feel the pinch. They were the people in Israel with resources, and Menahem knew how to compel them to raise the tribute money. Thus he bolstered up his rule with Assyrian support.(4)*

The focus of Gomer's infidelity concerns material goods, easy benefits, the profits she receives from her prostitution. Her pay seems to be more in the form of things than money; she runs off with strangers because of the ephemeral satisfaction of material benefits which she doesn't have. The prophet Hosea picks up on this metaphor initiating a theme found throughout the prophets concerning how the unfaithful run after worldly goods blind to the real riches which God has in store for them. To put it another way, true material goodness comes from God whereas the easy money, the glitter of gold, blinds people to the true source of wealth, as we read in Deutero-Isaiah: "Why do you spend your money for that which is not bread, and your labor for that which does not satisfy?" (Is.55:2).

Symbolizing this distortion in priorities about the true good, Hosea has Gomer saying — in looking for something better than what her husband can provide:

> *"I am going to court my lovers," she says*
> *"who give me my bread and water,*
> *my wool, my flax, my oil and my drink."*
>
> —Hos.2:5ff

Hosea and Yahweh, pained to their very souls, know that it was them who provided Gomer and her children, the sons and daughters of Israel, with all their real needs, while she runs off to strangers seeking the physical satisfactions of this world that appear more attractive. At home, all the basic goods are provided, but on the street with the foreigner the benefits seem more attractive, the pay-offs easier and quicker. The glitter of goods blinded her as to where true wealth ultimately comes from:

> *She would not acknowledge, not she,*
> *that I was the one who was giving her*
> *the corn, the wine, the oil,*
> *and [the ultimate irony] the one*
> *who freely gave her that silver and gold*
> *of which they have made Baals.*
>
> *—Hosea 2:5-8*
> *(emphasis added)*

The symbol here is not, therefore, pleasure with the "local" men who are promiscuous and who get their kicks out of temple prostitution, but **harloting with strangers**, the worship of strange gods, cavorting with foreign lovers who take advantage of Israel: the Assyrian empire. It is Ephraim's reliance on foreign powers that constitutes her worst sin... her adultery has turned into idolatry:

> *Ephraim is like a silly, witless dove*
> *calling on Egypt, turning to Assyria...*
> *Ephraim has built altar after altar*
> *they have only served him as occasion for sin.*
>
> *—Hosea 7:11, 8:11*

In the process, the whole country was "brought to ruin"(Hos.4). Clearly, the prophet describes Israel at a stage of moral disintegration considerably beyond even that described by Amos only a few years earlier. Where Amos was furious at the external class injustice in the society, Hosea takes us inside her soul to reveal to us the domestic breakdown of values and his pain as a loyal citizen — a faithful Jew — watching helplessly the downfall of a once proud kingdom, his beloved Israel. National integrity was gone, all semblances of community spirit and honor had vanished; at the highest levels the so-called "leaders" had sold out and looked only to their own welfare.

When king Menahem dies in 736 B.C., he is briefly succeeded on the throne by his son Pekahiah who four years later is assassinated by one of his chariot commanders, named Pekah, who takes over the throne of Israel. Pekah then links up with the king of Damascus, Rezin, with the intention of freeing themselves from Assyria's stranglehold. Because the empire is too strong, they decide instead to attack the much weaker state of Judah in what came to be called the Syro-Ephraimite war (an alliance of Aramaeans and Israelites against the Judeans) — but they fail to capture the city of Jerusalem.(5) In self-defense Ahaz, king of Judah, who is also involved in a sell-out to the Assyrians, offers to pay Tiglath-pileser a heavy tribute if he will only get these two "firebrands" (Pekah and Rezin) off his back(2 Kgs.16:5-9). The great king agrees and proceeds to occupy most of Israeli territory, leaving only the city of Samaria independent. In these events, we are watching the tragic decline of both kingdoms with Jew fighting Jew, internecine warfare in which the real enemy — the Assyrian empire — benefits and laughs as she watches the "street gangs" fight among themselves! Judean hatred of the Samaritans stems directly from this event.

After Pekah falls from power he is replaced by king Hoshea who becomes the last ruler of Israel, during the final decade of its political existence (733-722 B.C.). Hoshea's only political viability is as a vassal of the Assyrians since Israel is now totally in the hands of the empire. The moment Tiglath-pileser dies (in 727 B.C.), king Hoshea like Pekah before him presumptuously assumes he no longer has to pay tribute to Assyria and so he begins to politically cavort with Egypt, thereby sealing Israel's doom.(6) In anger, the new kings of Assyria retaliate: first Shalmanezer besieges Samaria and then, in 722 B.C., Sargon II occupies the capital, ending the history of Israel forever.

The fall of Samaria meant the complete cultural and religious dissolution of the northern kingdom. Emperor Sargon deported 27,000 of Israel's elite inhabitants — the wealthy, aristocratic and skilled — to northern Mesopotamia and Media. The depopulated land was filled with colonists from northern Syria and Babylonia, thereby completely breaking the national spirit, its culture absorbed into the Assyrian empire so that Israel "dissolved like salt in water."(7) They become known thereafter as the "Ten Lost Tribes," a people so merged into the life and religion of other nations that they lost their identity forever.

In spite of powerful words of condemnation from the prophet Hosea, we also catch the sense of his deep pathos at the loss of his beloved wife; his beloved country. He symbolizes this sadness by naming his daughter Lo-ruhamah which means "**Not Loved**" and his son Lo-ammi which means "**Not my people**," a sign of God's sad rejection of his own chosen ones because of their disloyalty and indifference. Though Yahweh has repeatedly called his wayward offspring, Israel and Judah, begging them to return home, they will not respond:

> *When Israel was a boy, I loved him.*
> *I called my son out of Egypt,*
> *But the more I called, the further he went from me...*
> *that I had lifted them like a little child to my cheek*
> *that I had bent down to feed them.*
> *Back they shall go to Egypt,*
> *And Assyria shall be their king;*
> *for they have refused to return to me.*
> *—Hosea 11:1-5*

The problem here goes beyond young people leaving home and their need to sow wild oats; indeed, it is more serious than a prodigal son who resists coming home to his father feeling he is not loved. At the heart of this sell-out to foreigners — this prostitution to the empires — is that what was initially just a pleasure becomes a true attraction to a false god. Whether the idol is a molten Mammon or the great City of Babylon, it becomes an adored little thing, as Gomer says, "**my** Baal". Hosea explains that what was originally just adultery with a stranger has become a total sell-out to foreign idolatry; "Words, words! False oaths! Alliances!"(Hos.10:3), as deals are cut, tributes paid, promises made... until finally Israel has lost her integrity as a nation. In selling her body she has also lost her soul.

Somoza's Prostitution Of Nicaragua & Chamorro's Search For A Patria

The parallels between ancient Israel and modern Nicaragua have to do not only with corrupt and despotic rulers like Menahem and Somoza, but with their sell-out to the empires — Assyria and the United States. Like ancient Assyria so America in modern times took from Nicaragua what it wanted and got from the dictatorship what it demanded: **total subservience**. As in the case with Assyria, so for the United States it was unnecessary to send in foreign troops (most of the time) because the local gendarmes, the National Guard, served that function as puppets of the empire, controlling the people against any possible rebellion. As long as Menahem and Somoza paid their respective tributes to Nineveh and Washington, the king and dictator could do what they pleased. Nor was this U.S. policy unique in the case of Nicaragua; it was the practice in many nations throughout the continent. As Pedro Joaquin Chamorro comments:

> *Afterward (i.e., after FDR's policy in 1934) North American politics would change, but the damage was done. Strong armies and strong men educated in the school of unlimited power, like Trujillo and Somoza (both children of the same system) occupied their places from which they imparted justice as the proconsuls of the new Rome, and acted like the ancient ones. They received unconditional support from their original tutors, allowing them to distort the very essence of democracy and the moral values of the Western Christian world.(8)*

There is also a close parallel between Hosea and Chamorro as citizen patriots who loved their countries in that they both sought to redeem their societies from the grips of those despots willing to sell the **patria** to the highest bidder. Both of them were middle class, religious, family men who considered their nation's leaders what is called in Latin America **vende-patria**, someone who is willing to sell out the nation's patrimony in exchange for the right to rule. Like Menahem and his landowners, so too, Somoza and his friends not only raped the land for its goods and sold them to foreigners, but commonly raped young Nicaraguan women as well. Thus their harloting with the United States led directly to brutalizing the Nicaraguan people and vice versa. That is why a man as moderate, even conservative as Chamorro, points to U.S. imperialism as the primary cause of Nicaragua's degradation.

After WW II, Anastasio Somoza Garcia (the father) sought to strengthen his control over the economy — vis-a-vis the traditional oligarchy who resented the dictatorship — by developing cotton production along the alluvial plains of the Pacific coast. To do so, he brought new entrepreneurs into the ruling elite, cotton producers like Alfonso Robelo. The condition was that they had to give Somoza their unconditional loyalty, pay him a percentage of their profits and operate under a series of state regulations that made it impossible for them to operate independently:

> *This new wealth was dominated by the Somoza family which had become synonymous with the "State". With this control over the expansion and diversification process, Somoza greatly increased his impact upon the social life of the country.(9)*

As a result of the expansion of cotton production, some 200,000 subsistence farmers living in the Pacific coastal area were driven off their lands, from Masaya to Chinandega. Forced to migrate, these poor **campesinos** moved to one of three places: to the eastern edges of the Zelaya as squatters, into the slums of the Pacific coast cities, or they became semi-slave workers and harvesters on the cotton plantations. No other single event in post WW II times so clearly reflects the boast of papa Somoza that **"Nicaragua es mi finca"** (Nicaragua is my farm).(10) The irony of this forced expulsion is that these embittered and alienated peasants became, in the 1970's, the first and most loyal recruits of the Sandinista revolution.

Given the extremity of exploitation of the land and repression of the people by the Somoza family, it is not surprising that the day would come, as it did on September 21, 1956, when a young poet patriot named Rigoberto López Pérez would put an end to the life of the old tyrant. His assassination of the dictator, as might be expected, was an act of self-sacrifice since he was instantly killed by Somoza's body-guards. But before his courageous act, he had written the following words which reflect the deep love of **patria** that marked the life of Chamorro as well as that of the Sandinistas:

> *The seed of Sandino's blood*
> *lashes the murderous rooftops;*
> *multiplied, in torrents*
> *it will cover exposed rooftops;*
> *and will insure, inevitable apocalypse.*
> *It will exterminate all of the murderers,*
> *and each and every one*
> *of the murderer's seed.*
>
> *Their treacherous embrace of Sandino*
> *is pregnant with biblical premonitions*
> *like the crime of Cain*
> *and the kiss of Judas.*
> *And then peace will reign*
> *and Nicaragua will fill with olive branches and voices*
> *that loft to the heavens*
> *an everlasting psalm of love.(11)*

That assassination would result in the deaths of dozens of other patriots who were known or suspected of opposition to the regime and as part of Somoza's sons' revenge for their father's death. Many more persons were tortured, including Pedro Joaquin Chamorro, who although not involved in the killing was a leading critic of the dictator who he had attacked indirectly many times in the columns of his newspaper, **La Prensa**. His torture took place on Somoza's own property, in his palatial home, sometimes referred to as "the atrium of Caiphas". In that house there were several special rooms, places used for torturing: the "sewing room" — where needles were driven under fingernails; "the well" — where repeated forced water submersion occurred; and, the "garden of the lions" — where (amazing as it may seem) tigers and panthers were kept to terrify and sometimes devour their victims.(12) The main purpose of the torture was to gain information about others plotting against the dictatorship. Though finally tried, convicted and banned, Pedro Joaquin and his wife Violeta escaped into Costa Rica across the San Juan River, where he continued his verbal resistance from exile.

In spite of all this, Chamorro's search for a true fatherland (**patria**) went on, a passionate love affair with his country; the dream of liberation from tyranny. The passion he felt about Nicaragua was so strong that one night Pedro Joaquin had a dream in which he was standing before.."a tribunal composed of seven men who called me before them to say to me, 'Citizen Chamorro, you are hereby condemned for searching for a **patria**.'"(13) This reflects the same passion of Augusto Cesar Sandino, about whom Chamorro wrote on occasion (with great care) in **La Prensa** after he returned to Nicaragua. In an editorial written in 1965, he referred to the hatred which the Somozas had for everything associated with Sandino, whose name could never be mentioned in Nicaragua:

> As it is natural on the anniversary of an illustrious man [i.e. Sandino] to revive his memory, so too it is natural that those guilty of his death would try to kill him (again) or that those parties or servants who took his life, should try to obliterate his memory.(14)

As is well-known, Pedro Joaquin Chamorro was not only not a political progressive, even less a leftist, but rather a conservative by tradition and class. Nonetheless, his struggle against Somoza had turned him into an outspoken Christian Democratic prophet. His love affair with Nicaragua was a radical, passionate commitment not only advocating the removal of the Somozas from power, but openly attacking U.S. imperialism as equally guilty of this crime against the Nicaraguan people, a system by which the Empire...

perpetuated in the country the status quo, backwardness, hu-
miliation, exploitation, alienation, dependency, order through
brute force, "reason" through the bullet, submission and death.
That invader (the USA) made Nicaragua what it is today, and
there will be no modification in substance or depth even if this
present satrap is replaced by another face which may appear
more benign or have more courteous and refined manners.
The (imperial) mold is what matters …(15)

In this regard, Gregorio Selser claims that Chamorro was very much like both "Zeledón and Sandino in their way and in their times."(16) To be sure, there were many differences between them: Sandino was a populist revolutionary who fought the United States with guns from the mountains; Chamorro, a bourgeois Catholic newspaper editor who attacked the Empire with his pen from Managua. Thus for his wife Violeta and the CIA to use **La Prensa** today in the service of reaction is not only disloyal to its founder's principles, it totally misunderstands his passionate search for a true **patria**, independent of imperial domination.

If the earthquake of 1972 marked the economic downfall of the Somoza dynasty because of all the international aid the Somozas stole for themselves and their friends; and if the election of 1974 marked the political end of Somoza's pseudo-democratic facade because of electoral fraud against UDEL (Chamorro's party); it is also true that the "spiritual" end of the dictatorship came in 1978 with the assassination of Pedro Joaquin Chamorro. After that, the middle class, Church, traditional oligarchy and many of those as yet uncommitted popular sectors openly turned against the dictatorship. Chamorro was murdered in the early morning hours of Jan.10, 1978 as he drove to **La Prensa** through the desolate earthquake zone of old Managua. Two cars overtook his, forcing him to stop. Its occupants climbed out and fired at point-blank range, killing him instantly, his body perforated with 30 gunshot wounds. From that spot, his body was carried back to his home in a seven-hour, pre-funeral procession in which 50,000 persons participated.(17)

Given the outspokenness of Chamorro and the vindictive
nature of Somoza, the two could not co-exist for long on the
same turf. It was a struggle that could only end as it did, with
the power of evil trampling down its arch-enemy. And con-
versely, it was inevitable that from the tomb of that fallen
martyr, the whole nation should rise up as a united people to

carry out the society's judgement against this corrupt system.(18)

From that date onward, neither the Carter administration nor the CIA knew exactly what to do with Somoza. As long as he remained in Nicaragua, no other alternative was possible. As a faithful lackey of the United States for so many years, they couldn't just eliminate him as the Agency had done with other undesirable leaders like Rafael Trujillo.(19) So they continued supporting the regime in a desultory fashion, urging the dictator to move up to Miami. Through the help of Archbishop Obando y Bravo, the United States began coordinating with its Christian Democratic friends in Venezuela to work out a compromise, what was called **"somocismo sin Somoza"**, a promise to support the Somoza system and his friends while removing the man himself from Managua. But Somoza's adamancy — claiming Nicaragua needed him — made it impossible for the Empire to employ its traditional methods of ruler-substitution. This impasse highlighted a key aspect of U.S. domination: hypocrisy. As prophet, Chamorro clarified the matter:

> *The politics of the United States is mistaken... the pretended rectification is a new error, perhaps more grave than the first. Because its intervening politics... has followed the (line) of non-intervention carried to its extreme of offering unconditional support to those it established in power through its political intervention... that is to intervene.(20)*

Reflection on Patriotism

Hosea's metaphor on the love relationship between Yahweh and Israel, just like Chamorro's love affair with Nicaragua, forces us to look at the nature of patriotism. For both prophets, love of country implied compassion for the poor and justice for the workers, whereas for Menahem and Somoza, the sell-out of the nation's patrimony to the empires was the means by which they continued in power. In other words, national adultery is the flip side of imperial idolatry. Many so-called patriotic citizens in the United States and Central America do not understand this connection and believe it is perfectly legitimate to exploit the poor and rip off the land... and still be loyal citizens. By contrast, the prophets are very clear that if you compromise on these principles, you are in fact destroying the **patria**. From the biblical perspective, *sincerity* is no indicator of loyalty to one's country, only the search for justice. No doubt, Somoza considered himself a loyal patriot while he was, in fact, destroying the social fabric of Nicaraguan society. As Jose Miranda says of Hosea:

> *A fundamental hermeneutical principle is at stake here... To know Yahweh is to achieve justice for the poor...[The] antithesis between "knowledge of God" and interhuman crimes demonstrates that the former is naturally understood to mean "justice among men." In Hosea we read:*
> *There is no goodness, no compassion,*
> *no knowledge of God in the country,*
> *only perjury and lies, slaughter, theft,*
> *adultery and violence, murder after murder.*
> *—Hos. 4:1b-2*
> *The synonymy between to-know-Yahweh and interhuman justice is here so taken for granted that this prophet of the early eighth century B.C. includes in his testimony all the previous centuries of Israelite tradition.(21)*

In the case of pre-revolutionary Cuba where the mafia no doubt assumed they were loyal to Cuba, as long as "patriotic" meant they could exploit women in their prostitution rings, use the country to move drugs into the U.S.A., make millions off illegal liquor sales and gambling... all with the approval of Fulgencio Batista, the dictator. When the Cuban revolution closed all that down, the mafia was furious, not because of communism but because Fidel Castro had outlawed their dishonest and corrupt operations. When they moved to Miami, the same **mafiosos** transferred their false patriotism to the United States because here they could cheat, rob, kill and make millions off of drugs and still be "patriotic". They don't care — any more than Batista or Somoza did — that American youth are being destroyed by their drugs. In their mind, "making a quick buck" is the American way even though under the banner of "patriotism" they are prostituting the body of American society.

Hosea's metaphor for Israel was a feminine model: his search for Gomer to be a true wife, not a prostitute. Right-wing repressive regimes in Latin America constantly talk about **patria** as in the patriotic slogan: "fatherland, family and God." Their view of a relationship to the nation is very macho, sexist and male-dominated, on behalf of which they make "**patria** propaganda". By contrast, the vision of nationhood held by the Sandinistas implies looking for a real companion, a true wife, in their relationship with Nicaragua. They even sing a song to this effect called "Nicaragua, Nicaragüita," the search for a **compañera** with whom they can forge a new future together as male and female equals. In doing so, they have clarified our theological search for an alternative to the adultery/idolatry model. The difference between the patriotism of Somoza and Chamorro is clear: the man with the sword was interested in selling his nation to the Empire; the man with the pen had a love affair with his People.

FOOTNOTES — CHAPTER 7

1   *The Westminster Bible*, "Introduction to the Prophet Hosea," <u>ibid</u>., p.1264.

2   Siegfried Herrmann, <u>ibid</u>., p.243ff. Cf.1Kgs.15:17-20.

3   <u>Ibid</u>., p.245.

4   <u>Ibid</u>., p.245.

5   <u>Ibid</u>., p.247.

6   Bailey & Kent, <u>Ibid</u>., p.196 (2Kgs.17:3-6).

7   <u>Ibid</u>., p.198 (2Kgs.17:24-33).

8   Pedro Joaquin Chamorro, *Estirpe Sangrienta: Los Somoza*, Ediciones El Pez y La Serpiente, Mexico, 1978, p.247.

9   EPICA, *Nicaragua: The People's Revolution*, Wash., D.C., 1980, p.4.

10   Walter LeFeber, Inev*itable Revolutions*, <u>ibid</u>., p.161.

11   EPICA, *Nicaragua: A People's Revolution*, <u>ibid</u>., p.4.

12   Chamorro, *Estirpe Sangrienta: Los Somoza*, <u>ibid</u>., Cf.Chapters 8, 9 and 10.

13   <u>Ibid</u>., Prologue by Gregorio Selser, Mexico, 1978, p.XVI.

14   <u>Ibid</u>., p.XVIII.

15   <u>Ibid</u>., Prologue p.XII-XIII (emphasis added).

16   Ibid., Prologue p.XIII.

17   EPICA, *Nicaragua: A People's Revolution,* ibid., p.16.

18   Ibid., p.18.

19   The CIA provided the guns with which Trujillo was assassinated to a group of high-level Dominican military officers. These guns were stored in a supermarket in the Gasque section of Santo Domingo named after its American owner, *Wimpy's.*

20   Chamorro, Estirpe *Sangrienta,* ibid., pp.247-248.

21   Jose P. Miranda, *Marx and the Bible,* Orbis, Maryknoll, New York, 1974, pp. 44-45.

CHAPTER 8
PRIDE

Jean-Marie Simon

Rios Montt Says, "I'm God's Choice"

Efraim Rios Montt, designated president of Guatemala (1982-83) is seen here preaching one of his Sunday sermons, saying of himself:"I'm God's choice, " while covering for the Indian massacre.

CHAPTER 8 PRIDE

*The Lord of Hosts planned it to prick every noble's pride
and bring the most honored men on earth into con-
tempt.*
—*Is. 23:9*

*Thus will I spoil the gross pride of Judah, the gross pride of
Jerusalem.*
*This wicked nation has refused to listen to my words;
they have followed*
other gods, serving them and bowing down to them.
—*Jer. 13:9-10*

In light of the tremendous discrepancy between a mighty empire
and a much weaker nation-state, it might seem understandable that the
weaker party would be vacillating and ambivalent towards the superpower; natural that its leaders would plot, plead and play political
games behind the back of Big Brother. But for the prophets, it is
precisely this false pride that comes before a fall; the absence of moral
integrity that determines the fate of a nation. This was particularly true
of (First) Isaiah (1), *an upper-class prophet* from an aristocratic back-
ground, yet a man of God whose role as the voice of conscience for
Judah was based on a deep spirituality. For him, the *third sin* (besides
class injustice and harloting with empires) which leads to God's
judgment on the Jewish kingdoms was **nationalistic pride**; that false
pride which vainly presumes it can challenge empires while in the end
capitulating before imperial pressure. The presumptuousness of King
Hezekiah before mighty Assyria is the focus of our biblical reflection.

In our day, we lift up this national sin of pride in relation to Mexico,
a middle-level actor in the Central American struggle; its ambivalence
between being an "independent intermediate power" versus a "sub-
imperial ally." On the one hand, Mexico with its apparent progressive
foreign policy could have played a crucial role in the present crisis in
terms of the thousands of refugees who fled into its territory in the
1980's from the terror in El Salvador and Guatemala. Challenged by its
prophet Sergio Mendez Arceo to return to the ways of God and humbly
stand with the poor, Mexico instead gave in to U.S. pressures because
of its financial sell-out and massive indebtedness to North American
capitalists. As in the case of Hezekiah, Mexico's leaders lacked the
integrity to stand on principle and because of false pride were unable
to serve as a protector against Guatemalan fascism and U.S. imperialism, causing thousands of refugees to flee further northward and
thousands of others to lose their lives.

Isaiah's Prophecy Against Judah For Hezekiah's Presumptuousness & Lack of Moral Integrity

During the reign of King Hezekiah, ruler of Judah between 714 and 696 B.C., his glory-seeking, intermittent intrigues and groveling repentance, Hezekiah represents for us the symbol of Judah's national capitulation as an intermediate power to the powerful Assyrian empire. Hezekiah first plots with Egypt and then with Babylon but when threatened comes running to the prophet (First) Isaiah pleading for divine intervention to save the nation, promising to amend his ways in order to stave off a political threat. In the face of this shallow faith and petty arrogance, Isaiah condemns those leaders who rebel against God:

> *Woe to those rebellious sons!*
> — *it is Yahweh who speaks.*
> *They carry out plans that are not mine*
> *and make alliances not inspired by me,*
> *and so add*
> *sin to sin.*
> — Is. 30:1

Judah's shock at the fall of Israel in 722 B.C. into the hands of the Assyrians had an immediate but not a lasting effect upon the people and rulers of the southern kingdom. Instead of any serious reassessment of the state of their nation, they decide to "play it cool" for a few years, paying tribute to Assyria while biding their time. As for Isaiah, his silence on the fall of Samaria while remarkable probably reflects his fear that almost anything he might do or say could push Judah "over the edge."(2) So he urges the Judeans to trust in God:

> *For thus said the Lord God, the Holy One of Israel,*
> *"In returning and rest you shall be saved;*
> *in quietness and in trust shall be your strength."*
> ***And you would not!***
>
> —Is. 30:15 (RSV)
> (emphasis added)

It is important to note how our modern liturgies usually omit this last line, leaving only the positive side of Isaiah's admonition. So often in the churches and synagogues in America today, "spirituality" implies reading only the easy word while rejecting the prophetic warning, the whole point of this text.

During the first nine years of his rule, king Hezekiah restrained himself, so that Assyria's suffocation of the Syrian rebellions in Hamath, Gath and Ashdod did not affect Judah. In part, he was able to do this because Judah was favored by its geographical location high in the hill country, away from the coastal plains and out of the line of the caravan routes to the East. On the other hand, Hezekiah's "quietness" did not arise from spiritual integrity but from his scheming tactic of waiting for the right moment in order to break away from Assyrian control. This is the context for Isaiah's famous reflection on the hollowness of the people versus the holiness of God:

> *What a wretched state I am in! I am lost,*
> *for I am a man of unclean lips*
> *and I live among a people of unclean lips,*
> *for my eyes have looked at the King, Yahweh Sabaoth.*
> *—Is. 6:5*

Over the next decade, two serious temptations lead Hezekiah to abandon his previous caution requiring all the powers of Isaiah to keep Judah from becoming enmeshed in alliances that could have resulted in the same disaster that had befallen Israel. The first temptation occurred around 711 B.C. when a delegation from king Shabaka of Egypt appeared in Jerusalem with a plan to establish a buffer zone of smaller states — Ashdod, Gath, Edom and Judah — between Egypt and Assyria to thwart any Assyrian attack. (3) Hezekiah, intrigued by the offer (one of the Big Powers was currying his favor!) faced a disgusted Isaiah who warned the king against coquetting with an imperial rival of Assyria, especially when Egypt was such a second-class power. Later, a representative of the king of Assyria would mock Hezekiah for even toying with the idea, warning him that Egypt was "a broken reed whose splintered end would pierce the hand of Judah itself"(Is. 36:6). Isaiah was so worried about Hezekiah's willingness to risk everything that for three years the prophet walked around Jerusalem **barefoot and naked**(Is. 20:1-6). His shocking symbolism, implying that one day Egypt would be led away barefoot and naked, made such an impact on the people it forced the king to desist from his folly, at least temporarily.

Secondly, in 705 B.C., after the dreaded Sargon II died and his son Sennacherib took over the throne of Assyria, Hezekiah was convinced that the time for Judah to "go independent" had arrived. The death of Sargon produced widespread dissension throughout the empire, requiring four years of hard political and military work for Sennacherib to re-unify it. His main trouble spot was Babylon, forcing the emperor to deploy his strongest garrisons there, far to the east near the Euphrates River. Hezekiah believed that this division of the Assyrian forces made it possible for the "impregnable" Jerusalem to become the center of a Western alliance,backed by Egypt.(4) Out of this presumptuousness, Hezekiah stopped paying his tribute money to Ninevah!(5) Isaiah, horrified, knowing that Sennacherib was the "master of the world" warned that these plotting schemes would only lead to disaster.

At that very time, king Hezekiah fell seriously ill with an abscess and it looked like he was going to die. Calling on Isaiah to save him, the prophet at first saw the sickness as a sign of God's displeasure because of Judah's flirtations with Egypt; so he told the king he could not save him. Hezekiah pleads with him, prays to Yahweh, promises to do penance. Eventually Isaiah relents and orders a cure which healed the boil.(6) Yet during his recovery, unknown to the prophet, another delegation arrives at court to offer its condolences: emissaries from Merodach-Baladan, leader of the rebel Babylon. The mission was, of course, political. The Babylonians hoped to encourage Judah to lead a Palestinian revolt against Assyria which would distract Sennacherib sufficiently to ensure them a victory. The plan failed and the revolt was put down. When Isaiah heard that Hezekiah had actually shown the visitors his weapon's arsenal, suggesting his willingness to become involved militarily, the prophet predicted (for the first time) that the instrument of Judah's fall would not come from the north (Assyria) but from the east (Babylon):

> *The time is coming, says the Lord, when everything in your house, and all that your fathers have amassed till the present day, will be carried away to Babylon; not a thing will be left.*
> —*Is. 39:6*

The proud and naive Hezekiah was actually pleased by this prophesy (Is. 39:8), reasoning in his egocentric way, that since it would take a long time for Babylon to replace Assyria as a world power, that would mean he could live out his life as a king in peace, his rule assured! Little did he know that at that very moment Sennacherib — having quelled Babylon — was returning home and would soon fall "like a thunderbolt" upon the Western alliance. The Assyrian forces easily took the Phoenician cities of Tyre and Sidon; then they moved against Philistia and finally against Edom, Moab and Ekron.(7) Hezekiah still felt he was safe with the backing of the Egyptians, but when Sennacherib defeated them and turned his forces eastward against the hill-country of Palestine, Jerusalem was in panic.

The Assyrian armies advanced until they had taken control of the entire countryside of Judah, not stopping until they stood at the very walls of the City of David. A debate then ensues, a warning and promise come to Hezekiah from a messenger of Sennacherib: "Do not let your God on whom you are relying deceive you when he says: 'Jerusalem shall not fall into the power of the king of Assyria.'" Hezekiah, terrified, turns to his "prayer-beads." Isaiah scoffs at his lack of faith and superficial repentance, but finally promises that Sennacherib "will not enter this city... Yahweh will protect it and save it"(Isa. 37:10; 33-35). A "miracle" then happens. The Bible says that a plague fell upon the Assyrian troops forcing them to withdraw, but we also know that Hezekiah paid an enormous tribute to Sennacherib — 30 talents of gold and silver; a sum equivalent to $22,800,000 today.(8) In addition, the king's own daughters were forced to become part of Sennacherib's harem along with many other spoils. Hezekiah had saved his throne and the city of Jerusalem but at a very high price. Although Judah would survive for another hundred years, the choice between confidence in God's Word and fear at the threat of the empire was clear: Hezekiah *had failed the test*.

Jewish society by the year 700 B.C. (after the crisis) was not only discredited and bankrupt, it was a disgrace internally as well. The prophets called the rulers "cannibals" because they ate up the people's livelihood (Micah 3:3). Judges and priests were corrupt and hypocritical; lust for money had utterly destroyed any sense of brotherhood, laws were for the benefit of the rich; drunkenness was widespread. Still, the leaders of Judah wouldn't practice justice nor see the folly of their ways.

> *Listen then to the word of the Lord, you arrogant men*
> *who rule this people in Jerusalem.*
> *You say, "we have made a treaty with Death*
> *and signed a pact with Sheol:*
> *so that, when the raging flood sweeps by, it shall not touch us;*
> *for we have taken refuge in lies..."*
>
> *—Is. 28:14-15*

Yet, given the near-disaster of an Assyrian takeover and under the prodding of Isaiah, Hezekiah in his last years did carry out a superficial religious reform, focusing primarily on the physical clean-up of the Temple with all its accumulated rubbish. For years, the Temple had been virtually abandoned, the priests discredited. Now, in addition to the cleansing, stone pillars and sacred poles were removed, idolatrous statues and altars to the Baalim were destroyed; an ancient brass serpent of Moses from the wilderness was discarded and Yahweh was restored as the national God.(9) This superficial cleansing and symbolic repentance were celebrated with great pomp and circumstance in the Temple, including the sacrifice of animals. To all this, the prophet responded in disgust:

> *Because this people approach me with their mouths*
> *and honor me with their lips*
> *while their hearts are far from me,*
> *and their religion is but a precept of men, learnt by rote,*
> *therefore I will again shock this people*
> *adding shock to shock:*
> *the wisdom of their wise men shall vanish*
> *and the discernment of the discerning shall be lost.*
> — *Isa. 29:13-14*

Judah's presumptuousness (Hezekiah's pride) before the Assyrian empire had disastrous consequences upon the nation and its people. It led to the betrayal of Judah's weaker neighbors who had relied on her support which proved to be nothing more than opportunism on Hezekiah's part. It also resulted in Judah's financial ruin through having to pay additional enormous tribute to Ninevah. Finally, he betrayed Judah's very existence by failing to trust in Yahweh rather than the empires which would ultimately do in the kingdom. Though Jerusalem would not fall for another century, its national pride was already undermined because its leaders had sold out on the principles of the covenant with God. In being willing to negotiate for a short-term success, Judah had lost the promise of God's protection...presaging its fall to Babylon.

Mendez Arceo's Witness Against Mexico For Echevarria's Vacillation Towards the USA

Since its independence from Spain in 1821, Mexico has been constantly torn between independent nationalism (true pride) and its artificial challenge of U.S. imperialism (false pride); between a commitment to the principles of its popular revolution and sell-out to wealthy elites allied to foreign capitalists. Because of its relatively larger size and thus greater hemispheric importance compared to its smaller and weaker neighbors to the south, Mexico has demonstrated the same kind of false pride and ambivalence we have just witnessed in ancient Judah, sometimes promising to defend its weaker neighbors against imperial aggression, sometimes capitulating before the super-power to their detriment. Today, this ambivalence can be seen in Mexico's schizophrenia between its liberal foreign policy and conservative domestic practice in which the only party in power — the Institutionalized Revolutionary Party (PRI) — has consistently repressed every popular challenge to its injustices.

Mexico's legitimate pride in her Aztec origins and modern revolutionary history (1910-1917) has often been vitiated by nationalistic presumptuousness which at times sought to absorb its smaller neighbors into a sub-imperial confederation or play cat-and-mouse power games with the United States. Emperor Agustín Iturbide (1821-1824) squandered the possibility of uniting the whole Central American Isthmus into a single federation under Mexico's leadership because of his imperialistic delusions of grandeur. His "Supreme Highness" Antonio de Santa Anna, with comparable megalomania, triggered the Mexican-American War as a result of his vicious repression of the Alamo, resulting in Mexico losing half of its territory (1841-1845). While it is true that Anglo-settler aggressiveness and Texan demands to maintain the practice of slavery (outlawed by Mexico) justified legitimate defense of its territory, Mexico failed to challenge the United States on **principles** giving the gringos an easy justification for their aggression.(10)

On the other hand, Mexico can boast of some of most outstanding leaders and revolutionary heros in the history of the hemisphere, north or south of the Rio Grande. Men like Benito Juárez and Emiliano Zapata had neither imperial pretensions nor took advantage of their power for personal gain. Yet every such exemplary witness of principle was undone by reactionary, money-grubbing leaders like Porfirio Díaz and Venustiano Carranza, who sold out on the people because of their alliances with wealthy landowners or American businessmen. Failure to concretize its vision of justice into law resulted in Mexico's revolution being undone by trusting in caretaker governments. What finally emerged out of the revolution in 1917 was...

> ...a defeated peasantry, a crippled and dependent labor movement, a wounded but victorious bourgeoisie, and, a divided Mexican people, a paper triumph—the 1917 Constitution.(11)

That initial compromise on principles led to Mexico's second and even more disastrous sell-out: the loss of economic independence to foreign corporations and banks, primarily those from the United States. During the presidency of Lázaro Cárdenas in the 1930's, a successful effort towards recovering its economic integrity through nationalizing its petroleum rights was begun. But Mexico was up against an extremely powerful and cunning imperial system which was bent on controlling it one way or another. While it was illegal for foreigners to own Mexican industries, the practice of "namelenders" or **prestanombres** developed in which Mexicans signed for companies that were actually controlled by foreigners.(12) By the end of WW II, foreign control over Mexico's economy was so extensive that gringos could actually decide what Mexico would import and export and which products could be produced locally.

From his vantage-point in Cuernavaca, the bishop of Morelos, Sergio Méndez Arceo — who like Isaiah is an upper-class prophet, the son of a lawyer and nephew of an archbishop, José Mora y del Río — had watched this process of national sell-out and political repression for years. From his episcopal seat in the diocese of Morelos, he could literally see both the power and poverty of Mexico's divided society, for it was there that Zapata's forces had been based and there that its modern elites often came to visit. Representatives from the country's "disgrace" and "virtue" often came to talk with the bishop, for he listened to both sides of Mexico's contradictory vision of society. On the one hand, Don Sergio was a man of letters, dignified, educated, an historian...and as such a close friend of presidents Lázaro Cárdenas, López Matos, Luis Echevarría and Miguel de la Madrid. On the other hand, angry students also came to talk, disgruntled peasants and the poor from all walks of life. As a Brazilian friend, Francisco Juliao, once correctly noted, the marginalized come because he listens..."to the cry of the people, to (those) without bread, without land, without work, without justice and without peace."(13)

The struggle between national dignity and foreign sell-out reached its culmination and catastrophe during the Summer and Fall of 1968. During the months of July, August and September, Mexican high school and university students carried out a series of peaceful protests, marching through the streets of downtown Mexico City. The number of participants in each march varied from between 50,000 to 300,000 persons as the students demanded: the freeing of political prisoners, the disbanding of the repressive police forces called the "granaderos", and the arrest and trial of those authorities guilty of atrocities in the prisons. Most of all, the students attacked the primary sin of the PRI: "**having sold out the country to American interests**."(14) Instead of making any concessions or even being willing to dialogue, the government responded with more and more repression.

The crisis that tipped the scales for the bishop and sent him into a dozen radical causes and open criticism of the nations' false pride and sell-out to the Empire was the slaughter at Tlatelolco in 1968. In a homily preached on September 28, some days before that terrible massacre, he said:

> *The lying makes my blood boil, the deformation of the truth, the cover-up of the facts, the cowardice, self-censorship, bribery and myopia exhibited by all the means of communication.(15)*

During those months of protest — August through October — Mendez Arceo repeatedly took the side of the students as representing the true voice of the Mexican people seeking justice and searching for national integrity.

The fateful night of October 2 was to produce a human slaughter at the Plaza de Tres Culturas (Three Cultures), known as the Tlatelolco housing project. Gathered there were thousands of people peacefully listening to speeches when silently and unnoticed the multitude was surrounded by 5,000 soldiers and dozens of plain-clothes policemen. Suddenly, at a signal, the military and police opened fire on the gathering, including sharpshooters from overhead helicopters and windows high up in the building project. At least 325 persons were killed and hundreds wounded, according to the *Manchester Guardian.* Some say that this tragedy was "as significant an event in Mexican history as Independence, the Reform and the Revolution"(16) because it revealed to all Mexicans the real nature of the PRI.

The underlying motive behind the massacre, however, was pressure from the United States on Mexican authorities because of the upcoming 1968 Olympics, scheduled to begin in Mexico City on October 15. The decision to use state violence was taken because leaders in both countries felt that mere dispersal of the crowd or blocking the marchers would not have ended the protests and might have projected a very negative image all during the games. Thus the price for preserving Mexico's international image as a liberal and open society was paid for with the lives of (at least) 325 of its own citizens! National pride and capitulation to Yankee pressure was revealed for what it really was: a sell-out on its own stated principles of justice and freedom in order to look good to the world.

> *Shame on you! you who call evil good and good evil,*
> *who turn darkness into light and light into darkness,*
> *who make bitter sweet and sweet bitter.*

*Shame on you! you who are wise in your own eyes
and prudent in your self-esteem.*

—*Is. 5:20-21*

President Echevarría of Mexico (1970-1976), like King Hezekiah, had dreams of making Mexico more independent from the United States, of carrying out social reforms and stabilizing the economy towards reducing the nation's terrible poverty. But Mexico's control by U.S. multinationals and the large number of its elites linked to North American interests compromised his idealistic plans at every step. At the beginning of his term, he laid out three objectives he hoped to accomplish during his six years in office: a) a "democratic opening" in which he would release the student prisoners from the Tlatelolco massacre; b) worker-peasant reforms in terms of increased wages; and c) economic improvement through technocratic and technological reforms (without any change in class relations).(17) The first failed when the students were again brutally repressed in 1971 and 1973; the second failed because the cost of living rose faster than the modest pay hikes; and the third failed because, as always, the PRI would only effect bureaucratic alterations not substantive change.

In sharp contrast with all this duplicity and double-talk, Don Sergio Méndez Arceo was a man of integrity. Though often called the "red bishop" by reactionary forces because of his support of radical causes and revolutionary movements, the bishop is in fact a political conservative by temperament, just as Isaiah was. Though often charged as being a radical, he refuses to locate himself ideologically, describing himself as a "free man" of God: "Rebel I have never been. I have been free, but not a rebel."(18) From whence, then, his radical positions? They come, as with the Hebrew prophets, from his deep commitment to the people and the truth. Don Sergio feels his call "to speak the truth" is an absolutely essential part of his Christian apostolate...an attribute so difficult for politicians, businessmen and presidents!

Following Tlatelolco, Don Sergio began lashing out at a whole series of injustices and hypocrisies in Mexico. He attacked capitalism as an "intrinsically perverse system" which helps builds basilicas even though the people are kept outside its buildings and benefits.(19) He criticized the Catholic hierarchy in Mexico for worrying so much about its own public image and lack of power that it refuses to stand by the people who are being exploited by the very system which the Church hopes will recognize it! The hierarchy reinforces its political marginalization by refusing to take stands on important political and social issues hoping it can get back into favor with the State by becoming a "spiritual" force. On the other hand, Don Sergio holds that the politicians are only interested in maintaining the *status quo* and as such are polarizing the society. Therefore, he cannot accept the letter of the Constitution which prohibits clergy from criticizing the State. Given this prophetic denunciation of both the Church and State, where does Don Sergio stand? He believes that the Gospel has a very special political dimension: **"to struggle for justice together with our oppressed brothers and sisters."**(20)

By 1972 the Mexican economy had stopped growing and the **peso** had to be devalued. One of the reasons for this stagnation was the growing government subsidy to private industry not being reinvested or transformed into better wages but used in league with foreign business interests to make more profit for the rich and in some cases for labor union leaders and the PRI itself.

> *The foreign debt is permitting foreigners to exercise increasing control over Mexico. Once in debt, more loans are needed to repay old ones, and to get these new loans, Mexico has to act in accordance with the desires of the lenders. If the lender doesn't like the project, no loan. Similarly, reliance on such credit increases the use of foreign imports, since many loans only serve to disguise installment buying.(21)*

By 1970, when it looked like Mexico was heading for bankruptcy, new oil discoveries gave the economy a shot in the arm. **Spending and borrowing from banks soared but not investment in new industry and business**. President Echevarria decided to pump life into the economy through massive government borrowing, thence converting dollars into **pesos**, nearly tripling the amount of cash in circulation.(22) Mexico's incredible indebtedness today — well over $100 billion — stems directly from that decision and its short-lived euphoria over oil. It was, in effect, like paying an incredible tribute to Assyria just as Hezekiah had been forced to do because of its economic sell-out and political arrogance.

When Central America exploded into three nearly simultaneous liberation struggles — Nicaragua (1979), El Salvador (1980) and Guatemala (1981) — forcing tens of thousands of refugees to flee northward into Mexican territory, that country's pride and ambivalence towards the Empire were put to the test. Within Mexico, a bureaucratic power struggle erupted between the ministries of Foreign Affairs and Interior over how to treat these refugees...and the hard-liners won. The massive influx of Salvadoran refugees exacerbated its already strained labor conditions in Mexico City and most were forced northward where Mexico collaborated with U.S. immigration officials along the border. On the other hand, Mexico's military governors in the south were even more troubled by the arrival of tens of thousands of Guatemalan refugees who settled right along the border and then began working with already impoverished and disgruntled Mexican peasants. As a result, the refugees were either turned over to Guatemalan authorities, isolated into refugee camps or forcibly relocated to Campeche.(23)

A few courageous witnesses to compassion and the truth defended the Guatemalan refugees trying to protect them from deportation. Bishop Samuel Ruiz mobilized the diocese of San Cristobal where parish teams served the refugees admirably by providing food, clothing, medicine, housing and sometimes jobs.(24) On the other hand, Méndez Arceo denounced Reagan's policy towards El Salvador, recognized the right of the Salvadoran people to struggle for justice, and served as president of the Mexican Christian Secretariat for Solidarity with El Salvador.(25) The refugees had literally forced Mexico to choose which side it was on...between these victims from the Third World and the Powers whose policies had caused them to flee. In the eyes of many observing this tragedy, *Mexico had failed the test.*

To its credit, Mexico did participate in the Contadora process which challenged the Reagan policy in Central America seeking to bring about peace by removing all foreign advisors and troops from the region. Yet that effort failed because none of the co-signatories (Mexico, Panama, Colombia or Venezuela) were prepared to openly challenge the Empire. Just as the pride of Mexico and its revolutionary roots had been called into question by the student protests at Tlatelolco in 1968, so once again they were challenged by these refugees flights from Central America in the 1980's. In both cases, these challenges to its integrity were compromised upon the altars of self-image and imperial subservience. As Don Sergio once said, the best place to analyze current politics is among the poor; the best place to understand the moral and theological issues of our day is within the **comunidades de base** because "they have no idols, no riches, no power."(26)

FOOTNOTES — CHAPTER 8

1   **(Historical Clarification of Isaiah)**
         There are three time periods and thus three authors (at least) contained within the prophecy: (*First*) Isaiah (Chps. 1-23; 28-39) which are from the 8th century B.C.; (*Second*) Deutero Isaiah (Chap. 40-55, plus likely 60-62) which are from the exilic period, that is, after the fall of Jerusalem; and (*Third*) Isaiah which is apocalyptic in nature and comes from the 4th century B.C. (Chps. 24-27 and 56-59; 63-66). Our focus here is on (First) Isaiah from the 8th century, particularly *during the reign of King Hezekiah* whose history is found primarily in Isaiah, Chps. 1, 28-31 and 36-39, including parallels found in 2 Kings 18-20.
         We divide this reflection on Hezekiah & First Isaiah into the following four periods in which a combination of biblical and historical dates appear to reinforce each other, though not precisely:

1. **Political Intrigue with Egypt**	715-706	BC
	Chaps. 18-20	
2. **Political Intrigue with Babylon**	705-702	BC
	Chaps. 29-30; 38-39	
3. **Assyria's Siege of Jerusalem**	701	BC
	Chaps. 32-33; 36-37	
4. **Pseudo-Religious Reform**	700-69	BC
	Historical references.	

2   Siegfried Herrmann, ibid., p. 255.

3   Bailey and Kent, ibid., p. 202.

4   Bailey & Kent, p. 204.

5   Martin Noth, *The History of Israel*, Harper & Row, New York, 1958, p. 266. In ancient oriental politics, a political break from dominant power always included the refusal to pay tribute and a rejection of the religious symbols of that power.

6   2 Kings 20 and Isa. 38:1-8.

7   Bailey & Kent, ibid., p. 206.

8 Bailey & Kent, ibid, pp. 207-208. The Cylinder of Sennacherib describes the tribute paid by Hezekiah to Assyria but mentions nothing of any plague. In addition, it describes the thousands of Jews taken into captivity along with spoils: innumerable horses, camels, oxen and sheep.

9 Bailey & Kent, ibid., pp. 213-215.

10 Philip Russell, *Mexico in Transition*, Colorado River Press, Austin, 1977, pp.15-19.

11 James Cockcroft, *Intellectual Precursors of the Mexican Revolution, 1900-1913*, Austin, University of Texas Press, 1968, p.235.

12 Philip Russell, op.cit., p.68.

13 Gabriela Videla, *Sergio Mendez Arceo: Un Senor Obispo*, (i.e., an honorable bishop), Correo del Sur, Cuernavaca, 1982, p.25.

14 Philip Russell, op.cit., p.133.

15 Gabriela Videla, *Sergio Mendez Arceo*, ibid., p.24.

16 Philip Russell, Ibid., p.134.

17 Ibid., p.56.

18 Gabriela Videla, op. cit., p.97.

19 Ibid., p.25.

20 Ibid., p.120.

21 Philip Russell, ibid., p.84.

22 Ibid., p.73.

23 L. Frank & P. Wheaton, *Indian Guatemala: Path to Liberation*, EPICA, Washington, D.C., p. 86. On one occasion, a group of 4,000 indigenous Guatemalans were trapped between Mexican & Guatemalan troops and turned over to the Guatemalan military. Nothing was heard of that group thereafter.

24 Ibid., p.86.

25 Gabriela Videla, op. cit., p.162. "Secretariado Cristiano Mexicano de Solidaridad con El Salvador."

26 Ibid., p.126.

PART III
EXILIC EXPERIENCE: PROMISE OF REDEMPTION FROM WITHIN BABYLONIAN CAPTIVITY

CHAPTER 9
DEATH

CHAPTER 9 DEATH

God was no longer merely a weak benefactor; Yahweh had become their enemy.

—Ralph Klein

God's "strange work" is not so much about judgement as it is of redemption, our conversion as U.S. citizens, our conscious-ness-raising as North Americans about our imperial idolatry.

—Philip Wheaton

The so-called "fall" of Jerusalem in 587 B.C. was, in fact, a holocaust: a *burning* of the City of David. Previously, Jerusalem had been surrounded and surrendered, even occupied and looted, but this final destruction before the Babylonian armies was a terrible end by fire.

In the fifth month, on the tenth day of the month, in the nineteenth year of Nebuchadnezzar king of Babylon, Nebuzara-dan, captain of the king's bodyguard, came to Jerusalem and set fire to the house of the Lord and the royal palace; all the houses in the city, including the mansion of Gedaliah, were burnt down.

—Jer.52:12-13

The city was left a burnt and barren skeleton of its former glory, a place now fit only for foxes, foreigners and those few Jews who returned to the dead body of the great city, like the faithful to Gethsemane, to lament over what once was. The walls and gates lay in ruins; the Temple and its sanctuary destroyed and desecrated; dead bodies lay every-where with the stench that goes with such a slaughter. Furthermore, all its leaders had been carried into exile. Even king Zedekiah had been captured, his sons executed before his eyes, and then his own eyes put out before he, too, was taken away into exile where he died in prison.

In addition to expressing the people's horror at the destruction of Jerusalem, their sad laments reflected an incredible despair over the loss of family and loved ones now gone, dead or in exile. Even worse, these lamentations take us into the dark hole of the Judean soul and their cry, "Why us, Oh God?"... "Why has this happened to us?" For the Jews these human questions went beyond personal grief and political tragedy, to those deeper, religious questions about their role as a Hebrew nation whose symbols were now gone or useless.(1)

The Book of Lamentations contains elements of the Jews' first search for theological answers about end-time in light of the fall of Jerusalem and their despair. These poems also reflect a deep shame at having become the scorn of their traditional enemies: the scoffing, scavenging bands of "Ammonites, Moabites, Philistines and Edomites (who) all swarmed in" plundering, mocking and settling old scores with a furious vengeance.(2) They wanted answers from God and thus the speculation is that these poems may "have been used — at public ceremonies on the site of the ruined temple."(3) It seemed as if they were in a bottomless pit with no one to pull them out. Their historic rescuer, Yahweh, had abandoned and forgotten them.

> *Still we strain our eyes*
> *looking in vain for help*
> *We have watched and watched*
> *for a nation powerless to save us.*
> *When we go out we take to by-ways*
> *to avoid the public streets*
> *our days are all but finished*
> ***our end has come**.*
>
> *—Lam 4:17-18*
> *(emphasis added)*

Between the Fall of 1981 and 1983, a scorched-earth pacification was carried out against the Indian villages in the highlands of Guatemala. The slaughter centered around what is called the Ixil triangle — the villages of Chajul, Nebaj and Cotzal — extending outward from there to cover the whole region of the Quiche. The murder of the inhabitants of one of some 44 villages which were totally destroyed — Santo Tomas Ixcan — was a burning, leading to the complete elimination of that community:

> *On February 15, 16 and 17, 1982, 150 persons from Santo Tomas Ixcan were massacred. At 11 p.m. on the night of the 15th, the national army arrived and fired on the houses. They pulled the people who were not killed in their homes out and killed them outside. Then they put all the cadavers in the church and burned them. The carbonized bones and ashes remained in the church. The national army burned everything. Now nothing and no one remains in this place.(4)*

When the holocaust of the highlands was over, at least 30,000 persons lay dead, some 50,000 remained unaccounted for and over 1 million persons had fled to other places inside Guatemala or across the border into Mexico, some moving on to Honduras, Belize and the United States.(5)

While this pacification was carried out by the Guatemalan military — including the use of the specially-trained killer patrols, the **kaibiles**, under the direction of General Benedicto Lucas, **the technique had been learned from the Americans out of their Vietnam experience**. Indeed, as mentioned earlier, this strategy was first applied to Guatemala in 1967-68 at the urging of the CIA and the Pentagon. Far more incriminating is the U.S. role in the 1981-83 counterinsurgency itself a cover-up of this Indian massacre via the support and collaboration provided by the Reagan administration. The President, together with evangelist Pat Robertson, recruited a former high-level Guatemalan military officer. General Efraím Ríos Montt, to serve as president of Guatemala during the period of the mass killings.(6) Placed in that position over the objections of the Guatemalan military, Ríos Montt — a self-styled "born-again" convert to the Church of the Word in Eureka, California — replaced the hated General Lucas García in order to officially "wipe the slate clean."(7) By temporarily reducing repression in Guatemala City, Ríos Montt presented Guatemala to the world as a more pacified country precisely at the moment when the main killing was going on in the highlands. As soon as the holocaust was over, in August 1983, Ríos Montt was removed from office and replaced by hardliner General Mejía Victores. He had served his function as a cover for the Indian slaughter.

While the guilty parties — Ronald Reagan, Ríos Montt and Mejía Victores — could walk away from their crimes (because who would know outside of Guatemala and who would dare mention the crime inside), **the Indians knew and have remembered every detail down to this day**. They remember that villagers were not merely shot and their houses burned but that sadistic torture preceded the final destructive acts, such as in the case of the massacre which occurred at San Bartolo in January, 1982:

> *The children's throats had been slit and sharply pointed sticks had been driven into them. Some people had been crucified and sticks driven into their mouths... Some young men had their testicles cut off, women were cut open and most were nude. I counted 100 dead in Tacachat and another 80 in Las Canoas. Altogether, I counted more than 300 dead.(8)*

Nor for many was that terrible holocaust the end of their suffering. Like the survivors in Jerusalem after its terrible burning, there was no security in the mountains to which they had fled because the refugees came under constant attack by the military who pursued them. In their desperate flight from death, there was no one to comfort or help them, no food or shelter; everything lay in ruins and now they had to watch their children starving to death.(9)

So the endtime in the highlands was very similar to that in Jerusalem, a time of lamentation and terrible questioning about their unknown future. Their cries were like those of the mothers of the holy innocents in Bethlehem, slaughtered by King Herod. A cry of lamentation which seemed to echo backward and forward in history across the centuries. Backward to Jerusalem after its fall in 587 B.C. with "Rachel weeping for her children, and refusing consolation, because they were no more" (Jer.31:15), and forward to the 1980's in Guatemala to the "the silent, warm weeping of Indian women without their husbands... the sad gaze of the children fixed there beyond memory..."(10) From 1984, we read from a Guatemalan poem:

Remember, O Lord, what has befallen us...
our inherited lands
have been turned over to strangers,
our homes to foreigners...
Around our necks is the yoke of those who drive us;
We are worn out, but allowed no rest...
The wives of Zion were ravished by the enemy,
the maidens in the cities of Judah...
The whole description by Jeremiah
in his lamentations
fell like a torrent
upon my heart.(11)

—Julia Esquivel

The Great Theological Question: Why Jerusalem Was Allowed to Fall? What was the Role of God in This Endtime of Israel?

Anguishing human questions and humiliating political uncertainties raised by the fall of Jerusalem pointed to profound theological questions about the future of Israel. The typical human cry in a time of tragedy, "Why did this happen to us?" and the traditional political question, "Who's responsible for this?" forced the Jews left behind in Judah to ask an even more disturbing theological question, "Does this mean that God has abandoned Israel?" As a people of God whose very *raison d'etre* was their covenant with Yahweh; as a people who had listened to prophetic warnings for two centuries from Amos, Hosea, Micah, Isaiah, Nahum, Habakkuk, Zephaniah and now Jeremiah,(12) the question was: *has God abandoned us?* It was clear that God was no longer their protector; it also seemed (in the religious understanding of the time) that Yahweh was *weaker* than the gods of other nations, like Marduk, god of the Babylonians.

The prophets and more specifically, the *Book of Lamentations* takes this question a step further, deepening the theological contradiction. Its author is convinced that the destruction of Jerusalem by the Babylonians was no fluke on God's part; it was not that God didn't care or was asleep (as in Elijah's encounter with the gods of Baal), but worse, that God intended that Jerusalem should fall! As one writer puts it, "worse yet, this was his plan, carried out with methodical, deliberate and unrelenting thoroughness in fulfillment of his frequently announced threats."(13) God was no longer merely a weak benefactor; **Yahweh had become their enemy**:

> *The Lord played the enemy's part*
> *and overwhelmed Israel.*
> *He overwhelmed all their towered mansions*
> *and brought down their strongholds in ruins.*
>
> —*Lam.2:15*

The theological problem they faced was the conflict between their traditional notions of God and what now seemed to be happening in history. No longer a national protector or personal talisman, Yahweh who once defended Israel against its enemies had now become an enemy, challenging the Jews' very idea of what it means to be "a god." Here was "our" god turning against the people, holding up a plumb-line to measure whether the Jewish nation of Judah was crooked or straight, and finding it very crooked indeed, had condemned Jerusalem right out of existence. Israel had failed the test; she had proven herself unworthy; her mission was finished!

One response to this pessimistic interpretation was "no", the Jews were merely being punished for their sins in order — in some unknown future — to be forgiven after sufficient time of suffering and proper repentance.

> *We ourselves have sinned and rebelled,*
> *and thou hast not forgiven.*

In anger, thou hast turned and pursued us
and slain without pity...(so)
Let us examine our path, let us ponder it
and return to Yahweh.
Let us stretch out our hearts and hands
to God in heaven.

—Lam.3:42-43; 40-41

The problem with this simplistic moral-theological syllogism: "you have sinned/you must repent/you will be forgiven" is that these mourners in Jerusalem were the poor, ordinary folk who had been left behind; people without wealth or power, those citizens who hadn't made the political decisions for which Jerusalem was being condemned. How could they be held responsible? The principle fault lay with the king, the priests and court prophets who should have but didn't warn them, indeed, who collaborated with the system (Lam.2:14; 4:13)! Further-more, the fall of Jerusalem represented that kind of traumatic shock which always accompanies a historical tragedy; unlike the death of a given individual, here a whole way of life had perished.

Yet, what difference did placing blame on anyone make now? Now, that all was lost and the society had come to an end! What good does it do to blame anyone when there is no nation; now that Judah is finished; since there was no future for the Jews? There they were, balancing on history's tightrope between a dead past and an unborn future, lost in the hopelessness of their present, meaningless situation. If Israel no longer has a mission in life; if the Jewish community has lost its purpose... then what was the meaning of life itself? This is why their personal loss and political tragedy lay so heavy on their hearts. And yet, these same mourners knew that God was still there; that somehow Yahweh still loved them...

The Lord's love is surely not spent
nor has his compassion failed;
they are new every morning,
so great is his constancy.

—Lam.3:22

The sufferers could go no further than this hope against hope at the moment. This was the limit of Lamentations' reach: the writer of these painful poems knew God was still there, but their pain was too great; as in Guatemala today, the loss too poignant. All they had were grief and questions. As we read about the conditions of the people at the end

of the holocaust in the highlands of Guatemala, emptiness and
lamentation is all that comes through when the Indians speak. And yet,
though all they had were sorrow and doubts; still their sad cries are
directed to God:

> *Why do you forget us so long*
> *and forsake us these many days?*
> *—Lam.5:20*

> *Lord, you conquered me,*
> *because you continue to be*
> *stronger than I.*
>
> *—Julia Esquivel, p. 41*

Significance of Societal Death for the Empire Vs. the People; Necessity of a Political-Theological Reflection

We must pursue these unanswered questions of the Judeans and
Guatemalans because on them hangs the nature of God's call for
Central America today as for the Jews of old. The physical disaster and
their despair not only raise questions about the nature of God but about
how to proceed and move forward in light of this *endtime*. The hardest
and most immediate reality for both peoples — Judeans and Guatemalans — was that the Empire was still in control, so that any question
about the future had to begin from that hard imperial reality and in the
context of apparent powerlessness of the people to change that!

During the post exilic period in Judah, the Babylonian empire was
omnipresent; everything came from it and depended on it. Judah was
now Babylon's colony; Jerusalem was ruled by Gedeliah, an imperial
puppet governor. Nebuchadnezzar had no thought, however, of
depopulating Judah and letting it fall back into a jungle, but only of
breaking the power of the people to ever revolt again. Think about the
significance of that purpose. **This is precisely the goal of modern
pacification!** Ancient Babylon and modern America use exactly the
same strategy and tactics to destroy all possibility of future resistance:
scorch the earth, kill massively, brutally torture, exile all potential
dissidents and then "rebuild" on the basis of fear and intimidation.(14)
This is precisely the model of U.S. pacification in Vietnam and in the
highlands of Guatemala... "a necessary evil" in order to maintain
imperial control!

The effect upon the people is, of course, absolutely devastating:
personally, socially, politically and theologically disastrous; a time of

societal death. In the highlands of Guatemala, after the fire and torture and the burnings... there was, for those still alive, only flight and panic. In the mountains, they were hunted down, killed or starved into submission. In the destroyed areas, strategic hamlets were set up as in Vietnam, places for women and children, constantly patrolled by Guatemalan soldiers, often surrounded by barbed-wire with tall look-out towers manned by ever-watchful guards. For the men and boys, civilian "defense patrols" were created in which they had to serve under threat of death to spy on and repress their own people. This pacification strategy also aims at eradicating from the soul of the children all traces of Indianness: no indigenous clothing, only Spanish language; the outlawing of all Indian rites and traditional customs. The plan is *ethnocide*: the blotting out of their past history; the tearing out of their culture by the entrails.(15) In modern Quiche as in ancient Jerusalem, the impact on the people was physical, cultural, religious death: a total *endtime*.

These two pivotal years — 587 B.C. and 1980 A.D. — are not merely moments of transition from the old to the new, but because of the systematic attempt to destroy their culture and faith in God and to replace that with imperial idolatry, represent a complete historical disjuncture which demand radical theological answers. Babylonian captivity and the occupation of Judah imprinted itself upon the mind of the Jew forever: the absolute mercilessness of imperial power; the total disruption of the exilic experience; and then the need to rethink everything they once believed about themselves, the Word of God and their faith. So too in Guatemala, the Indians call this scorched earth pacification by the **kaibiles** and the American Empire in 1982-83 comparable only to one other experience in their long history: the Spanish conquest and its decimation of the Mayan civilization. When biblically oriented Americans read about the Babylonian captivity, it is only an interesting bible story whereas for those Jews it meant death and destruction. When we Americans read about the holocaust in the highlands of Guatemala, it is only interesting news whereas for these Indians it meant death and destruction.

Thus their hard question *WHY?* Why had God allowed this horrible thing to happen was not for them an interesting philosophical discussion, it was an essential faith question in their desperate need to survive and move forward. The theologian Walter Brueggemann is therefore correct in noting that **this date 587 B.C. was a pivotal moment in this dialectic history from death-to-life**. The fall of Jerusalem was the end of their previous history; the exile the beginning of a totally new life. He is correct in saying that the Jews had to divest themselves of the past and take hold of the future:

> *(Judah) had to let go of the old world of king and temple that God had now taken from it. It had to receive from God's hand a new world which it did not believe possible and which was not the one it would have preferred or chosen.(16)*

But then, Brueggemann contradicts himself when he says that his concern is not with the political, cultural and historical implications of that crucial moment in time; he merely wants to make symbolic comparisons:

> *Our interest, however, is not in the descriptive character of a historical event. Rather, our study is organized around "587" now treated as **metaphor**!(17)*

This represents a significant retreat from the point he makes about the nature of that date "587" being pivotal as it is critical to our search for meaning in the *corresponding pivotal moment of "1980"*. Why his shift away from the historical? We must search for an answer to *his avoidance of the historical presence* in which the people are crying to God for help and God is using the prophets to confront them in history with an absolute crisis. Brueggemann certainly recognizes the rising crisis in our modern world as he notes that "God's work at transforming our world is apparent in the rise of the Third World Nations"(18) and when he "envisions the destruction of idols and the emergence of new community, will inevitably evoke resistance [from the powers]."(19) The problem, we think, lies precisely *in his separation of history from metaphor.* The answer to his avoidance of the historical encounter may be found in his statement about who he thinks we are, as the faithful in America:

> *the loss of authority of the dynasty and temple is analogous to the loss of certainty, dominance and legitimacy **in our own time**.(20)*

Brueggemann is comparing us North Americans with the Jews in ancient Palestine at the time of the exile. That is a false parallel, because **we are not Judah or the Jews, but citizens of Babylon, the cause of the problem**. While we the people can also be considered in some ways caught in a modern "Babylonian captivity" ourselves, we must find our answers to this injustice as those who benefit from a system *which is complicit with Central America's holocaust.*

His avoidance stems, it would appear, from two concerns: one *pastoral,* that of showing how the prophets helped the Jews deal with grief at the loss of their nation; and another *historical,* to show the prophets' concern about building links between the old and the new. The problem with these two legitimate concerns is that if God was the author of the fall of Jerusalem and if Yahweh intended that the Jews' old life should end, then pastoral adjustment is not the primary focus of the prophets, but rather their liberation: God was forcing a new life upon the Jews!

Behind this rupture and how to deal with it theologically involves what the Danish philosopher Soren Kierkegaard calls responding to the divine demand to choose — **"either/or"** — which side are we on, life or death? That is not merely to move through a moment of crisis as when a loved one dies but in the smashing of all false hope the Jews might still have about the glory of the old kingdom and new promises from the idolatry of the empire.(21) This is precisely the problem in Central America today — faced as they are by the diabolical strategy of U.S. imperialism — not merely how can they survive their terrible trial and suffering, but how can they use the present crisis and their faith to clarify once and for all the impossibility of depending on some new face cloaking the old order (like Cerezo or Duarte) or of believing in the new promises of the Empire! Both are siren songs which will only lead to further suffering and disenchantment. End-time in the physical/historical sense is thus intended by God **to force an end to all false hope about returning to the old orders**.

Consider this same distinction in our own unresolved crisis of Vietnam. We too have to deal with that event in terms of both the individual and collective tragedy it represents. At first, most Americans didn't want to deal with Vietnam at all, so we shunned the reality and rejected the victims, that is, our veterans returning from that holocaust. "Let's just put the whole thing behind us and move on" many said. But neither the reality of Indochina nor the suffering of our Vets went away. So, finally, we got around to dealing with Vietnam **at the pastoral level**, in several ways: we built the Veterans and ourselves a "wailing wall" — the Vietnam Memorial in Washington, D. C. — where we could grieve.(22) Next, we honored the Vets themselves, which we should have done years earlier but couldn't because of our ambivalence and guilt over the deed in the first place. Thirdly, we produced a whole rash of films about Vietnam, so the American people could "live the reality" vicariously. The best motive behind all these films and film-makers is to be found in the movie "Platoon" which basically argues that we should never do that kind of thing again. No doubt all of these are therapeutic to a point; all pastorally valid.

But by concentrating on pastoral adjustment we still fail to look at the structural cause behind our misadventure in Vietnam... **U.S. imperialism!** We went to Vietnam because we saw ourselves as the self-appointed guardians of an anti-communist ideology wherein we had to destroy all such movements anywhere in the world. The United States has never accepted the legitimacy of Third World uprisings against despots and colonialism but rather has labelled them all as communist-inspired. In fact, French colonialism was already dead in Indochina when we first went there in 1954-56 to shore it up. A democratic victory by Ho Chi Minh, espousing a constitution almost identical to our own, would have brought peace and justice to Vietnam compared to what had preceded it.(23) But we had to stop it and if possible destroy it simply because it was "communistic." Our arrogance in not even consulting with the South Vietnamese leaders on the wisdom or way of being in Vietnam is a further indication of our imperial arrogance. It is a subject we always avoid! **Until we deal with the United States as empire, we will never get Vietnam out of our soul**. This is why the present Central American situation is so critical to our own salvation as a people...because it makes the imperial issue absolutely clear.

Societal Death as the Strange Work of God in History

To find answers to these questions, we turn to what the prophets call the "strange work" of God in the process of the fall of Jerusalem and the war in Central America today. "Strange work" because Judah's tragic end wasn't merely a harsh judgement but something ultimately liberating for the Jewish people; "strange" because Babylon's triumph over the Jews initiates a process which ultimately leads to her own demise. Thus we read at the end of Jeremiah's book a strange citation which he directs at his historian or scribe, to whom he says:

> *When you have finished the book, tie a stone to it and throw it into the Euphrates, and then, say, "so shall Babylon sink, never to rise again after the disaster which I shall bring upon her.*
> —Jer.51:63-64

We believe it is part of God's "strange work" in Central America today that the Empire's systematic aggression and domination of the region

may be precisely **the preparation for its liberation while sig-
nalling the Empire's own eventual demise!**

The answers we are seeking about the implications of the death of
a society — reflected in the book of **Lamentations** — as they apply
to the questions raised by the Central American crisis and the role of
the Empire — may be found in two female prophets from Guatemala.
One of these "**quetzal** *prophets*"(24) is a woman named Rigoberta
Menchu — an oral transmitter of the Mayan tradition — who uses a
strange Indian term which was unclear to us at first... -**Xibalba**- (She-
bal-ba). Because of the way she used it in an interview about the
Guatemalan military, it was clear she was referring to them in a very
demonic way. As many people know, Rigoberta was forced (along with
other Indians) to watch Guatemalan soldiers torture and murder her
mother before her very eyes... in order to force her to cry out so they
could kill her too. We assumed that the word referred to that diabolical
behavior.

But there was something else, something more behind this curious
symbolic word. We discovered that in Mayan thought, the base of the
western quadrant of each pyramid is called Xibalba, representing
symbolically night and darkness and behind them metaphorically evil
and death.(25) This means that beyond Rigoberta's mother's death as
tragedy and the horror of her father being burned to death in the
Spanish Embassy fire-bombing, lay a deeper historical meaning and
metaphysical implication. Re-reading the *Popul Vuh* (the Mayan bible
(26), we realized that the term Xibalba refers not so much to evil deeds
as to a transcendental struggle between the forces of good and evil over
control of the world. Written shortly after the Spanish conquest, as a
great parable on the ultimate victory of the Mayan peoples over all
imperial **conquistadores**, it represents the same "strange work" of
God we find in Jeremiah: the apparent triumph of imperial evil in the
Babylonian destruction of Jerusalem only to be countered by Yahweh's
reversal as in the resurrection of Israel in exile, metaphorically depicted
by the Valley of the Dry Bones (Ezekiel 37). Life from death.

The other **quetzal** *prophetess,* Julia Esquivel, draws the connection
between this transcendental struggle and the role of the United States
today as a modern Babylonian empire. But her "strange work" is not
so much about judgement as it is of redemption, our conversion as U.S.
citizens, our consciousness-raising as North Americans about our
imperial idolatry. She writes of her dismay in trying to make Americans
understand and failing, how she is called by God to return time and
again until those of us who can hear, those of the faithful remnant who
will listen, are converted and convinced.

Then, in tears, I prostrated myself
and cried out: "Lord, what can we do?"
If they have no time
to hear the truth
and even less to seek it for themselves?
They are a people too ignorant and too comfortable.
Come to me, Lord, I wish to die among my people!"

Without strength, I waited for the answer.
After a long silence
and a heavy darkness...
He who sits on the throne
to judge the nations
spoke in a soft whisper
in the recesses of my heart:

"You have to denounce their idolatry
in good times and in bad
Force them to hear the truth,
for what is impossible to men,
is possible for God!"(27)

From both women, we hear anew the ancient warning of God's wrath and promise of an ultimate triumph so unique to the prophets, and yet as the book of Lamentations reminds us, the search for answers will only come out of a deep sadness and painful loss. In spite of all their experience with death, tragedy and separation, these two prophetic women have begun to provide us answers about the strange work of God in history that ultimately leads to societal redemption: the rebirth of the nation of Israel and the promise of liberation for Central America. But this word of hope within despair comes with a warning to the citizens of the Empire that her end is coming, and yet with that dying the hope for a new beginning in America.

FOOTNOTES — CHAPTER 9

1   Ralph W. Klein, *Israel in Exile*, Fortress Press, Philadelphia, 1979, p.5. "The old symbols had been rendered useless...the old institutions no longer functioned."

2   Bailey & Kent, op.cita, p.252.

3   Ibid., p.9

4   Frank & Wheaton, *Indian Guatemala: Path to Liberation,* EPICA, Washington, D. C. 1984, p.70.

5   Ibid., pp.70-92. See especially p.92 with sources. These figures have since been verified approximately by WOLA, Washington D.C. by data gathered in 1986-87.

6   Frank & Wheaton, *Indian Guatemala,* Ibid., p.72.

7   Rafael Mondragon, *De Indios y Cristianos en Guatemala,* COPEC-CECOPE, Mexico, 1983, p.46.

8   Guatemalan Church in Exile, "Guatemalan Indians: Beyond the Myth", *Managua,* Feb.-March., 1984, pp.23-24. Quote from Frank & Wheaton, *Indian Guatemala,* op.cita, p.71.

9   Frank & Wheaton, op.cita, pp.84-86. The great majority of refugees displaced to other cities also starved and were forced to beg in the streets of Guatemala's cities.

10   Julia Esquivel, *Threatened with Resurrection,* op.cita, p.59.

11   Ibid., p.101.

12   The pre-exilic prophets.

13   Ralph Klein, op.cita, p.12.

14   Bailey & Kent, op.cita, p.248. The purpose of pacification by the Babylonians was identical to that of modern pacification as devised by the United States in Vietnam and employed in Guatemala and El Salvador in the 1980's.

15   Frank & Wheaton, op.cita, p.81.

16   Walter Brueggemann, *Hopeful Imagination,* Fortress Press, Philadelphia, 1986., p.4.

17   Ibid., pp.3-4.

18   Ibid., p.6.

19   Ibid., p.5.

20   Ibid., p.6.

21   Soren Kierkegaard, *Either/Or*, Princeton University Press, Princeton, NJ, 1946, "Ancient Tragedical Motive As Reflected in the Modern," p.121, "the spectator has lost his compassion, but compassion is in a subjective as well as an objective sense, the precise expression of the tragic," i.e., **not to see the real problem and yourself as a causal agent in it.**

22   Elizabeth O'Connor, *Cry Pain, Cry Hope*, Word Books, Waco, Texas, 1987. Her reflection on the Vietnam Memorial as a modern wailing wall was made during her book party at the Potter's House in Washington, D.C. in 1987.

23   *The Indochina Story*, Committee of Concerned Asia Scholars, Bantam Books, New York, 1970, pp.22-23. "In 1945, as the war ended, the Democratic Republic of Vietnam had declared its independence from France in a document borrowing heavily from the American Declaration of 1776."

24   The *quetzal* is the national bird of Guatemala which cannot live in captivity symbolizing the Guatemalan people's determination to be free from both the local oppression of the military and imperial captivity.

25   Thomas & Wheaton, op.cita, pp.103-105, including a diagram of the Mayan pyramid.

26   *Popul Vuh*, the Mayan bible, is based upon the Ketchichal "sayings" which were written before the Conquest, but the *Popul Vuh* follows it, appearing around 1535ff. In the many battles between the sons of the Mayans and the Xibalba, sometimes one side sometimes the other wins, while the dead sons of the Mayans are often revived (resurrected) from the dead.

27   Julia Esquivel, op.cita, pp.89 and 91.

CHAPTER 10
LAND

A Guatemalan indian woman with her baby harvesting crops. As they say, "Sown to be eaten, it is the sustenance of the people made of maize. Sown to make money, it means famine for the people made of maize." *Men of Maize*, Miguel Angel Asturias

CHAPTER 10 LAND

Babylonian captivity is affirmed by Jeremiah as a way the
promise to the Jews will be fulfilled—in dialectical terms: the
end must come so that the future could begin.

—Ralph Klein

It is blood and pain that will water and make fertile new and
continually more numerous seeds... to build a more just and
human society.

—Oscar Romero

The most striking political and theological parallel between ancient
Judah and modern Central America is to be found in the apparently
contradictory promise of God through Jeremiah to the Jews just before
the fall of Jerusalem: "Submit to the Empire/Return to the Land." This
dialectic thesis finds its closest application in El Salvador where we have
witnessed since 1980 a mass exodus of refugees coming to the United
States, and more recently, their return as they begin to "repopulate"
their land. This dynamic of exile and return while the Empire is still in
power, this "**vay ven**" from their homeland to Babylon and back home
again is a foretaste of that ultimate promise of God that the people of
El Salvador shall fully inherit the land through this present "submission"
to the Empire. The prophets were claiming that this Babylonian
captivity would eventually lead to liberation!

They will be carried off to Babylon and stay there until the day
I fetch them back— it is Yahweh who speaks. Then I shall bring
them back and restore them to this place.

—Jer.27:22

Our focus is not on the exile in this section but on **the promise
of land because of the imperial occupation of their homeland**. In
the next chapter, we will deal with exile and the challenge of
Babylonian captivity as interpreted by the prophet Ezekiel. Here, we
are concentrating on life in Judah between the first and second attacks
by the armies of Nebuchadnezzar, during that decade from 596 to 587
B.C.(1) It was then when the witness and the word of Jeremiah found
its fullest expression in his contradictory message: "this is the end/here
is your future."

In parallel fashion, we are focusing here on those who have been
living in El Salvador these last nine years, that is, since the United States
began its aggressive involvement in Salvadoran politics under Jimmy
Carter until the present under Ronald Reagan (1979-1987 A.D.). At the

outset of this period, Mon.Oscar Arnulfo Romero carried out a very similar ministry to that of Jeremiah in the sense of this thesis "submit and return," not withstanding the fact that he was murdered after only three years of having been named archbishop. In this parallel, we are trying to understand the meaning of the prophetic promise of "return" as a result of divine judgement executed through imperial aggression. While it is true that the Salvadoran crisis was created by domestic forces of oppression and exploitation — i.e., by the military and oligarchy — it is the U.S. empire which is now in control of El Salvador and which through its aggression and exposure is helping liberate it. This does not in the least diminish the importance of the role of the revolutionary and democratic forces inside El Salvador; to the contrary, — they have greatly enhanced the contradiction.

Before we examine this strange irony and apparent contradiction, we must first ground our reflection in the unique ministries of these two prophets — Jeremiah and Oscar Romero — whose lives and messages form the basis for our assertion. These men of God had two unique characteristics in common: their *vicarious suffering* on behalf of their people, and, their prophetic message directed primarily *to the people* and increasingly less and less against the State and Empire.

The first common element in the lives of both prophets is their vicarious suffering in behalf of their people; their participation in the misery, shame and danger of their people — when such courage and boldness wasn't required by their station and calling. The deaths of Jeremiah in Egypt in 581 B.C. and of Oscar Romero in 1980 A.D. stemmed directly from this radical commitment to their people.(2) However much some biblicists would say that such suffering is predetermined, that is, required by Yahweh because they had been called to be prophets, still the choice to follow that call or not was still theirs to make . Beyond that, we are not referring to the mere call to be ministers of God, but to their **passionate identification with their people in dangerous situations and in the face of ruthless power**. Note the passion and pathos in each of these two men of God:

> *Let my eyes stream with tears,*
> *ceaselessly, day and night,*
> *For the virgin daughter of my people*
> *has been broken in pieces...*
> *Oh, the writhing of my bowels*
> *   and the throbbing of my heart!*
> *I cannot keep silence.*

> *—Jer.14:17; 4:19*

I ask the Lord during the week, while I receive the cries of the people and the sorrow of so much crime, the disgrace of so much violence, to give me the fitting word to console, to denounce, to call to repentance. And though I continue to be a voice that cries in the desert, I know that the church is making the effort to fulfill its mission.(3)

— *Oscar Romero*

Both prophets were deeply religious men; both held positions of national influence; and both openly criticized the role of Empire in relation to the suffering of their people. During their respective ministries, both prophets were repeatedly threatened with death and both were offered exile in foreign states which they refused... preferring to remain with the poor in the land.(4) Both of them spoke repeatedly against those in power(5) from public forums, including the temple of God.(6) And both were chastised by high-level religious peers as traitors to the nation and false prophets of God. In the case of Jeremiah we read:

I hear so many disparaging me,
' "Terror from every side!"
Denounce him! Let us denounce him!'
All those who used to be my friends
watched for my downfall...

—*Jer.20:10*

Mons.Romero had his detractors as well; those who accused him of being a false prophet, including his fellow bishops:

You're dividing the country. You're confusing the nation... We know your underhanded maneuvers. And then you appear as the victim, as if they're doing you every wrong. We're on to you...(7)

On the other hand, while they walked with their people-in-suffering, neither prophet ever softened his strong message of judgement and warning which they were called to proclaim. In spite of the pending disaster and obvious implications of this encounter between the Word and the idolatry, the people affirmed their prophecies. You can't fool the poor for long; they know how to distinguish a true prophet from a false one: true prophets don't capitulate before power; they speak the truth; they are consistent in both ministry and message.

While prophets are sensitive to the people's suffering that does not mean that their primary work is "a tale and voice of grief"(8); rather, it is a demand to push forward and never give up the struggle. Indeed, the prophetic word becomes stronger and clearer under adversity because of their passion for the people.

Prophets for the people, not merely against the System

A second similarity between these two men of God—Jeremiah and Oscar Romero — reflects a shift which we note between the pre- and post-exilic prophets in which the latter begin to direct their message **more and more towards the people and less and less against the corrupt powers**. This shift, particularly notable in Jeremiah and Ezekiel — who bridge the exilic process — reflects their growing concern about the people as the judgement falls upon the kingdom of Judah and their warnings become realities. This shift represents a movement on God's part from judge to redeemer and confirms the fact that the Word is not "absolute" but responds to historical exigencies and listens to the signs of the times!

And yet, these two prophets were not "populists" in the common usage of that word. The image of the all too familiar preacher or politician who dazzles his audience, is idolized by his congregation or blindly followed by party loyalists. On the contrary, these two prophets were often despised and hated because they spoke truth to power, astonishing even their admirers with the harshness and boldness of their message. They attacked the shibboleths of their day; those slogans used by the ruling class to keep the people in line through false hopes and superficial promises. As prophets of the people, part of their responsibility included challenging institutional religion when it tried to mask injustices at the national level.

Both were drawn into unavoidable encounters with the false prophets of their day. In the present crisis in Central America we have seen such reactionary priests, neutral pastors and opportunistic evangelists, who use religion to justify the imperial order. Some of this is the fruit of Western Christendom and its traditional sell-out to the powers that be; some of it is the product of North American missionary teaching; and sometimes, more crudely, because it is safer or produces economic advantages. Being anti-communist and pro-Yankee is, in many countries of Latin America and the Caribbean, almost a guarantee for success. It is not strange to discover that such pastoral patriots are used by the Empire as counter-revolutionaries, as in Nicaragua. Of them, the voice of Jeremiah speaks loud and clear, proving that this isn't some modern "political" development, but an age-old phenomenon by which clergy down through the centuries have used religion to justify the **status quo**:

> *For all, high and low,*
> *are out for ill-gotten gain;*
> *prophets and priests are frauds,*
> *everyone of them;*
> *they heal my people's wounds, but skin-deep only,*
> *with their saying, "All is well."*
> *All well? Nothing is well!*
>
> *Are they ashamed when they practice their abominations?-*
> *Ashamed? not they!*
> *They can never be put down nor ashamed.*
> *Therefore they shall fall with a great crash,*
> *and be brought to the ground on the day of reckoning.*
> *—Jer.8:10-17*

After his consecration as Archbishop of San Salvador, something drastic happened to Oscar Romero, changing him from a conservative Catholic bishop into a prophet of the people. His "conversion" happened on March 12, 1977, the day Padre Rutilio Grande was murdered in cold blood by members of a Salvadoran death squad on his way from Aguilares to the little village of Paisnal.(9) That State-approved murder of a priest of the Church produced a terrible conflict in Romero's soul, for Padre Rutilio was his best friend. As Archbishop, Oscar Romero faced a fundamental moral crisis: he was supposed to bless the State (that is the military, oligarchy) which murdered his own priests and tortured his people with impunity. He often spoke out about what he considered to be the worst sin in all of El Salvador: "institutionalized violence",(10) a sin which the Catholic Church in Latin America has overlooked for centuries. He could no longer be pastorally sympathetic towards the suffering of his people and also bless and condone the actions of the system. Deep down in his soul, he made a choice which would have momentous implications in the months to come: **to take the side of the people against this unjust State**. Although he would do this from within his religious role as archbishop and as part of his ecclesial responsibilities, still the choice was clear. Many of Mons. Romero's admirers today only want to praise him for his inspiring words or lament his tragic death without dealing with this fundamental choice, crucial for any true prophet: between pleasing the system and serving the people.

In taking this stand, Romero by his words and example intensified the polarization in the Salvadoran society, a fundamental division in the country caused by poverty, class injustice and military repression. Because he spoke the truth and held it up to the light of day, the people — so hungry for some honesty — poured into the cathedral in greater numbers every Sunday to hear the Word of God; to listen to his homilies. His peers, his friends in government, even those from the American embassy warned him of the danger he was in; of the risk he was taking by being so outspoken. But spiritually it was too late for him to turn back. The shock of all those deaths; the constant contact with one horrible killing and sadistic murder after another from 1977 onward, were screaming out like Abel's blood a message of protest a hundred times louder than all the reasonable words of caution coming from those defending the *status quo*. Romero had made his decision: he would stand with the people and witness out of that primary commitment.

> *I believe it my duty to make it as pastor of a people suffering injustice. It is a duty placed on me by the gospel, for which I am ready to face trial and prison, even though they would only add another injustice... (finishing by quoting Isaiah 32:17). Peace can only be the product of justice."(11)*

After only three short years of vicarious suffering and speaking the truth, Oscar Romero had become a prophet of the people of El Salvador for which they paid him their greatest honor... the right to be their spokesperson: "the voice of the voiceless."

Contradictory Promise: Submit to the Empire/Receive the Land

In light of these similarities in their personalities, let us now examine Jeremiah's seemingly contradictory promise: "Yes to Exile/Yes to the Land."(12)

> *But if any nation submits to the yoke of the King of Babylon and serves him, I will leave them on their own soil, says the Lord; they shall cultivate it and live there.*
>
> *—Jer. 27:11*

Remember that our focus here is on the Jews while they are still in Jerusalem between the two Babylonian attacks in 596 and 587 B.C. During those years, Jeremiah took an unusual stand for a Jew: he welcomed the pending collapse of the kingdom of Judah to the

Babylonians as the inevitable judgement of God. For that stance, he was considered a traitor to the Jewish state and its nationalistic religion. He was thrown into prison as a national-security risk; as a false prophet who had capitulated to the idolatrous Babylonian empire. Just how difficult Jeremiah's position was can be appreciated if we were to apply his perspective to the situation in El Salvador today. It would be like Mons. Romero saying "submit to U.S. imperialism" for only then is the recovery of your freedom possible! That sounds like a contradiction in terms. It doesn't make any sense. Empires are to be resisted... especially by the people who are being oppressed by them. Thus in the Exodus event, Yahweh responded to the cry of the people, challenged the Egyptian oppression and the enslavement of the Hebrews and assured them of liberation and a promised land. Though audacious, that sounded to the Hebrew slaves like a consistent political and theological position. It reminds us of the cry of the Zealots in Jesus's day: free Palestine from Roman tyranny!

We are convinced that this is precisely why the primary metaphor used in liberation theology in Latin America today to illustrate and inspire the struggle for liberation is the Exodus. Certainly for many people in Central America that event seems like the logical biblical paradigm for those suffering under U.S. imperial captivity. **But this is not the thesis of the exilic prophets**! Why not? Because the real liberation Jeremiah sought was not escape from the Babylonians — freedom from foreign domination — but something more radical: liberation *from their own captivity;* conformity to the *status quo;* belief in the Empire's promises; sell-out on the Word of God!

To demonstrate his point, Jeremiah placed a wooden yoke around his neck — the kind used for oxen — and paraded around with it on his shoulders, calling on the Jews to "submit to Babylon'" as an ox must submit to its taskmaster. The Jews were furious, scandalized, asking as they mocked Jeremiah, "What, us proud Jews, submit to Nebuchadnezzar? Never!" Challenging the prophet, Hananiah pulled the wooden yoke off of Jeremiah's neck, saying: "God says that I will break the yoke of Nebuchadnezzar king of Babylon...off the neck of all nations within two years" (Jer. 28:11). After a long talk with God, Jeremiah returned with *an iron yoke* around his neck and condemned Hananiah because he "preached rebellion against the Lord" in not *fully* submitting to Babylon. He also warned that Hananiah would die that same year, which is what happened. For Jeremiah, the crux of the issue was the Jews' own arrogance and sin; their own false hope and lack of faith. False prophets who he said, preach "Peace, peace, when there is no peace" (Jer. 6:14). For Jeremiah, there would be no quick solution, no easy forgiveness; as we Christians say, no "cheap" grace; no escape from the wrath of God's anger... Jerusalem would fall!(13) As one expert on the Exile reflects:

> *A call to submit to Babylon, to say yes to the reality and appropriateness of God's judgement— that was Jeremiah's and God's word as the shades of exile fell... Surrender to Babylon was the only logical and theological consequence to be drawn from an analysis of Judah's idolatrous infidelity.(14)*

On the other hand, towards the end of this interim period when the armies of Babylon were literally pounding against the walls of Jerusalem, when its fall was imminent, Jeremiah from his prison cell — mocked and berated as a traitor to the Judean cause — issued a message of hope! He purchased a plot of land from his cousin Hanamel in the town of Anathoth; bought it according to the Hebrew law of redemption (Cf.Lev. 25:25). As a kinsman-redeemer, the prophet agreed to pay the appropriate price; had his friend Baruch draw up the legal deeds to the property; signed them; and ordered the documents be placed in an earthen jar and buried in the ground...**in anticipation of that future date when the Jews would return to inherit the land promised them from the beginning**. He does this, mind you, at the very moment when Jerusalem is about to be destroyed and all its leaders sent into exile!

> *The time will come when houses, fields, and vineyards will again be bought and sold in this land... O Lord God, thou has made the heavens and the earth by thy great strength... nothing is impossible for thee*
>
> *.—Jer. 32:6-25*

This is clearly one of the most radical symbols of hope to be found in Hebrew scriptures but it is presented in *dialectical* terms not in *direct revolutionary* terms: Babylonian captivity is affirmed as the way the promise to the Jews will be fulfilled; the end must come so that the future could begin.

In the case of Oscar Romero's role in El Salvador we must ask seriously whether there is a corresponding parallel to this Jeremedic contradiction "Yes to the Empire/Yes to the Land"? Remember, mass repression in El Salvador and the mass exodus from it had not yet begun...they would follow Romero's death as horrors authorized and orchestrated by the Empire. Yet can we really assert that Romero was calling, as Jeremiah had, for the Salvadoran people to "submit to Babylon"? At first glance, it doesn't seem so. Certainly, he doesn't say so in specific terms and indeed, at one point towards the end of his life, he openly challenged the Empire by telling President Carter not to send military aid to El Salvador. On the other hand, if we recall that Romero often spoke about the necessity of many people and priests to die in order to build a new El Salvador, and, that he realized that the United States was taking control of his beloved country, then it is legitimate to advance the thesis that Romero did see such suffering and occupation as "submitting" to Babylon. And that he saw it in a dialectical way, for he made repeated references to the people "returning to the land" when the oligarchy and imperialists were gone.

> *It is blood and pain that will water and make fertile new and continually more numerous seeds — Salvadorans who will awaken to the responsibility they have to build a more just and human society— and that will bear fruit in the accomplishment of the daring, urgent and radical structural reforms that our nation needs.(15)*

Let us probe this assertion more carefully. In the first place, Romero affirms the theme "Yes to Exile" in the sense that he called on both the faithful and the hierarchy — indeed on the oligarchy and military as well— to leave their old ways: their old institutional prejudices; the old system of exploitation; the traditional practice of the military to use repression. In terms of the Church, Romero openly challenged the hierarchically-run *ecclesia* which was forever blessing military weapons and oligarchic businesses. He opted, instead, for the people of El Salvador and especially for the emerging Church of the Poor, affirming the Catholic bishops' statement about making "a preferential option for the poor". They were his priority and the criteria for his moral judgements in terms of what was and wasn't important in his ministry.

For his stance, Archbishop Romero ran into public conflict with other bishops in the country and specifically a challenge from Bishop Aparicio (as Jeremiah had been by Hananiah). In May, 1979, a majority of the bishops led by Aparicio sent a document to Rome entitled "Political-Religious Situation in El Salvador" which read...

> *...The pastoral practice emanating from the archdiocese (Romero)... incites to class struggle, to the radicalization of the peasantry and the laboring class, to revolution and taking power for the establishment of a socialist government of peas-*

ants and laborers. It manipulates the Bible, adulterates the figure of Jesus Christ our Lord, portraying him as a subversive and revolutionary, and political leader... Grass-roots communities dare to criticize bishops.(16)

In response, Romero went on quietly affirming the popular church, defending the persecuted, defining the "magisterium of the Church" as *being the people of God.*(17) By encouraging the **comunidades de bases** (CEBs),he was arguing for the emergence of a new Church, a community of the faithful within the "captive" institutional Church, even as the bishops were trying to force the CEBs to conform to the rule of the hierarchy. Similarly, in terms of the ruling class, he told them to give up some of their riches and their land, and most of all to stop their repression of the people:

> *But all this takes nothing away from the fundamental fact that in our country the children of God are being murdered with impunity, especially the poor. The favored of God, for whom at Puebla we made a preferential choice.(18)*

In all these ways, he was calling for a transformation of the society from within this captivity of traditional structures and even from within the Babylonian captivity of the Empire. While he said that the extreme situation in El Salvador made-popular uprising justifiable — "An insurrection is legitimate in the very exceptional case of evident and prolonged tyranny..."(19) yet what he was really arguing for in conversations with both the right and the left in El Salvador was the creation of a new society; a conversion from the old order to the "new man & new woman". Thus he referred repeatedly to Padre Rafael Palacios and all the other priests who were murdered by the death squads because of their identification with the poor and their servant ministries...

> *In him we see **the new man** and the zeal he had to make those new men that Latin America needs today, not just by **changing** structures but by **changing hearts**. It is the voice of conversion, the voice of genuine evangelization.(20)*

In terms of the second aspect — Return to the Land — the parallel with Jeremiah's words is once again borne out in the sense that Mons. Romero, by publicly rejecting the old order, was thereby rejecting reformist solutions and false promises, and in this way, was calling for the genuine liberation of the society. For instance, in terms of the political and agrarian reforms being espoused by the U.S. Embassy in the fall of 1979, Mons. Romero was very skeptical. On October 10, five days before the coup which removed Gen. Humberto Romero from power, he was visited by U.S. Ambassador Devine who asked him how he saw "the situation" and what he thought was "the solution" (that's how ambassadors talk!). Mons. Romero responded that for any change to be real it had to be a true one, not a false promise, as he said, "an option for **genuine** democracy."(21) In light of all the pseudo-democracy and contrived electoral processes which have dominated El Salvador since 1979, his skepticism was justified. After the coup of October 15, when the 1st. Junta was in office (though not in power) and the killings were increasing every day, Romero wondered publicly in his homily on Nov.4 whether "the security forces were not trying to weaken the new government, robbing it of its credibility by their brutality."(22)

For the archbishop, pseudo-reforms and artificial power only meant more shedding of blood in the country. By Dec. 9, it was obvious to him and many other Salvadorans that the old-guard military was back in control of the Armed Forces and the oligarchy of the media, and that the United States was complicit in this process. The U.S. Embassy's choice for head of the army was Col. Jose Garcia who quickly pushed aside the leader of the so-called "younger officers", Col. Majano, which meant (for Mons. Romero) that "the days of the Junta were num-bered."(23) The point is that **an essential part of any prophetic message is to challenge false promises and false hopes if any real change is to occur**. In this, Oscar Romero was as adamant as Jeremiah that only fundamental change could redeem the situation in El Salvador. Proof that the whole reformist orchestration by Washington D.C was a charade came on January 22, 1980 when a huge, peaceful march involving at least 100,000 persons — including workers, campesinos, students, professionals and religious — warned against a repeat of the massacre of 1932 when some 30,000 persons were killed.(24) What happened was to become a foreshadowing of pre-cisely another such tragedy. Suddenly, army troops and plain-clothes-men opened fired on the participants, shooting and killing indiscrimi-nately. From that moment on, Romero knew that the path to any new future for El Salvador would not be through some peaceful coup or superficial reform but by the "way of the cross."

And worse was yet to come...again, not referring to his own death, which Romero now knew was inevitable, but to the increasingly evident role of the U.S. Empire in the affairs of El Salvador. By early

February, he learned from the newspapers that President Jimmy Carter was planning to send military aid to El Salvador (not just anti-riot gear as before). So he wrote a letter of protest to the American head of State, imploring him — in the name of his stated concern about human rights **not to send such military aid and not to intervene directly into Salvadoran affairs**, for it would only result in increased suffering by the innocent.(25). The Vatican (true to form) was very upset by this prophetic message that sought peace so Rome strongly chastised the archbishop for daring to challenge the President of the United States. Through its ambassador to El Salvador, Robert White, Washington was polite but firm: the weapons were necessary to stop the communist rebellion and thus were needed to maintain "peace" in the country. It was the old imperial adage: **si vos paccem para bellum**: "if you want peace, prepare for war," that ancient slogan of the Pax Romana now resurrected by the Pax Americana.

At the same time, the oligarchy went forward with its plans to assassinate the archbishop. Though Oscar Romero knew that his time was coming, he became in those last days almost serene, like Jeremiah, in his conviction that with the U.S. takeover of El Salvador and all the disaster that implied for the people a larger judgement would befall El Salvador leading to eventual liberation. In the final weeks of his life, Oscar Romero made repeated references to **a return to the land** and the birth of a new society:

> *How beautiful our country would be if we all lived this plan of God each one busy in his or her job, without pretensions of dominating anyone, simply earning and eating with justice the bread that the family needs.(26)*

Romero emphasized that his words were not "political" in the sense of calling for a popular uprising, but "theological" that is they were meant to enlighten the ways of the land.(27)

Yet this philosophical perspective and hopeful vision for the future did not diminish his anger at the rising slaughter of the people going on during February and March, 1980. He increasingly turned his wrath against the systemic actors from the oligarchy, military and Empire:

> *Woe to the power when they do not take into account the power of God, the only powerful one! When they try to torture, to kill, to massacre so as to subjugate people to their power. What terrible idolatry is being offered to the god of power, the god of money! So many victims, so much blood, for which God, the*

true God, the author of human life, will charge a high price to these idolaters of power!(28)

Oscar Romero now knew that the power of the Empire and the evil of the military could not be stopped. He knew that there would be no easy passage across a "Red Sea" by which the children of El Salvador could pass unscathed as in the Exodus, protected by the mighty arm of God. He knew that the people would have to follow the Judean experience — the destruction of their country and exile into Babylonian captivity — in order to be finally rescued, returned and redeemed. He knew that they would only inherit the land through personal sacrifice and societal crucifixion. In his final homily, he talked once again about the land and of the good earth he himself was about to enter. Indeed, he was reading from the Gospel of John about the promise of the seed buried in the soil at the very moment that the evil ones entered the chapel that evening of March 24, 1980 and shot him down in cold blood:

> *Unless the grain of wheat falls to the earth and dies, it remains only a grain. But if it dies, it bears much fruit...*
> —Jn. 12:23-26

Romero's insight into the suffering and death of the Salvadoran people was, like the vision of Jeremiah, a dialectic perspective arising from his profound understanding of historical contradiction. Knowing there was no escape from the judgement of God against the old order, he also knew that the coming of the Empire to take over and dominate Salvadoran life would imply the inevitable demise of that old system. Ironically, the United States' desperate effort to secure its hegemony over Central America has undercut the Salvadoran oligarchy and remade the Salvadoran military in its own image... thus **exposing the Empire for what it really is: a more efficient death machine**. That exposure and arrogance will lead in time to its downfall and thus to the eventual return of the people to the land and the recovery of the nation's true sovereignty. As Jeremiah had clarified the issue so many centuries ago, arrogance is the real stumbling block of imperialism.

> *My quarrel is with you, "Arrogance"!*
> *It is the Lord Yahweh Sabaoth who speaks:*
> *your day has come,*
> *the time when I must punish you*
> *"Arrogance" will stumble, she will fall,*
> *no one will lift her up:*

I will light a fire inside her towns;
it shall devour all her surroundings.
   —Jer. 50:31-32

Thus our thesis is that the logical paradigm for Central America today is not the Exodus event but **the Exilic experience**. The liberation of the Isthmus is even now coming to pass, not directly but dialectically through the power and presumption of the Empire itself, as Jeremiah knew would eventually happen to Babylon. It is precisely because Romero recognized that this domination by the United States would lead to its downfall that he was more concerned about the transformation of the Salvadoran people into "new men & new women" in preparation for the building of a new society. "Yes to the Exile" is not an affirmation of the Empire but of God's use of the Empire to bring about repentance and return to the land. This is the "strange work" of God in Central America today.

FOOTNOTES — CHAPTER 10

1   The Babylonian crown prince Nebuchadnezzar defeated the Egyptian armies under Pharaoh Necho in 604 B.C. at the battle of Carchemish after which Babylon became master of the West-lands, including Palestine. The Babylonians attacked Jerusalem in 596 B.C. but were unable to break its fortifications and so retreated. They returned after Judah's renewed flirting with Egypt and this time in 587 B.C. penetrated the walls and destroyed the City of David.

2   Jeremiah refused to go to Babylon but was later forced to go to Egypt with his friend Baruch by Judeans who had murdered governor Gedeliah who feared the Babylonians. The prophet died there though we do not know the exact date. Cf. Siegfried Herrmann, Ibid., p.292.

3   James Brockman, *The Word Remains*, Orbis, Maryknoll, 1983, p.216.

4   Jeremiah was threatened with death under both kings Jehoiakim (Jer.26:8) and Zedekiah (Jer.32:2-3; 34:5); and, he could have gone to Babylon as privileged exile. Romero was often attacked by Bishop Marco Rene Revelo and threatened by Major Roberto D'Aubuisson (Cf.J.Brockman, pp.84-87; and Wheaton: *The Agrarian Reform in El Salvador*) and he was invited on February 15, 1980, by Miguel D'Escoto to spend time in Nicaragua.

5   Jeremiah openly attacked kings Jehoiakim, Zedekiah and Gedeliah as well as Nebuchadnezzar, king of Babylon. Romero openly criticized General Humberto Romero, General Garcia and acting head of Government Hector Dada (2nd Junta), as well as President Jimmy Carter.

6   Jeremiah used both the king's palace and the Temple; Romero, the Cathedral in San Salvador where his homilies became the principle instrument of national communication. Both men spoke publicly and wrote constantly, combining a ministry of word and action.

7   James Brockman, op.cita, p.101.

8   Walter Brueggemann, *Hopeful Imagination*, ibid., chap.2, as on p.33... "Jeremiah's testimony is a tale of grief... a voice of deep grief". It is not that the prophet didn't grieve with his people, but that his message is so much more than that.

9   James Brockman, ibid., pp. 8-11.

10   Ibid., p.129

11   Ibid., p.113

12   Ralph Klein in his book — *Israel in Exile* has been the most helpful in our understanding of this contradiction. He uses a similar phrase: "saying Yes to Exile — and No!," Cf. Ch.3.

13   The tragedy of Jewish leadership in Palestine today is that they see everything in terms of foreign enemies; nothing of their own captivity and sell-out to the American Empire!

14   Ralph Klein, op cit., pp. 49-50.

15   James Brockman, ibid., p. 201.

16   Ibid., p. 163.

17   Ibid.

18   Ibid., p. 164.

19 Ibid., p. 173.

20 Ibid., p. 161.

21 Ibid., p. 180.

22 Ibid., p. 184.

23 Ibid., p. 193.

24 The peasant-worker strike of 1932 was led by Farabundo Marti. In the massacre all the leaders of that movement were summarily tried and executed. The number of persons murdered in 1932 and 1980-81 is almost the same: *30,000 lives!*

25 Romero read the letter he was planning on sending to Pres. Carter during his homily on Feb. 17, asking for the people's approval. They gave it wholeheartedly, so that the request went from the Salvadoran people to the president of the Empire.

26 James Brockman, ibid., p. 210.

27 Ibid, pp. 207 and 210.

28 Ibid., pp. 209 and 210.

CHAPTER 11
LIFE

Orlando Valenzuela

Many young Nicaraguan women have gone to the front to defend the new life coming from their bodies and from the Sandinista revolution.

CHAPTER 11 LIFE

Son of man, I have appointed you as watchman to the House of Israel. When you hear a word from my mouth, warn them in my name...

The Lord Yahweh says this to the land of Israel: Finished! The end is coming for the four quarters of the land. Now all is over with you; I mean to unleash my anger on you, and judge you as your conduct deserves and force you to answer for all your filthy practices...

I shall make a covenant of peace with them, an eternal covenant with them. I shall resettle them and increase them; I shall settle my sanctuary among them forever. I shall make my home above them; I will be their God and they shall be my people.

—Ez.33: 7; 7:5-7; 37:26-28

Watchman! What hour is it of the night?
Watchman! What hour is it of the night?

Managua surrounded by a huge concentration-camp barbed wire
its decomposing body breaking into bits
*   buzzards over the City Bank*
Another Managua: block after block after block, leveled flat!
*   "Behold I make all things new...*
*   and our crime is to announce a Paradise.*
Monopolies are only since the Neolithic Age.
*   The Kingdom of God is at hand*
the City of Communion, brothers
*   Only the dead are reborn.(1)*

—*Ernesto Cardenal*

The biblical promise of liberation and the emergence of new life for Israel and Nicaragua begins with the prophets' unrelenting insistence that the old orders in Jerusalem and Managua must first fall. Not only must Zedekiah and Somoza leave but the whole corrupt structure of their kingly and dictatorial systems must come down. Furthermore, the watchman prophets must be just as vigilant in the new age to warn the people of the new temptations they face within the more sophisticated captivity of Babylon. They are, then, watchmen over the discontinuity between the old and the new: Jeremiah and Ezekiel for the Jews; Ernesto Cardenal and Miguel D'Escoto for the Nicaraguan people today.(2) All four watchmen are adamant that no reform of the old order is possible — the tyranny must go — thereby the people of God can be liberated to move forward in history towards a new life.

This new life is born within the context of contradiction: both Judeans and Nicaraguans are "liberated" *from national despotism into imperial captivity;* into the grips of a far more powerful, sophisticated and subtle tyranny than before. As the Brazilian educator Paolo Freire says, liberation means moving from "one limit situation to another,"(3) except that in this case the new oppressor (the Empire) is forced to become directly involved because the local despots (Zedekiah and Somoza) can no longer keep things under control. So the dangers and temptations are now even more formidable because the evil of the empire is more insidious: imperialism will be less visible, more covert, more deceptive... enticing the people into a false sense of peace and prosperity.

Ironically, this new captivity actually helped the exiled and subjugated peoples of God move forward towards fuller liberation because the sophistication of imperial domination steels their resolve, sharpens their skills, disciplines their organizations and broadens their vision.

> *The exile therefore was for the Jews a period of radical transformation. It wrought a fundamental change in their point of view, so that instead of being provincial and local in their interests they became interested in the whole world. The impression then stamped upon the national character has never faded out. The Jews have from that day to this become citizens of the world.(4)*

For the Jews in Babylon, the exile produced the synagogue, the diaspora and the return to Jerusalem. For Nicaraguans, pressure from the Empire forced the issue of Indian autonomy, the inclusion of all sectors of society into the political process, and the integration of the Church of the Poor into the revolution. In both cases, imperial domination strengthened the people's determination to be free.

On the other hand, the new captivity exposed the empires for what they really are: *enemies of the people* because of having to operate more openly and directly, using their own forces and resources; exposing as never before their lies and arrogance. The real challenge facing both ancient Jew and modern Nicaraguan is their ability to forge a new society within the parameters and pressures laid down by the imperial design.

For the Empire, the great threat of any new experiment in liberation is not external, that is, military aggression against the Empire (though that will be charged) but *the vision that something other than Babylon is possible*. For the Empire everything "out there" — in liberated territory — is considered to be chaos and repression. As Ernesto Cardenal reflects with great insight, it is an imperial crime even to think about building a paradise on earth; a new society of justice and peace. Thus Babylon never allowed the Jews to return to Judah to apply the new experiments in life which they were developing in captivity just as the United States is doing everything in its power to undercut and destroy the creative programs of the Sandinista revolution. As Larry Kuenning warned us back in 1978:

> *Babylon denies that this is an assault against the world. In Babylon the name of "world" is given only to the creations of Marduk; anything else belongs to the domain of Tiamat and can only be called chaos. The Babylonian empire, the domain of Marduk, is to be defended against the threat of the chaos outside; the chaos itself contains nothing to be defended. Far from being defended, Tiamat must be killed, and when this does not mean literally killing whoever and whatever threatens the orderly system of Babylon, it means at least preventing such threats from having any life of their own outside the structures of the great city.(5)*

Reagan's real fear is not that Nicaragua poses a military threat to the United States, as in his "domino theory"(6), but that it might succeed in and of itself, thus destroying the mythology which says "nothing good can come of revolution and socialism." So imperialism must forever confine and destabilize every progressive alternative so it does not become an inspiration for other liberation efforts.

The Old Order & The New Spirit in Nicaragua

The most apt metaphor used by Ezekiel to describe the old order of the Judean kingdom — the reign of Zedekiah — was that of a rotten building with crumbling walls.

> *Instead of my people rebuilding the wall, these men come and slap on plaster. Tell these plasterers: it will rain hard... and down will come the wall. Will not people ask: where is the plaster you slapped on it?... I mean to shatter the wall you slapped with plaster, to throw it down and lay its foundations bare.*
> —*Ez.13:11-14*

The prophet was not just condemning a single, corrupt leader like King Zedekiah but the whole unjust system which Judah had become. For

Ezekiel, ancient Judah was like the walls of a house eaten away from inside by termites; it was a crumbling structure that could not be saved by external whitewashing.

So too, the old order in Nicaragua represented by the Somoza dynasty was a rickety old building daubed with plaster and whitewash on the outside to make it look good while inside it was hollow and evil. On July 21, 1979, when a group of Nicaraguans along with a few North Americans took over the Nicaraguan embassy and ambassador's residence in Washington, D.C., they found whole rooms, indeed entire sections of those buildings filled with trash!(7) Accumulated rubbish from years of decadent living and indifference to detail: old papers, clothes, gifts... junk. The old cronies of the dictator had used the front rooms for "show", elegant diplomatic receptions, while just underneath the floor and behind the walls was nothing but trash and decay.

So too, the mighty National Guard, those bullies who protected the dictator and repressed the Nicaraguan people, so powerful looking and proud on the outside were vain and corrupt on the inside because of so many years of privilege and power. "Since Somoza's criterion for promotion to high Guardia ranks eliminated the most competent and popular officers from high positions and since total loyalty rather than combat ability was the primary requisite for being given command"(8)... the Guard was only *efficient in brutality* and therefore hated by the people. Notwithstanding all the Guard's modern equipment, U.S. training and unlimited funding...

> *The Guard was an empty, rotted shell. It delighted in its reputation of toughness, but its officers had grown fat and lazy from corruption. The Guard's toughness, moreover, had been proved by the murder and brutalizing of women, children and unarmed men.(9)*

These forces and their leaders make up the core of the present *contra* army, that corrupt and repressive force Ronald Reagan euphemistically calls "freedom fighters."

This is why the end of the old Somoza dynasty came so quickly and easily in July, 1979, when the Sandinista forces and the Nicaraguan people poured into Managua *en masse* while the cowardly National Guard soldiers desperately tried to change into civilian clothes and flee for their lives. It was the fall not merely of an old order, but of an evil one. As one heroic priest who died fighting Somoza, padre Gaspar García Laviana, said: "Somocismo is sin, and to free ourselves of that oppression is to free ourselves of sin."(10) The fall of the dynasty was thus a time of rejoicing:

As the joyous music and instructions continued into the day,
people poured out into the streets. Truck loads of "muchachos"
headed for Managua. Church bells rang in the border towns
and refugees began crossing into territorio libre— free territory
— proclaimed by signs at the border.(11)

The new replaced the old like the coming of the light of day ends
the night of darkness and sin. Once Jerusalem and Managua had fallen
and the old despotism had ended, the prophets themselves could once
again speak; could announce the good news; could proclaim the
promise of God — hope for future history. Early after his call, Ezekiel
had been silenced by God as a sign against the rebellious Jews who
would not, therefore, be allowed to hear the Word of God. "I am going
to make your tongue stick to the roof of your mouth; you will be
dumb"(Ez.4:26). But now that the old order was finished and Jerusalem
had fallen, Ezekiel could speak once again: "The city had been taken...
(the Lord) had opened my mouth... and I was no longer dumb"(Ez.33:21-
22).

A similar thing happened in Managua in September, 1979. A
conference was held at the Catholic University, a dialogue between
Marxists and Christians (now that the peace had come, the lion and the
lamb could lay down together). The principal speaker on the first
evening of that event was Commander Jaime Wheelock, Nicaragua's
expert on agrarian reform. But the podium microphone wouldn't work,
so Padre Alvaro Arguello asked him to simply speak loudly so the
hundreds gathered there could hear. Wheelock apologized, saying he
would do his best, but it was hard to speak out since they had been
"silent" for ten years speaking only in whispers. But that night he spoke
out for the first time in a decade loud and clear, announcing the new
day of hope for Nicaragua wherein communists and Christians could
work together for the People, serving them and bringing new life and
justice to the country.(12)

In the same spirit, the first national program of the new government
was a literacy campaign by which all Nicaraguans might learn to speak
and read and write. The campaign would, moreover, be held in three
languages: first in Spanish, and then throughout the Zelaya and Atlantic
coast in English and Mosquito. In rural areas the illiteracy rate was
estimated at 75-80 percent, and, for women in many villages, sometimes 100 percent.(13) Within five weeks of the Sandinista victory, plans
for a Literacy Crusade were begun under the direction of Fernando
Cardenal. Influenced by Paolo Freire's pedagogical methods, the
planners hoped to provide one literacy teacher for every five campesinos. The volunteers worked in the fields with their pupils during the
day and taught them at night. By the end of the Crusade it is estimated

that 500,000 people who previously could not read were basically literate: Nicaragua had found its collective voice.(14)

This newfound voice was not only a revolutionary one, it was above all — in the spirit of the prophets — a *moral voice*. In any revolutionary experiment as in any imperial conquest, the question is "how will the people be treated," or more specifically, "their enemies." In Nicaragua there would be no revenge; the policy was that everyone was free as long as they did not engage in counterrevolutionary activities. Some of that began to happen in 1979 and some political prisoners were taken in. But the real test came one day, early in the revolution, when Commander Tomás Borge came upon a man on the street who had been his torturer and had murdered Borge's wife. The man stopped dead in his tracks, uncertain what was to be his fate. The commander looked at him hard for a moment, and then went up to him, embraced him and forgave him.(15) The new word of the revolution was also a biblical word of new life: the sins of the old order had been forgiven. Said Borge: "Our vengeance towards our enemies will be to pardon, it is the best of all vengeances."(15)

Prophetic Faith in a Foreign Environment: The Mobility of God

The positive side of this contradictory history of exile and liberation was the prophetic revelation that God was in the midst of this process; indeed, that Yahweh was present in the exile... in that foreign environment. Remember that Ezekiel the priest had been taken into captivity with all those Jews exiled to Babylon in 596 B.C., that is, in the first exile. So from the Psalmist pondering over how the Jews could "worship God in a foreign land"(Ps.137:4), emerged the first theological question about Yahweh being able to operate in captivity now that "his throne" in the Temple in Jerusalem had been destroyed. God had always been associated with the Temple — the holy place — so that the theological question for the exiles was posed in rather crude geographical terms: *Can the Holy One of Israel be in this unholy place of Babylon?* Indeed, the prophet's vision about this new revelation came to him at the very beginning of his ministry "among the exiles beside the river Chebar" in Babylon (Ez.1.1). Ezekiel answers this question with his amazing metaphor about the *mobility of God* which affirms in a very dramatic way that Yahweh can operate outside of the holy of holies in Jerusalem. Furthermore, the metaphor takes the rather mechanistic way the Jews had of looking at God as something fixed in time and space and turned it into a marvelous science-fiction instrument of movement.

In the center, four animals in human form; each had four faces and four wings, facing in all four directions... but they went *straight forward. The were mounted on glittering wheels, wheels within wheels, which went forward in all four directions at once **but kept their course unswervingly.***

—*Ez.chap.1*
(emphasis added)

There was an unconscious fear among the Jewish exiles that if God were removed from a fixed place in Jerusalem to a foreign environment that the fixed covenant principles of justice and forgiveness would also become ungrounded and fluid; they would lose their absoluteness. Therefore, Ezekiel's emphasis that for all God's marvelous mobility Yahweh would remain the same in substance, that God would "keep his course unswervingly." The Jews were wrestling, of course, with their own moral uncertainties about being there in Babylon without a Temple and without the old societal mores (now that Judah was gone); they were afraid they might stray from the Word and start living and thinking like Babylonians. The moral-theological question was therefore situationally valid: *Can we continue to be faithful Jews in this Babylonian captivity?*

This is an equally valid question for Nicaraguans today living within a socialist revolution under pressures of a U.S. imperial war just as it is for the exiles who live in these United States. The question today is posed, however, not in personal-spiritual terms but in political-geographical terms: Can Christianity survive within the foreign environment of a socialist revolution? At the crude level of religious freedom, U.S. propaganda declares falsely that there is religious persecution in revolutionary Nicaragua. That is a lie, of course, contradicted by the fact that on every Sunday since July 19, 1979, some 350 religious services have been held in Managua alone without interruption nor harassment. At a more sophisticated level, both the Empire and the Vatican claim that there is a life-and-death impasse between the Sandinista government and the Catholic hierarchy suggesting that the revolution is anti-religious just as Marxism is atheistic and therefore that God cannot operate freely in Nicaragua; i.e., that Yahweh has no mobility in a socialist society!

This was *not* the position of the Catholic Church in Managua at the beginning of the revolution, that is, before the Empire began to put pressure on Archbishop Obando y Bravo in 1981. In the fall of 1979, the Catholic episcopate (the collective body of bishops) issued a positive statement about the revolution:

We believe that this word can be of service to the people of God, animating them in their commitment, and helping them discern what is the work of the Holy Spirit in the revolutionary process.(16)

Nor, in the beginning, did the Sandinistas see any fundamental conflict between the revolution and the Church, for certainly all kinds of Christians — Catholics, Evangelicals and Pentecostals — had openly participated in the revolutionary overthrow of the Somoza dictatorship.(17) Furthermore, until the fall of the tyrant, dozens of Christian Base Communities had used Catholic parishes as a base for their anti-Somoza activities: carrying medical supplies, messages to the Sandinistas and helping those pursued by the National Guard to hide or escape. The man considered by many to be the hard-line ideologue of the Sandinista revolution, Tomás Borge, when speaking about the potential relationship between the Church and the new State held that there was real potential for good relations between the two *at the spiritual level!*

> *...understanding from the outset that there was no contradiction between being a Christian and being a revolutionary made incarnate a political and spiritual potential whose recent dimensions are only now beginning to be transcended.(18)*

This euphoria continued at the popular level during 1980 although Obando y Bravo and some of the other bishops had begun to pull back at the institutional level. For instance, when the Base Communities (CBs) were asked to leave the parishes, most of those Christians chose to help rebuild Nicaragua from within the revolutionary organizations rather than "as welfare agents" of the Church. This led to a certain "distancing" between the institutional Church and the CBs (under the leadership of CEPA), though no open break took place during 1980. Indeed, at the personal level, many prominent Christians were joining the revolutionary government, such as Roberto Arguello, president of the Supreme Court, who said:

> *As I see it, this revolution meshes very well with Christianity, especially insofar as it aims to benefit the poor and favors the most marginal groups in the country. Everything the revolution has done has been for the poor at the expense of those who are better off. That's where I see a great deal of overlap between the revolution and Christianity, in the love the gospel shows toward workers, the humble people.(19)*

This commitment of Christians participating in the Sandinista government and the revolutionary process was not limited to a few notables like Ernesto Cardenal, Miguel D'Escoto, Fernando Cardenal, Carlos Tunnermann, Alvaro Arguello, etc. etc., but included Christians from all classes and walks of life. It was a meeting of minds and hearts over the *project of the revolution not around ideological principles.*

This was precisely the concern of the United States, which saw this salutary relationship as a serious threat to the Empire's ideology, for as technocrats say, "this doesn't compute." In the U.S. script about socialist revolutions, written by anti-communistic prejudice and U.S. propaganda, *there has to be a fundamental conflict between Church and a revolutionary State as well as between Christians and Marxists, yet that simply wasn't happening in Nicaragua.* There was no repression of the Church; Christians were joining the revolutionary process; there was no fundamental theoretical clash between the goals of the Revolution and the Gospel. As such, the Sandinista experiment represented a serious threat to the Empire's ideology; it broke the stereotype; it unmasked the mythology of the East/West conflict; most seriously, *it produced hope about the possibility of a creative alternative outside the Empire!*

As soon as Ronald Reagan entered the office of the presidency of the United States, he initiated his policy of destabilizing and discrediting the Nicaraguan government and immediately labeled the Sandinista revolution "a Marxist-Leninist totalitarian state." By November 1981, he had appropriated $19 million from discretionary funds to supply the *contras* and ordered the CIA to coordinate their activities.(20) The good image of the revolution already building in international circles had to be destroyed; the progress being made at the social levels inside Nicaragua had to be de-stabilized and the attention of the American people had to be diverted to a made-in-the-USA *contra* war. The U.S. answer to the revolution — war and propaganda — was put into full operation. To counter this new breath of life which the revolution had brought to Central America, the United States would offer up its alternatives: lies and killings: this creative revolution would have to be destroyed because Marduk demanded it.

New Heart of Flesh in Nicaragua: Creating New Men and New Women

God's whole purpose in bringing down Jerusalem and forcing the Jews into exile was redemptive: to restore life to a dead or dying Israel. But this meant that the old ways, attitudes and practices had to be replaced by their opposites. Thus Ezekiel's theophanic vision about a new Israel involved a cleansing, a conversion and a rebirth at both personal and societal levels:

> *I shall pour clean water on you and you will be cleansed; I shall cleanse you of all your defilement and all your idols. **I shall give you a new heart, and put a new spirit in you**; I shall remove the heart of stone from your bodies and give you a heart of flesh instead. I shall put my spirit within you... You will live*

*in the land which I gave to your ancestors. You shall be my
people and I will be your God.*

—Ez.36:25-28

While the Sandinista struggle triumphed on July 19, 1979, the end
of the fighting only marked the beginning of the real revolution, the
building of a new society. By 1980 — that pivotal year in Central
American history — the conversion of the Nicaraguan people, the
rebirth of a society with a heart of flesh and spirit of love was becoming
a reality. But any such "rebirth" has to be incarnated into concrete
expressions of new life. This has been the story of the Sandinista
revolution over these past eight years. Yet this societal transformation
has almost gone unnoticed by most U.S. citizens because of U.S.
propaganda. But those who have visited Nicaragua personally and
participated in some way in any one of dozens of these new projects
of life, know the changes are real. These projects stand as proof of the
revolution's creativity and effectiveness despite the negative aspects of
Nicaraguan society caused by the *contra* war: hunger, long food lines,
lack of all kinds of consumer products, black-marketing, rampant
inflation, brown-outs and water shortages. In the midst of all this
hardship and the Empire's attempt to discredit and to strangle the
revolution, all kinds of new forms of life have emerged. It is important
to list some of these achievements as signs of this new life, and to
understand that these developments do not exist in the other countries
of the region:

EXAMPLES OF NEW LIFE UNDER THE SANDINISTAS
(Not found in other Central American Countries)

- Literacy programs *for the whole country in three languages*
- Health projects, public clinics and *preventive medicine for everyone*
- Indian *participation in the Council of State and autonomy*
- No repression or harassment *of Base Christian Communities or their leaders*
- National Trade Unions which *are not influenced by U.S. trade unionism* (AIFLD)(23)
- Widespread *land distribution to the peasants worked as cooperatives*
- Freedom of *movement in the country (except in the war zones)*
- Government support *of women's organization in combating machismo*
- Encouragement *of the culture of poor and marginal groups*
- Education through *high school for all who want it* (also available in Costa Rica)

- A new Constitution which gives equal power to all classes and recognizes Nicaragua *as a multi-ethnic society with equal rights for all minorities*

These powerful signs of new life are facilely dismissed by U.S. propaganda saying that they have been obtained at the loss of political and personal freedom in what is nothing but a totalitarian state. As the New Testament says, "by their fruits you shall know them" whether one is good and the other bad. In Central America, one need only compare this incredible record of the Sandinista revolution with life in Honduras, El Salvador and Guatemala... the three pawns of the Empire in the region. By every criteria these other societies fail to measure up, indeed, have become increasingly repressive societies. While there is no question that there are avowed Marxists in the Sandinista government and that its project is pro-socialist, this means on behalf of the peasants and the workers to whom the revolution gives "preferential option"... the same goal sought by the Catholic Church in its declaration at Puebla in 1978, " a preferential option for the poor." Nicaragua's leading poet-prophet explains why in Nicaragua these two presumably antagonistic entities — Church and Revolution — are, under the Sandinista banner, coming together:

> *What most radicalized us politically were the Gospels. At mass, we discussed the Gospels with the peasants in the form of a dialogue, and they began to understand in the essence of the divine message the heralding of God's kingdom. Which is the establishment on earth of a just society, without exploiters and exploited...(21)*
>
> —*Ernesto Cardenal*

The political uniqueness of the Sandinista revolution is found in what Guilio Girardi calls an inductive model of Marxism "which has allowed us to incorporate revolutionary Christianity and democratic institutions into a socialist framework."(22) From the prophetic perspective, the uniqueness of the Sandinista experiment is found in its priority of the people over proscriptive ideology.

Life Beyond Human Capability: The Role of the Demonic

In the exilic experience, the question of the future went beyond the issue of life to that of resurrection, and therefore to the difference between human will and the spirit of God. At the basic level of survival, both the Jews of Judah and in Babylon were going to "make it." Those in Judah still had a few crops, herds, vineyards so they could survive "off the land." Those in Babylon were starting from scratch but Babylon was rich and there were possibilities if one worked hard. Thus in terms of mere existence, human will and determination were sufficient for the Jews. But in terms of the *political* future of Israel and even more uncertain the religious role of Israel as the chosen people of God, the Jews felt completely helpless. These matters were in a very real sense "out of their hands." It is within this context of the political and missional nature of Israel's future that the prophet Ezekiel posed his greatest theological question to the Son of Man:

"Can these bones live?"

The hand of Yahweh was laid on me, and he carried me away by the spirit... and set me down in the middle of a valley, a valley full of bones. He made me walk up and down among them. There were vast quantities of these bones on the ground the whole length of the valley; and they were quite dried up. He said to me, "Son of man, can these bones live? I said, You know, Lord Yahweh". He said, "Prophesy over these bones. Say, "Dry bones, hear the word of Yahweh."

—*Ez. 37:1-4*

The question posed to the Jews in the exile: What is your role as the faithful people of God living in this Babylonian captivity? We raise the question not rhetorically but because at the political level any answer of about what to do with imperialism seems *beyond our human capabilities*. In the face of the United States' indifference and adamancy, of its lying and covertness, we in the solidarity movement in the States often feel powerless. At the beginning of the revolution, the Sandinistas along with many Nicaraguans felt that "they could do it"; that they could create a new Nicaragua and make the revolution work...that it was within the grasp of their human determination and revolutionary capabilities. But by late 1983, Ezekiel's question from the Valley of the Dry Bones began to loom as more and more important. Given the incredible power of the Empire, its diabolical distortion of the truth and the extent of the suffering by the whole society, many Nicaraguans began to ask themselves: "Can these bones live?" "Can this revolution survive?"

We imagine that Augusto César Sandino must have felt the same way at times back in those years when he was struggling against the U.S. Marines and all the power of the Empire (1927-1933). There was no question that they could survive in the mountains, but they must have wondered at times, "How long can this struggle go on?" and "Will we ever be able to raise up a new Nicaragua out of these ashes?" Just when they thought they had prevailed and the Marines were withdrawn,

Sandino came down from the mountains to sign a peace treaty and betrayed by the Empire's agent, Anastasio Somoza, he was murdered. The National Guard then proceeded to destroy or imprison the remainder of Sandino's forces, and his dream remained buried there in the mountains of Segovia for more than 30 years. Even as late as 1973, after the earthquake, there was hardly anyone in Nicaragua — at least publicly who would have answered Ezekiel's question positively, "Yes, Sandino's bones can live again."(22) And yet it happened and today the Sandinista revolution is a reality! In light of that earlier "death and resurrection" history, one has to recognize that there was more operating in that long process than just human will. The victory over Somoza was certainly the product of a whole people rising up against an evil tyrant, and yet, aspects of it — like the takeover of the National Palace — were indeed political "miracles." As they say in Nicaragua today, "*Gracias a Dios y la Revolucion*"!(23)

When the Jews returned to Jerusalem to rebuild the city and repossess the land, just as when the Nicaraguans returned to Managua and repossessed their land... the forces of evil were still around. Indeed, since then, the Empire has done everything in its power to bring down the revolution... everything except invade with U.S. troops. America's use of *contra* forces is symbolically significant in light of Ezekiel's warning to the Jews that the very same thing would happen to them. That an evil horde would sweep down "from the north", Gog from Magog, to try and undo what God had ordained. The promise was given that God would frustrate this incursion and challenge such profanity:

> *I will turn you round, Gog, lead you on, and bring you from the farthest north to attack the mountains of Israel. I will break the bow in your left hand and dash the arrows out of your right. You will be killed on the mountains of Israel (of Nicaragua), you and all your hordes, and the nations with you...I will no longer allow my holy name to be profaned; the nations shall learn that I am Yahweh, holy in Israel (holy in Nicaragua).*
> —*Ez. 39:1-7*

In light of the recognition that Nicaragua was facing more than an imperial enemy, that she was struggling against a demonic force caused that other Sandinista prophet Miguel D'Escoto, to initiate his strategy for defeating that force on a spiritual plane. His feeling that Nicaragua was up against truly evil forces began in 1983 when the Pope visited the country but refused to pray — even at the request of distraught mothers — for the souls of those civilians and Sandinista soldiers who had been killed by the *contras*. That extremely un-pastoral and indeed clearly political act was reinforced that same year when Ronald Reagan warned he was going to pressure the Nicaraguan people making them suffer until the Sandinistas "cry uncle." In 1984, the Pope named Archbishop Obando y Bravo cardinal of all Central America, a post which normally should have been given to any number of other bishops more qualified than he. As many in Nicaragua said, Obando became cardinal only "thanks to the revolution." Not only was his first mass held with *somocistas* in Miami but none of the Central American bishops attended his second mass held in Managua. The whole thing was diabolical and clearly represented a total political capitulation of Obando to the will of the Empire. It is no wonder, then, that Miguel D'Escoto felt Nicaragua was dealing with more than anti-communism and a *contra* war; that they were facing *demonic powers*.

As a result, in August 1985, Padre Miguel D'Escoto — foreign minister of the Sandinista government, (24) laid aside his responsibilities of state, took off his fine clothes, and initiated what he called an "Evangelical Insurrection" : thirty days of prayer and fasting to see if he could cast out this evil spirit. Some of the poor campesinos who joined Padre Miguel in his vigil, reflected:

— *These weapons are more powerful than Reagan's weapons;*
— *Father, with such gestures, empires tremble;*
— *Our only weapon is the defense of God;*
— *Such prophetic resistance is a sign of great hope...(25)*

In February 1986, with the *contras* continuing their murderous attacks (since the beginning of their war having killed over 14,000 persons), Padre Miguel began a *via crucis* from Jalapa to Managua (326 kms.), a religious procession covering 25-30 kilometers a day, including 15 stations of the cross along the way and involving over 100,000 persons. At its conclusion, a mass was held in the Plaza of the Revolution on the steps of the old gutted and roofless Cathedral during which Miguel launched a diatribe against the Archbishop, speaking to him in very personal terms, saying:

— *Your hands are stained with the blood of the Nicaraguan people;*
— *You have betrayed your people by supporting the* **contras** *and* **contra** *aid;*
— *Do not celebrate mass nor leave the country until you have repented of your sins.*
— *"Miguel Obando"...the Lord and our people seek your repentance.(26)*

Because neither ancient Jews nor modern Nicaraguans can do very much directly to challenge an empire or change imperial intent, alternatives necessarily had to involve more than human will. They required a reliance on the power of the Spirit and faith in God as sovereign over history. When Nicaraguans pleaded with us Americans as friends visiting their country to go back and do all we can to stop this *contra* madness — and much has certainly been done — we often felt the matter was beyond our human capabilities. While we believed that the forces of Gog would eventually be defeated or withdrawn and while we believed the Nicaraguan revolution would ultimately triumph, yet we are also aware that we are dealing with powerful, demonic forces here in the United States. As we watched what was happening in Nicaragua and all of Central America we were reminded of the demonic forces which crucified the Lord of history, and how they eventually brought about their own undoing:

> *On that cross, he dislodged the principalities and powers from their throne like an old garment; he made a public spectacle of them and led them as captives in his triumphal procession.*
> *—Col.2:15*

Looking at the exilic history of the Jews in Babylonian captivity and at the struggle of Nicaragua to rise up from its evil past and build a new society, we realize as we watch life emerge from death that it takes more than human will to redeem this world from evil. Not long ago, we passed a slogan painted on a wall in the town of Masatepe, Nicaragua, over which a drawing was painted depicting a woman weeping over the body of Jesus which had been machine-gunned and lay dead at her feet. The saying read:

> *From this pain neither hatred nor vengeance is born,*
> *but only the will to defend the resurrection of Nicaragua(27)*

FOOTNOTES—CHAPTER 11

1   Ernesto Cardenal, *Zero Hour and Other Documentary Poems*, New Directions, New York, 1980, "Oracle Over Managua," pp. 62 and 68. Somoza erected a barbed-wire fence around the huge area of destruction in old downtown Managua.

2   W. Brueggemann, op.cita, p. 51, "The two of them — Jeremiah and Ezekiel — are the only ones we know about who ministered across the discontinuity, that is, before and after 587." Similarly, Cardenal and D'Escoto across the discontinuity before and after 1979-1980.

3   Philip Wheaton, "Towards the Societal Transformation of America's Imperialist Environment," Inter-American Foundation paper, Dec. 1975., Wash. D.C., "The Thought of Paolo Freire," p. 61.

> *When anyone challenges capitalism and imperialism as contradictory to our best interests, as North Americans we are accused of being disloyal. This proves what we said before about capitalism having won out over democracy. It also indicates that we have reached our U.S. "limit situation". In other words, any changes or adjustments within the parameters of capitalism is more or less acceptable, while any challenge of the system itself is prohibited..."*

4   Bailey & Kent, op. cita, p. 259.

5   Larry Kuenning, *Exiles in Babylon*, Publishers of the Truth, Cambridge, Mass. 1978, p. 28. Marduk (Hebrew: Merodach) was the chief god of the Babylonians and kings took their names from him. In Babylonian creation stories, Tiamat is the chaos monster.

6   The "domino theory" of Central America was advanced through a pro-Reagan propaganda video widely distributed in 1981 called "Attack on the Americas."

7   A group of some 30 Nicaraguans and 5 Americans occupied the embassy and residence two days after the Sandinista victory with permission of the Sandinista government.

8   Richard Millet, *Guardians of the Dynasty*, Orbis, Maryknoll, N.Y. 1979, p. 243.

9   Walter Le Febre, *Inevitable Revolutions*, op.cita, pp.236-37.

10   Nicaraguac, *Los Cristianos y La Revolucion*, Ministerio de Cultura, Managua, April-June, 1981,. p. 68. Padre Gaspar García Laviana was a Spanish priest who joined the Sandinistas and died fighting the Somoza dynasty. These words were spoken on Dec. 11, 1978.

11   EPICA Task Force, *Nicaragua: A People's Revolution*, Wash D.C., 1980, p. 71.

12   The authors of *Nicaragua: A People's Revolution*, Philip Wheaton and Ivonne Dilling were present at this event at UDC in Managua, September, 1979.

13   Rosset and Vandermeer, *The Nicaragua Reader*, "Education for Change," Grove Press, New York, 1983, p. 334

14   Ibid., p. 337

15   Ibid, "Our Vengeance", by Tomás Borge, p.167.

16   *Pastoral Message from the Nicaraguan Episcopate*, Managua, Nov. 16, 1979, signed by Archbishop Obando y Bravo and the other bishops of the Episcopal Conference.

17   EPICA, *Nicaragua: A People's Revolution*, opus cita, p.56.

18   Nicaraguac, ibid., p. 183, from a conversation between Tomás Borge and Fernando Cardenal in the film "Gracias a Dios y a la Revolucion"

19   Teófilo Cabestrero, *Revolutionaries for the Gospel*, Orbis, 1986, p.7.

20   The announcement of the appropriation of the $19 million in CIA funds was not made until late January and early February, 1982 but the first contra offensive entitled "Red Christmas" began in November 1981.

21   *Christianity & Crisis*, Sept. 14, 1987, "Nicaragua Eight Years Later" by Alan Reding, p.280.

22   One of the authors, Philip Wheaton, visited Managua in 1973 and talked secretly with a Sandinista supporter, but under carefully controlled conditions.

23   "Thanks to God and the Revolution" is a very common expression Nicaragua, used by Sandinistas as well as by Christians, expressing their dual gratitude.

24   A Maryknoll priest who studied in the United States, Padre Miguel has been ordered by the Pope not to celebrate mass because he is serving in the Sandinista government.

25   *Amanecer*, Fall, 1985, Centro Valdivieso, Managua, p.8.

26   *Amanecer*, Fall, 1985, Centro Valdivieso, ibid., p.8.

27   There is an eschatological undergirding among the Sandinistas which is fundamentally biblical and in no way comes from any Marxist ideology nor is forced by the government.

CHAPTER 12
PATH

Struggle to overthrow the old tyranny and build new societies in Nicaragua, El Salvador & Guatemala seen as the only path to peace: "Happy are those who work for peace because they shall be known as children of God," —Mt.5:9

Comfort, comfort my people;
it is the voice of your God;
speak tenderly to Jerusalem
to be of good heart, tell her
that she has fulfilled her term of bondage
that her penalty is paid;
she has received from the hand of Yahweh
double measure for all her sins.

A voice cries in the wilderness,
prepare a way *for Yahweh.*
Make a straight highway for our God
across the desert.

—Is.40:1-3 (N.E.,J)

For Israel the captivity in Egypt and in Babylonia implied times of forging hope and the necessary dynamism for that liberating moment when they would be needed. The tasks of the Church are others; also the functions of theology. It is time to **prepare the ground** *for the seeding, the conception, a growing within the mother's womb; it is not yet time for birth. The Church is urged on to a confrontation with the imperial State.(1)*
—Leonardo Boff

The call of Deutero-Isaiah and Leonardo Boff to "prepare the way", and "prepare the ground" is something absolutely clear to people in the Third World, and more specifically to those who live in Central America today. They understand why this slow seeding time and terrible birth pains are necessary and what they are waiting for: return to the land; repossession of the patrimony promised to them by God since time immemorial. They understand that "across the desert" means from their present Babylonian captivity to a promised land no longer dominated by oligarchs and multinational corporations nor under the sway of the Empire to the north.

North Americans don't understand the need for this suffering preparation for fundamental change which goes to the roots of the problem because we live in an affluent society which is full of materialistic "life". Those in Latin America and the Caribbean do understand suffering because they live in perpetual poverty and must find a way out of their existence of death whatever it costs and however long it takes. In one sense we too are "exiles in Babylon" as they are, but the difference is they can feel it and taste it every day as pain and hopelessness, whereas for us it is still largely a theoretical concept. They have a great deal to teach us because they are already "on their way" while we have hardly begun the long, hard journey that awaits us.

While the promise of return was clearly announced by Isaiah to the Jews in Babylon, his good news wasn't enough... they wanted to know *When?* Because Deutero-Isaiah was written between 550 and 540 B.C.(2), some 10 to 20 years before the first Jews would return to Judah in 532 B.C., the good news was too vague, too far off to give them any real hope.

> *However joyful his message and however soaring his lyrical poetry, we dare not overlook the fact that Second Isaiah and his message probably seemed unbelievable to his original audience.(3)*

Babylon was still a powerful empire and the Jews still in captivity. While storm clouds were gathering on Babylon's horizon just as they are for the United States today, its leaders scoffed at such warnings as most American experts do now. Both mock "prophets of doom" who talk of an imminent crash of the Tower of Babel or Wall Street's stock market, saying who takes such pessimistic prognostications seriously? Isaiah's words were not a blueprint about when precisely this return would occur, they were only promises; his was not a plan of action but a voice crying in the wilderness. Yet, for us to know that Isaiah's prophecy in fact came true a decade or two later is reassuring, especially for Central Americans today, who still see no end to their suffering.

In light of their anguish, the question remains: How long can the Nicaraguans hold out? Can the Salvadoran people suffer much more and still survive? Will there be anything left of the Mayan culture after another decade of ethnocide in Guatemala? What, in fact, will Honduras be like after another ten years of military occupation by foreign troops? Still, the promise of Yahweh is repeated in Isaiah over and over again: "I, God, can do it!" "I will keep my promise!" "My people shall return and inherit the land!" Whenever we human beings face such impossible situations as those in Central America today, when we cannot see any way our hopes will be fulfilled... we turn to God. But in the Exilic experience it is not to await miracles but the fulfillment of the Word... and that means *along the path laid out by Yahweh.*

This is why the much heralded words of Isaiah 40 "Comfort, comfort my people" are not for everyone. Just because they are beautiful and inspiring phrases does not mean that we in the West can claim them; that we have any right to them. Mostly, we don't even really want them except to read them poetically, to reflect on them inspirationally. That is, we are not prepared to receive them in terms of all the suffering they portend; all the loss and dispossession which exile implies. So when Isaiah offers the Jews in Babylon the comfort of God, it is for those who have paid a great price... as the prophet said, "double for all your sins." These words are not for everyone but for the sufferers, exiles, the persecuted and poor, yes, even for the dead who have already sacrificed everything that this promise of return and rest might come to pass.

On Understanding the Nature of Redemption: Trial of the Nations

In the days of the Babylonian captivity as in today's Central American captivity by the United States, the question is the same: who ultimately controls history? Who has the last word? As the faithful remnant, our answer is not to say "God, of course" in some simplistic or mechanistic way, but rather to realize that precisely the opposite is what the empires think even if they do not say so publicly... *that they are in control of history.* That presumption is why we are engaged today in a monumental struggle between the East and the West over who will control the world and thus human history. This is why a trial is presently underway... what the prophets call "the trial of the nations":(4)

> *Second Isaiah deals with such questions in a series of trial speeches between Yahweh and the nations or their gods. These speeches are a defense of Yahweh's claim to rule history and a radical denial of the counterclaim of the gods.(5)*

The first trial has to do with *longevity...* how long can any empire last? To put this question into perspective we ask ourselves: Where is mighty Babylon today...indeed, it had been forgotten for 500 years before Jesus of Nazareth was even born! Where, then is mighty Rome? which did away with that carpenter and yet, who lives on while Rome is nothing but a crumbling relic? For that matter where is the mighty Nazi Germany which ruled Europe and imperial Japan which ruled the Far East only 40 years ago? And while England is still there, clearly Great Britain no longer rules the waves! Yet, despite all these striking examples, most Americans believe it can never happen to us, that we will never fall. Foolish mankind which presumes eternity while the historical clock of the immediate ticks relentlessly on to finite endtimes.

The second trial involves the *arrogance of power...* the notion that we in America are superior to other nations; that power and wealth make us substantively better. In the Bible, Yahweh sees the good and folly in every nation and on that basis weighs each on the scales of justice and truth whether it should survive. On that divine balance, the United States is getting into deeper and deeper trouble, highlighted by the policy of Ronald Reagan and his lack of respect for the Family of Nations. His administration rejected the World Court at the Hague (consider the case of Nicaragua and the *contra* war which found against the USA).(6) His administration doesn't respect the United Nations now because it is so influenced by "insignificant" Third World countries (consider the fact that the United States has pulled out of UNESCO). As a result of such arrogance, the Family of Nations which once admired America for her principles now has us on trial, judged not only by our refusal to abide by the rules of international behavior but because of our attitude of superiority towards them; our arrogance.

The third trial involves *the poor of the Third World* who judge us because our affluence, greed and gluttony means that they suffer, go hungry and die. This is why walls all over Asia, Africa and Latin America, even in the mid-East, read "Yankee go home!" Many Americans assume such graffiti represents the extreme attitude of a few crazy leftists, whereas in reality the sentiment is widespread and growing. Americans don't understand that the slogan is not directed at us as a people but *at our imperial policies* which daily impact their lives in the form of malnutrition, joblessness and despair. If a given imperial structure — like, say, the IMF — decides to increase the interest of its loans, set up a new tariff barrier, freeze wages, raise prices... it is done without any thought to the suffering such policies will cause millions of people. This indifference to the suffering of others is why we are being judged by the poor.

The *final trial* is a curious one since it has to do with our own military surrogates in Central America, those military elites who do our bidding and receive our aid... and yet, who have us on trial. We are not referring here to our political puppets — like Duarte in El Salvador, Azcona in Honduras or Cerezo in Guatemala — for they are mere pawns in the Empire's game. Rather, we are referring to those military leaders who have real power, who repress their people and take orders from Washington. They, too, have us on trial! Why do you suppose the Honduran military secretly rose up and overthrew Washington's chief man in Tegucigalpa, General Gustavo Alvarez?(7) Why do you suppose General Mejía Victores in Guatemala ordered our man, President Efrain Ríos Montt, to leave the country and then refused to head up our regional military organization CONDECA?(8) Why do you suppose our man in El Salvador, General José Garcia, resisted U.S. efforts to impose the Pentagon's model of counterinsurgency upon that country?(9) And why do you suppose the pragmatic and opportunistic General Manuel Noriega of Panama has been so steadfastly resisting U.S. pressure for him to resign after collaborating with us for so many years?(10) The reason is, because like our surrogates in South Vietnam, General Ky and President Thieu, we employ these leaders for our purposes and then discard them when they are no longer useful to us. So... they go along with our imperial policies at the official level while playing games behind our backs... because they do not trust us. Because we have no respect even for our reactionary military allies in Central America, we are in effect being judged even by them. And so the trial of the nations goes on.

High Price of Redemption & What It Has Accomplished

On the other hand, there is a solution to all this madness and imperial domination, what the Bible calls "*substitutional redemption.*"(11) In biblical revelation and theology, this is a key concept, based on the notion that the sacrifice of one person can save another from sin, error or even tragedy. There are many forms this redemption can take. One involves the redeeming of a relative who has been sold into slavery, that is, you can buy another person out of debt-slavery by paying a price (Lev.25:47-55). Similarly, if a person is forced by poverty to sell his land, a kinsman can buy it back, thus redeeming it for the true owner (Jer.32:7-8). Still a third form of redemption involves the widow of a deceased relative who, if she has no male heir, can become his wife, thus redeeming her honor (Ruth 3:12-13). But the most important example of this kind of sacrificial redemption involves redeeming a nation which has been sold into captivity or forced into exile... for which God will pay the price of redemption:

> *Do not be afraid, Jacob, poor worm,*
> *Israel, puny mite.*
> *I will help you it is Yahweh who speaks —*
> *the Holy One of Israel is your redeemer...*
>
> *Do not be afraid, for I have redeemed you;*
> *I have called you by your name, you are mine...*
> *I give Egypt for your ransom,*
> *and exchange Cush and Seba for you...*
> *I give men in exchange for you,*

peoples in return for your life.

—*Is.41:14; 43:1-5*
(emphasis added)

Throughout the Bible, God uses the blood of innocent victims to both condemn and redeem, as in the case of Abel's blood for Cain's life (Gen.4) or Naboth's blood in bringing down the reign of Ahab and Jezebel (1 Kgs.21). Despots and empires assume that the moment a killing is done, that's the end of the matter, whereas in fact such a crime is merely the beginning of a dialectic process of condemnation and redemption. In the Bible, the shedding of someone's blood means the whole world dies (Talmud) whereas the other way around, in the Gospel, Jesus Christ redeems the whole world through the shedding of his blood on Calvary:

According to the Law, almost everything has to be purified with blood, and there is no redemption save through the shedding of blood.

—*Heb.9:22-23*

What does this mean in terms of all the innocent people who have been murdered in Central America since 1978? Quite simply, that those thousands of Guatemalans, Nicaraguans and Salvadorans who have been murdered by their military under tacit approval of the United States, *have paid the price for its redemption.* Consider what this price has been in human terms, by conservative estimates:

Guatemala	*40,000 including 30,000 Indians between 1981-83*
El Salvador	*60,000 plus another 10,000 disappeared and presumed dead*
Nicaragua	*54,000 - 40,000 under Somoza and 16,000 by the contras*
Honduras	*200 in 1981-82 and another 100 from 1983 to present.*
TOTAL, 1978-88	*154,200 since 1978(12)— actual figures are probably much higher.*

This is the price — 154,200 lives — which Central America has had to pay to keep the oligarchs in power and maintain U.S. hegemony over the region!

Yet if this is the *price required* by the evil ones and the Empire, then the reverse of this divine equation of condemnation and redemption is also valid: this price is also the *sacrifice offered* by those who gave their lives in the process of serving their people and refusing to bow the knee before the idols of despotism and imperialism. Deutero-Isaiah speaks about what the theologians call "*nominal substitution*", that is, I can substitute myself for you, give my life for yours... "no greater love can a person have than that she lays down her life for another" (Jn.15:13). Yet, because those 154,200 lives belong to God who created them and loved them and suffered when they died, their dying is God's sacrifice towards redeeming Central America from its sin and debt, saying to the people "your penalty is paid."

If this is so, then we can legitimately affirm that these 154,200 human beings beloved of God who were beaten, raped, tortured, burnt, dismembered and disappeared... this horrendous human sacrifice... *has bought the redemption of Central America!* — This means that the price for the return of the people to their homelands has already been paid, indeed, as the prophet says, "double for your sins." Therefore, the exiles can go home right now and occupy the land, for their deed to it has been "signed, sealed and delivered" in the blood of their sacrificed sisters and brothers!

> *Because they live*
> *today, tomorrow and always*
> *on the streets, baptized with their blood*
> *and in the air which gathered up their cry,*
> *in the jungle that hid their shadows,*
> *in the river that gathered up their laughter,*
> *in the ocean that holds their secrets,*
> *in the craters of the volcanos*
> *Pyramids of the New Day*
> *which swallowed up their ashes.(13)*

On Following the Right Path... of Integrity

Deutero-Isaiah now picks up on another theme first introduced by Ezekiel — the New Exodus — returning home to Jerusalem as "a glorious way" across the desert; as a "path of rejoicing." In sharp contrast to the first Exodus where the Hebrews' flight from Egypt involved a tortuous, uncertain wandering for years through the Sinai desert, this time there would be no murmuring along the way against Yahweh, they would go "straight home" to Jerusalem across the desert!(14) Where during the trek through the Sinai wilderness, nature seemed to be against them at every turn, this time she would collaborate by making the way easy and their burdens light:

> *Yes, you will leave with joy*
> *and be led away in safety.*
> *Mountains and hills will break into joyful cries before you*
> *and all the trees of the countryside clap their hands.*
> *Cypress will grow instead of thorns,*
> *myrtle instead of briars:*
> *And it shall be to the Lord for a name*
> *For an everlasting sign that shall not be cut off.*
> *—Is.55:12-13*

The great difference between this New Exodus and the old one is that instead of the Promised Land being a goal or the "end", it is now *a way of returning*, the very process of getting there now becomes the central issue... *following the right path*. Admonished by the prophets that they must have a "new heart of flesh" or else "going home" would mean nothing, they first had to become changed persons. In the Exodus, the focus was entirely on the goal... if they could just get to the Promised Land (for us Christians: find the Holy Grail)... they would have their reward. As we say today, "just keep your eyes on the prize." But external success without attention to how one gets there can be as disastrous for us as it was for the Hebrews. The Hebrews' indifference to morals and methods — their vicious manner of occupying, conquering, possessing and dominating the land and-peoples of Canaan would prove disastrous and lead to the eventual downfall of Israel and Judah. This same blindness by the Jews about Palestinians today may also prove disastrous for this latest enterprise of getting to the Promised Land. Because they don't care how they treat the Palestinians or how many Arabs they kill, the Jews are corrupting their own great dream; indeed, they may even lose their prize— their birthright to the holy land — because they trust in the great Empire rather than in the Word of God!

There is a comparable parallel for our situation in the United States vis-a-vis Central America. For us Americans, "winning" is our obsession... success, even though we compromise on principles. "Obtaining the goal" not only corrupts our national politics and our business integrity, but even our national sports and clearly our personal ambition. By only focussing on the prize we lose our perspective, so that expediency has become the by-word in the country: "Whatever it takes, do it... don't ask questions, just get the job done." Such a philosophy may seem like "innocent pragmatism" but in fact it implies a contract with the Devil. Whether we are talking about the coach who looks the other way on student grades, or corporations entering into "sweetheart deals", or Ronald Reagan lying about Nicaragua in order to accomplish his foreign policy goals... all are examples of selling our souls.

To the contrary, those in Central America struggling for liberation as well as those of us who take the side of the Empire's victims in this country... we *have to tell the truth; we have to play it straight!* This contrast between personal honor and imperial deceit is ultimately not merely "politics", for upon it human lives depend. Take the case of Augusto Cesar Sandino, a man who though called "a bandit" by Washington never lied; he was *a man of absolute integrity*. There's a story about Sandino that appeared in *The New York Times* in 1930 which reported that Sandino had received a check for $60,000 from the "Committee Pro-Hands Off Nicaragua" to come down from the Segovia mountains and stop fighting. The purpose of this false report-was, it seems, to create divisions among those groups supporting Sandino, particularly the Communist Party of Mexico and the Anti-Imperialist League of the Americas. Sandino not only denied that he had ever received such a check, but he charged that the false information must have been planted by Yankee agents to discredit the revolution. When demands were made to produce a copy of the check, those in the States charging the pay-off equivocated saying "the investigation is secret" and refused to allow a copy of the check to be seen.(14) The point is that the difference between Sandinista honesty and imperial deceit was evident from that very beginning of this long, sordid history and has continued down to this very day.

> *Listen to me, you who know what integrity means,*
> *people who take my laws to heart:*
> *do not fear the taunts of men,*
> *nor be dismayed by their insults,*
> *for the moth shall eat them like garments,*
> *the grub devour them like wool,*
> *but my integrity will remain forever,*
> *and my salvation for all generations.*
>
> —Is.51:7-8

We in the solidarity and sanctuary movements have learned this same kind of honesty from the exiles, victims of U.S. imperialism. They tell us the truth while Washington lies. Because we suffer from a liberal tendency to believe whatever our government tells us, for a number of years we had to wrestle with our consciences... until we realized that it was the agents of the Empire who were lying to us whereas these poor and persecuted victims from Central America almost always told us the truth. This opinion was verified when we went down to the region to see for ourselves. Our first reaction was that we had learned a valuable lesson about believing in people rather than in politicians, but in time we realized that empires always lie and their lying regularly implies death to the innocent. This means that telling the truth is more than a moral principle or an ethical rule of thumb; it is a matter of life and death... and as such, that speaking the truth is the only way we can get back to the Promised Land.

The Promise of Return Requires Walking Through the Fire
Just as Babylon had no intention of letting the Jews return to Judah, so the United States has no intention of letting the exiles from Central America inherit their land, even though it has been paid for twice over by the sacrifice of the blood of their people. Yet because the promise of such inheritance comes from God, today's imperial obstinacy, like Pharaoh's refusal to listen to the Word of Yahweh, is leading to the Empire's own destruction. The warning against them has already been spoken in that famous "handwriting on the wall" from the prophet Daniel: "Mene, Mene, Tekel, Pharsin"...

> *God has measured your arrogant ways,*
> *God has set an endtime for it,*
> *God has weighed the Empire and found it wanting,*
> *God will divide your kingdom and give it to the Medes and*
> *Persians.*
>
> *—Dan.5:25-28*

Foolish America like arrogant Babylon is always looking around to discover some "enemy" that might attack her from outside and destroy her... as Reagan says: "they will advance from one country after another in Central America until they cross Mexico itself and stand at our very borders." In fact, there is no such external enemy, in terms of either intention or ability to challenge us because we are far too powerful. But there is a threat. While the war-mongers preach "national security", warn against "international terrorists" and decry a "communist conspiracy", the termites of our real demise are eating away at our moral integrity from within. The *enemy is us* to the degree that we have swallowed and digested the imperial idolatry and its lies. Like ancient Babylon, the United States cannot be defeated by any outside force, but she can easily fall apart from the inside by her own hand, brought down by her own foolishness and arrogance:

> *Cyrus did not find his victory over Babylon difficult. To begin with, he did not even make a personal appearance. In 539 he ordered his commander Gobryas to attack: Nabonidus fell. Babylon came into Persian hands virtually without a struggle. It seems that the priests of Marduk welcomed the conquerors as liberators, for they (from inside) brought an end to Nabonidus' rule. Finally, Cyrus himself entered the city in a triumphal procession.(15)*

During those last years before Babylon fell, the issue of loyalty became increasingly important, until it resulted in having to pledge an oath to the king or face death. The prophet Daniel reflects back on those days, on the arrogance of Babylon and the price one would have to pay to resist the "abomination of desolation"(16) — in our day the worship of the idol of imperialism. As the king of Babylon demanded more and more loyalty, requiring all dissidents to bow down and "cry uncle", when they refused they were imprisoned or killed; (in America we are imprisoned; in Central America they are murdered).

Now Daniel had three friends, each of them representing in our day, the faithful in Nicaragua, El Salvador and Guatemala. Their names were Hananiah, Mishael and Azariah, of whom you probably have not heard, for they were not revolutionaries or heroes; they were not priests or poets... just ordinary folks like you and me, faithful Jews who were trying to survive the empire's madness since so many had already been killed or disappeared. To protect themselves, they decided to adopt pseudonyms, fake names which you may well have heard of: Shadrach, Mishach and Abednego. When the king of Babylon heard that they wouldn't bow down and worship the idols of the Empire — "national security", "maximization of profit" and "the materialistic American way of life" — he ordered them cast into the fiery furnace and burned alive. Upon hearing their sentence of death, they spoke up faithfully and fearlessly, saying:

> *If our God, the one we serve, is able to save us from the burning fiery furnace and from your power, O king, he will save us; and*

*even if he does not, then you must know, O king, that we will
not serve your god or worship the statue you have erected. These
words infuriated King Nebuchadnezzar... and he gave orders
for them to be thrown into the fiery furnace.*

—Dn.3:16-21

We know for sure that Daniel's three friends did not recant and
remained faithful to the end. Whether they physically survived the
flames of the fiery furnace or not we do not know, for they disappeared
and have not been seen since. But because they could say *Basta!* until
the end, many others have learned how to say *Presente!* to this day.

One of the great prophets of Latin America, Leonardo Boff, who
speaks for the whole continent, recalls this episode of Daniel's three
friends when he speaks about our need to be converted to a radical faith
commitment. He says this about our call to the Covenant:

> *Who is with me, is with me **in the fire**; who is far from me, will
> be found far from the kingdom.(17)*

This intriguing phrase was apparently an apocryphal saying of St.
Thomas Aquinas though it may well have been an authentic saying of
Jesus of Nazareth. It says, in effect, whoever refuses to bow the knee
to the kingdoms of this world and their idols, will of necessity have to
pass through the fire of the Empire's wrath, just as Nicaragua, El
Salvador and Guatemala are now doing. Although they are no threat to
the empire, their refusal to capitulate constitutes a fundamental
danger... *because they have the audacity to dream of a better way.* Thus
Leonardo Boff says of Nicaragua and its willingness to stand up to the
North American empire, that it is "an example for all Christians in Latin
America and in the Third World involved in the revolutionary process"... because "there is a theological dimension in (such) human
solidarity."(18)

This theological dimension implies something more than helping
our poor neighbor and even more than protesting against our
government's unjust practices in Central America; it involves what we
in the Sanctuary movement call *accompaniment,* walking along with
these imperial victims wherever they need us, wherever it may lead us.
It involves more than the old Indian phrase — "to experience our
situation you must walk a hundred miles in our moccasins" — it
requires of us learning how to listen, how to follow, how to be judged
and how to sing and dance with them... alo*ng the way!* It demands a
new heart and a new vision, inter-American solidarity in which no one

oppresses and no one controls. Americans who think they have made it to the "top of the mountain" or those religious idealists dreaming of some other kingdom not of this world... both have to learn a new song which is coming from our Central American sisters and brothers: *how to walk together.* That is the only way to reach the new Jerusalem.

FOOTNOTES — CHAPTER 12

1   Leonardo Boff, *Teólogia Desde El Cautiverio*, Indo-American Press, Bogota, opus cita, p.23.

2   Deutero or Second Isaiah refers to chapters 40-55 of the book of the prophet Isaiah who is not at all related to 1st. Isaiah, who wrote considerably before the fall of Jerusalem. Cf. Roy F. Melugin, *The Formation of Isaiah 40-55*, BZAW 141, Berlin: Walter Gruyter, 1976 and C.R. North, *The Second Isaiah*, Oxford, 1964.

3   Ralph Klein, *Israel in Exile*, op.cita, pp. 97-98.

4   Ibid, pp. 99-104.

5   Ibid., p.101.

6   When the World Court found in favor of Nicaragua in terms of U.S. aggression, the Reagan administration simply disavowed the authority of the Court over U.S. affairs.

7   *Honduras Update*, Vol.3, Nos.2-3, Nov.-Dec., 1984, "Honduras: a Journalism of Silence," p.8.

8   Frank & Wheaton, *Indian Guatemala*, opus cita, pp. 93-94.

9   Ray Bonner, *Weakness & Deceit*, Times Books, New York, N.Y., 1984, pp.311-312:

> *...This was underscored in early 1983, when Lieutenant Colonel Ochoa staged a rebellion, refusing to obey any further orders issued by the minister of defense, General Garcia, (rather, obeying the Pentagon). Reagan administration officials maintained that Magaña ended the rebellion and ob-*

*tained Garcia's resignation... (but, in fact) **Garcia was forced out.***

10 EPICA, *Panama: Sovereignty For A Land Divided,* Washington, D.C., 1976, pp. 54-56. In the *coup* attempt against Gen. Torrijos while he was in Mexico in Dec. 1969, he returned through the help of Lt. Col. Noriega, then based in David, Panama. There was evident U.S. backing of that *coup* attempt so that although Col. Noriega was head of G-2 (military intelligence) and thus had close workings with U.S. military intelligence, he was from then on suspicious of and antagonistic toward U.S. maneuvers against Panama.

11 Ralph Klein, <u>opus cita</u>, pp. 109-110.

12 These figures represent conservative estimates by Americas Watch and the national solidarity networks: CISPES, NISGUA & The Nicaraguan Network, September, 1987.

13 Julia Esquivel, *Threatened by Resurrection,* <u>opus cita</u>, p.61.

14 Augusto C. Sandino, *El pensamiento vivo,* Tomo 2, Editorial Nueva Nicaragua, Letter to Hernan Laborde, Secretary General of the Communist Party of Mexico, January 8, 1930, pp.41-43.

15 Siegfreid Hermann, *A History of Israel,* <u>opus cita</u>, p.295.

16 The Book of Daniel was written at a very late date, probably about 168 B.C., during the Greek empire after the death of Alexander the Great during the rule of Antiochus Epiphanes (175-163 B.C.). The "abomination of desolation" refers to his setting up a statue of Jupiter in the Holy of Holies. However, Daniel (who belongs to neither the Minor or Major prophets) attempts to heighten the impact of his metaphor by referring back in history to a former notable, namely, the despised Nebuchadnezzar who destroyed Jerusalem in the 6th century B.C. However, for our purposes, the parallel to the implications of imperial idolatry is quite apt. In this case, Antiochus broke down the walls of the sanctuary, desecrating it by placing a pagan statue of Jupiter inside the Temple. This is an apocalyptic prophesy in which such idolatry not only causes the desolation of Jewish society but ultimately the downfall of Antiochus, i.e., symbolically of the Babylonian empire.

17   Leonardo Boff, *Jesucristo el Liberador*, Ed. Sal Terrae, Santander, Spain, 1983, p.79.

18   Centro Valdivieso, *Amanecer*, No. 49, May 1987, "Interview with Leonardo Boff," p. 39.

PART IV
JUDGEMENT & PROMISE IN AMERICA: ROLE OF THE FAITHFUL REMNANT

CHAPTER 13
AMERICA AS EMPIRE IS ACCURSED: IMPERIAL IDOLATRY REQUIRES A STATE THEOLOGY

Guatemalan Indian women and children held as captives in "Model Villages" as part of U.S. Pacification strategy is symptomatic of why U.S. imperialism is accursed by God.

*The process of combining and formulating all those elements of American imperialism into a coherent global strategy that could be implemented as policy was guided by several traditional axioms... Those arguments produced scintillating rhetoric; but the consequential dialogue, while less effervescent, concerned the **means not the whether** of empire.(1)*
   —*William Appleman Williams*

See, I set before you today a blessing and a curse: a blessing if you obey the commandment of Yahweh our God that I enjoin on you today; a curse if you disobey the commandments of Yahweh your God and leave the way I have marked out for you today, by going after other gods you have not known.
   —*Dt.11:26-28*

In light of our examination of the history of U.S. imperialism in Central America, what does this portend for us in terms of our own future in the United States? What are the implications of our imperial practices and the pain and suffering they have caused our brothers and sisters south of the border? While many Americans may not care, for a growing number of us in the religious and solidarity communities "the Horror is starting already to scratch its way into our brain" as W.H. Auden has said,(2) causing us mounting disquiet. We ask ourselves...

*Without the **contra** forces— galvanized, funded, directed and empowered by the CIA — those 16,000 unarmed Nicaragua civilians murdered to date by the FDN would be alive today. Isn't the Empire, then, the real enemy of the people of Central America?*

Such concern may have been expressed initially only as hard questions but the faithful remnant who have read their Shakespeare and Bible know that a nation which murders cannot-easily wipe the blood off its hands nor does the blood shed upon this good earth stop screaming up to heaven simply because the *Washington Post* decides to no longer carry stories about El Salvador. The Central American crisis has become our Achilles heel; that "little irritation" down there is growing; the infection is spreading and soon it will cause a cancer in the whole U.S. body politic.

The naiveté of the American people about their nation being only a democracy whereas our political, military and economic leaders are absolutely clear about the imperial role of the United States never ceases to amaze and sometimes confound us. Given the relatively high level of education and intelligence in America, our scientific genius and religious knowledge, this incredible political blindness is clearly the by-product of self-deception — believing our own propaganda and accepting our leaders' doublespeak at face value. Let's be honest: *we deceive ourselves.* We put down other empires as a kind of lower species — like the British who still play around with kings and queens and all that pomp and circumstance — and yet, at least they have always been quite straight-forward about their imperialism, "Hail Britannia, Britannia rules the waves" representing imperial honesty. We Americans, on the other hand, dissemble; we pretend we're not what we are and the danger of such misrepresentation, as Appleman Williams has said, is that we become accursed through self-deception.

Our task in this fourth part of *Empire & the Word* is to ascertain how this conflict affects us as North Americans, both negatively and positively. How is it for us as a people both "a blessing and a curse"? What is our responsibility as the faithful remnant living inside the Empire in light of this catastrophe? We sometimes say that this nation *is us*, the American people, but that's only half true. We are also part of an imperial system, an economic and political idolatry, which has blinded us, seduced and corrupted us.

On the other hand, for the faithful who are beginning to admit that the problem is a systemic one — America as empire is accursed — have begun to look closely at the ugly side of our system, and find it to be a national portrait of Dorian Grey.(3) We realize that our reality and theirs in Central America are interrelated and that we can only break out of our curse when we come to accept the judgement enclosed within this crisis... that we Americans are at fault for the suffering and dying in the hemisphere.

Spiritual Evils of Imperialism & Empire as Idolatry

When we say that America is accursed, it sounds like a throw-back to that vindictive view of God found at places in Hebrew scriptures — the flood, Sodom & Gomorrah, the fall of Jerusalem — a notion which many modern-day Jews and Christians find abhorrent and literalistic. We would argue, to the contrary, that the nature of God as merciful does not preclude the element of divine wrath on human deeds of darkness and dialectically, that such negative events are part of the redemptive process. Because we see the Spirit operating *dialectically through history and humankind,* our assertion of God as Judge also means that Yahweh is Redeemer saving us through such judgement. Our assertion that this nation is accursed stems from a very objective view that this nation has been sucked into *the structural evils of imperialism* — greed, war and lying — without most Americans realizing it. In the process, that imperial side of our American system has led to attitudes and practices which are damnable to God and murderous to our brothers and sisters in Central America.

Greed & Our Worship of Mammon. We have not attempted in this book to analyze capitalism but merely to highlight certain aspects of it which impinge upon our theme *Empire & the Word*. There is an obvious connection, of course, between our greed and Central America's suffering, namely, the linkage between U.S. corporations and their national oligarchies; a linkage reinforced by our geo-political priorities. The question for most Americans who think about this connection is: Where does that line of demarcation lie between legitimate profit-making-and gross exploitation; between wanting to make a living and using people as things... whether here in the United States or overseas? Theoretically, some would claim that any concentration of wealth in a few hands necessarily leads to the abuse of others. But for us, it is the explicit philosophy of "maximization of profits" that causes the real suffering, for within that goal there is no limit to corruption, aggrandizement of power and the exploitation of people.

How, specifically, does such greed lead to the idolatry of money...to the worship of Mammon? We have already discussed the case of the United Fruit Company (UFCo) in Guatemala and the negative impact which the decision by the Dulles brothers to overthrow President Arbenz in 1954 had upon the people there. UFCo's affirmation of the thesis "maximization of profits" and the arbitrary assumption of its right to hold on indefinitely to fallow land even when Guatemalan peasants were starving to death represents a perfect example of how the idol Mammon demands human life as a sacrifice to satisfy her greed.

The question for us then, as the American people, is how are *we* related to this equation of economic exploitation using this example (UFCo's profit) and its resulting death (Guatemala's impoverishment)? The answer is threefold: through inexpensive bananas in our supermarkets; through the assumption that presumably whatever is sold by UFCo improves the U.S. economy; and through the overthrow of Arbenz which kept Central America "open" for more capitalist investment and profit-making. During the weeks following the 1954 destabilization, the propaganda package sold to the American people was that the United States (through the CIA) had "saved the American way of life by stopping communism" in Guatemala. While the American people had nothing to do with that act of gross injustice, we became inextricably and structurally linked to it, indeed, most Americans applauded the intervention at the time. As a direct result of that act, which installed a military dictatorship in Guatemala which has persisted to this day, it is estimated that between 1954 and 1980 (before the recent holocaust), some 100,000 Guatemalan civilians-were brutally tortured, murdered or disappeared by a dynasty of military administrations.(4)

Many U.S. businessmen and even our elected representatives — both Democrats and Republicans — would, to this day, affirm that the action taken by the Dulles brothers in 1954 was necessary in order to maintain a "stable climate for U.S. investment," which in this case has meant a fascist way of life for an entire society over a period of three decades! These U.S. leaders would argue, further, that the U.S. government had to intervene because Arbenz' goal of giving land to Guatemala's poor not only threatened UFCo's investment and thus could have weakened the capitalist system there, but might well have become an inspiration for similar rebellions elsewhere in the Isthmus... thus threatening our whole American way of life in the Continent!

If we transfer this philosophy to the workplace where it becomes incarnated into deeds — at Wall Street's stock exchange — we can begin to see how it translates into an idolatry for us the people. There, the worshippers of Mammon gaze up at the ticker-tape monitors and watch with fascination the rising and falling of the numbers next to the coded figures of the corporations on which they wager their bets, i.e., buy and sell stock. As they engage in this intriguing game of chance with the goddess of profit and loss; as they "play the game," it makes absolutely no difference to those who play the stock market, the disaster and death which the Dulles brothers' action would bring upon the Guatemalan people through deprivation of land, lack of food, starvation and the repression that resulted from the CIA invasion. Indeed, after 1954, UFCo's stock went up, which was very good for UFCo, its stockholders and presumably for the U.S. economy. In other words, *we Americans benefitted directly from the suffering and death which ensued in Guatemala.* This is how we are structurally tied into the monetary mechanism called the "maximization of profits" and into the death machine which this policy implies for Third World peoples:

Each day false prophets
invited the inhabitants
of the Unchaste City
to kneel before the idols
of gluttony,
money

and death:
Idolaters from all nations
were being converted to the American Way of Life.(5)

The idolatry of money becomes a reality because whether consciously
or unconsciously we are willing to sacrifice the poor upon the altar of
our greed. This is why it is scientifically accurate to say that many
Americans worship Mammon.

National Security & Our Worship of War. Tied into this
corporate greed and national profit-making is the fear that others less
fortunate in the world might try to take our wealth and advantages away
from us and thus the need for "national security." The hawks among us
assume that the primary threats facing us today come not so much from
the Soviet Union (the Cold War doctrine) but from Third World
rebellions which though indigenous and even justifiable "may be
toying with Marxism and might go leftist." This fear completely masks
the reality, namely, that after WW II hard-liners in our government
decided to "play it safe" by perpetuating oligarchies, military dictatorships and colonial systems in order to prevent such potential moves "to
the left." At the same time, the Soviet Union moved to support popular
resistance movements and Third World rebellions against the old,
repressive orders. Thus, in spite of the virtues of the American system
and the shortcomings of the Russian system, the United States has
consistently lost out because we have been trying *to hold back the tide
of history.* Since we made the whole world our supposed "sphere of
influence", our imperial megalomania saw everything that happened
everywhere in the world — any disturbance, protest, truly free election
or revolution — as a direct threat to our interests and thus as potentially
undermining our national security. Our sin and shame in Central
America today stem directly from this monumental stupidity, this
colossal misreading of history.

Some pro-imperialists among us would argue that the uprisings in
our hemisphere were indeed a threat and to this day they will hang their
entire argument on the Cuban missile crisis. Clearly, that crisis could
legitimately be deemed a real threat to our national security... unless we
look more closely at its cause and outcome. The primary concern of the
Soviet Union was the protection of the Cuban revolution against
another Bay of Pigs invasion. When President Kennedy agreed the
United States would not repeat such an overthrow attempt, the Russians
withdrew. How do we know, however, that the Soviets might not have
used the missiles against us? Simply because any such act of aggression
would have resulted in a devastating counter-attack upon their own

territory. Even a liberal historian like Peter Wyden acknowledges that the 1962 Cuban missile crisis grew out of our own foolishness, not out of Russia's evil intent...

> *If the CIA, acting out of control and independently, had not escalated its plan against Fidel Castro from a modest guerrilla operation into a full-fledged invasion. President Kennedy would not have suffered an humiliating, almost grotesque defeat.*
>
> *If Kennedy had not been thoroughly defeated by Castro on the beaches in 1961, Nikita Khrushchev almost certainly would not have dared to precipitate the Cuban Missile Crisis of 1962 — the crisis which, in the words of former CIA Director William E. Colby, pushed the world "as close to Armageddon" as it has ever come....*
>
> *Hindsight improves with the years. Right after the event, President Kennedy found it impossible to explain. He asked his special counsel, Theodore C. Sorensen, the central question still being asked around the world: How could I have been so stupid to let them go ahead?"(6)*

This evaluation suggests, however, that the White House made a tactical error in this one unique case, creating an unnecessary though real national security threat. We would argue that U.S. reaction to the Cuban revolution is not unique but rather quite comparable to every other uprising in the hemisphere since WW II. Every time since 1945 that a united people or a majority of a population has risen up to overthrow a despotic regime, class injustice or colonial oppression, U.S. imperialism has seen it as a "communist threat." Consider the following incidents as proof of the consistency in America's reaction:

1947	*National Security Act passed by Congress under Truman*
1950-54	*Joseph McCarthy phobia against potential communists in the USA*
1954	*CIA-backed invasion of Guatemala & overthrow of democracy*
1961	*Abortive CIA-backed Bay of Pigs invasion of Cuba*
1963	*Destabilization of democracy under Jagan in Guyana.*

1964	*U.S..Brazilian military overthrow of Joao Goulart in Brazil*
1964	*Destabilization of the Bosch government and democracy Dominican Republic.*
1967-68	*CIA-backed scorched earth-slaughter Lake Izabal, Guatemala*
1968-72	*Police training by the United States at IPA headquarters in Wash., D.C.*
1971	*CIA destruction of the Tupamaros organization in Uruguay*
1972	*Installation of a military dictatorship in Argentina*
1973	*Overthrow of the democracy of Salvador Allende in Chile*
1975-76	*Use of CONDECA forces on behalf of Somoza in Nicaragua*
1977	*Destabilization of the Michael Manley democracy through IMF in Jamaica*
1979-80	*False coup land re-militarization of El Salvador under U.S. direction*
1981	*Contra war begins against Nicaragua organized and funded by the CIA*
1982-83	*Counterinsurgency massacre of the Indians in the Quiche, Guatemala*
1983	*U.S. invasion of Grenada*
1983-84	*U.S. militarization of Honduras and regional training operations*

In the name of National Security, the United States has literally turned the hemisphere into a place of constant war and deepening repression. Under the banner of anti-communism, we have come to worship the god of War as the only way to maintain U.S. domination over the hemisphere and the *Gran Caribe*.

Since Vietnam, however, we have had to operate more covertly, pretending the United States was not directly involved, deceiving the American people. Washington has used both foreign troops and foreign territory to accomplish this dirty work, using other countries as bases from which to launch our aggressions: from Puerto Rico into the Dominican Republic, from Guatemala into Cuba, from Honduras today into Nicaragua, etc... We plan and play war from other countries in order to hide what we are doing from the American people. A well-known Washington correspondent reflects on how the Pentagon and

CIA "plan war" using Central America as their field of operations. He describes how, on one occasion, CIA director William Casey set off...

> *with several aides aboard a small "special mission" aircraft for a secret two-day trip to Central America. "He was off with his boys to plan war," Woodward writes, catching just the boyish belligerence of the man...(7)*

The problem with empires "playing war" on someone else's turf is that *others get hurt.* In Vietnam the *greatest* crime committed by the United States was not sending over 57,000 American boys to their deaths but the slaughter of over one million Vietnamese civilians. Today, out of our counterinsurgency base in Honduras thousands have already been killed in El Salvador and Nicaragua. Our military leaders, like those of any empire, assume they have the right to invade, make war and kill...in the name of *patria y gloria.*

This is how we have come to worship the gods of War. No doubt, we will finally leave Central America one day just as we did Vietnam without any victory or anything we can be proud of.. leaving behind only disaster, death and destabilized societies that can barely survive thereafter. "We the people" must understand that such tragedies have become a way of life for the Empire. Therein lies the proof of our imperial idolatry, our worship of the gods of war.

U.S. Propaganda & Our Worship of the Lie. If profiteering leads to the worship of Mammon and national security phobia to the worship of War, the most insidious aspect of U.S. imperialism is the selling of these evils to the American people under the guise of the good life and true patriotism. Many Americans think of "propaganda" as something only the Nazis did during WW II or as the exclusive practice today of the socialist bloc countries and the Soviet Union. But no one has a corner on this mechanism of governments deceiving their own people. Since the Watergate scandal and more recently the Iran-Contragate scandal, we Americans have become aware of just how systematically and intentionally we have been lied to.

The selling of this LIE is always predicated, of course, on a "higher cause" — saving American democracy or Western civilization, if not the whole world from total destruction by the evil enemy! In the process, not only has the White House often applied extreme pressure on the national media to remain silent on delicate issues, but argues its case on the basis that *truth represents a serious threat to our "national security!"* Perhaps even more insidious, because it is usually self-motivated, has been the extraordinary numbers of TV programs and movie plots based on stopping the "communist threat" and towards that end justifying the most vile practices, blatantly or subtly arguing that lying, killing and war are perfectly justified *under these circumstances*.

The goal of government in getting us to acquiesce to the LIE is that it allows the Empire to implement its political and military policies without popular opposition. The White House uses propaganda to convince us to accept a particular foreign policy which, if we knew the truth, we would reject. They do this through the creation of incidents, U.S.-fabricated events, making us believe that something has happened "out there," something extremely dangerous to our national well-being, some outrageous act of aggression against us for which we must defend ourselves. Consider these examples:

1898   *The Sinking of the U.S.S. Maine* in the harbor of Havana, Cuba, in 1898 was a set-up, a planned explosion, in order to incite the American people to outrage and thereby to make them open to a declaration of war against Spain through the battle-cry, "Remember the Maine!" But that explosion was not caused by a Spanish mine but it was an internal charge from within the battleship, a created incident. Only a few people knew, like William Randolph Hearst, who was directly involved in the story and propaganda which infuriated the American public and took us into-that imperial war. (8)

1964   T*he Gulf of Tonkin Attack* in Vietnam never happened. The U.S. Navy attacks against North Vietnamese positions in July & August 1964 produced counter-attacks by N. Vietnamese torpedo boats against U.S. destroyers. But on the evening of August 4, 1964 when the destroyers Maddox and Turner Joy reported radar sightings of patrol boats and announced they were being attacked, in fact the commander of the Maddox sent a message to the Pentagon expressing doubts there had been any attack. Yet the so-called Gulf of Tonkin incident was used by Pres. Johnson to order hundreds of thousands of U.S. troops to Vietnam, a massive escalation over previous U.S. involvement.(9)

1983   *Sandinista aggression against Honduras.* Outside of reaction to U.S.- contra aggression into Nicaraguan territory, the Sandinista forces have never threatened nor attacked any Honduran troops. Cross border pursuit of contras who initiate hostilities is authorized by the United Nations; it's called "hot pursuit". Furthermore, these contra forces led by old Somoza National Guardsmen have initiated all the cross-border aggressions and incursions. Repeatedly, the Sandinistas have tried to sit down with the Honduran government to negotiate a border peace but the United States has not allowed it.(10)

In each of these cases, deception was the key element in persuading the American people to go along with an imperial strategy under the assumption that the United States was being threatened. We never were in any of these cases. Spain was absolutely no threat to us; it was a dying empire which had virtually been put into its grave eighty years earlier. The Vietnamese (unlike the Japanese in WW II) had no plans for expansion outside their borders but were merely trying to liberate themselves from a dying French colonial empire. The Sandinistas were even a lesser threat to the security of this nation given their extremely small size and population. Constant charges by the United States that the Sandinistas were providing the FMLN in El Salvador with arms was never substantiated. In each case, the United States enters the picture to either perpetuate the old order of death or to bring a new system of domination into being. DEATH is the by-product of this imperial idolatry.

Rationalizing the Lie leads to Demonic Possession

If the structural evils of the Empire must be cloaked by the LIE, the question is what are the implications of such deception for the American people? What happens to our society and way of life when our government compromises on the truth and how do evil policies overseas affect our domestic reality? To be sure, we the people are up against sophisticated methods used to confuse and convince us: the elements of *time* (the Guatemalan coup happened a long time ago!); *distance* (where is Grenada anyway?); *ignorance* (I really can't tell the difference between a Nicaraguan *contra* and a Salvadoran *guerrilla*); and, *the lie* (communism is the cause of all the turmoil in Central America). But if challenging these arguments is difficult, the implications of not doing so may well be disastrous for America as well as for our own moral integrity.

Take, for example, the MyLai incident in Vietnam. In that case, U.S. troops belonging to Task Force Barker moved into a small group of hamlets known as MyLai in Quang Ngai province in South Vietnam on

March 16, 1968. It was a typical "search and destroy" mission but in this case there were no armed combatants, no one fired on them and the U.S. troops found there only unarmed women, children and old men. On that morning, 50-60 American soldiers murdered some 500 villagers in cold blood! The massacre was not reported for some time and when it did leak out, high level officers covered it up along with the combat troops involved in the crime. It was a classic example of capitulation to group pressure and fear; of going along with a lie.

The author of a book entitled *People of the Lie*, a noted psychiatrist Dr. M. Scott Peck, describes the interconnection between this social pathology of justifying crimes against the "out-group" and our larger imperial policy.

> *A less benign but practically universal form of group narcissism is what might be called "enemy creation," or hatred of the "out-group." We can see this naturally occurring in children as they first learn to develop groups. The groups become cliques. Those who do not belong to the group (club or clique) are despised as being inferior or evil or both. If a group does not already have an enemy, it will most likely create one in short order. Task Force Barker, of course, had a predesignated enemy: the Viet Cong. But the Viet Cong were largely indigenous to South Vietnamese People, from whom they were often impossible to distinguish. Almost inevitably the specified enemy was generalized to include all Vietnamese so that the average American soldier did not just hate the Viet Cong, he hated "Gooks" in general.(11)*

We would argue that the government's lying about Vietnam was in fact a causal factor in the MyLai tragedy: because our leaders lie... therefore, *ME LIE*. In other words, the soldiers' cover-up of that crime was intimately related to President Johnson's lying about Tonkin Bay which legitimized a massive increase in the numbers of troops sent to Vietnam. All U.S. soldiers sent there were trained to hate the Viet Cong — the enemy, and then they were placed in a situation where they couldn't distinguish between the soldiers and the people, so their hatred/fear was expanded to include everyone in the "out-group" i.e., all Vietnamese people. When the soldiers reached MyLai, it was as part of a combat experience in which some of their buddies had already been killed, so that they were filled with rage and seeking revenge. They took out those feelings on the unarmed and defenseless segment of the hated population. Thus, we can see how U.S. propaganda which labels a whole people as "communist" and thus worthy of death can easily lead to mass-murder. It seems impossible to separate the MyLai tragedy from the overall policies and propaganda of the U.S. government at the time. How else to explain how "good" God-fearing American boys could end up slaughtering defenseless old men, women and children in cold blood?

Have we learned our lesson from Vietnam? Obviously not, since the same syndrome has dominated the policies of the White House under Reagan with respect to Nicaragua, Guatemala and El Salvador: selling the war in Central America on the basis of the same Lie. Once the Reagan administration had labelled the Sandinistas "communists" then they could be legitimately murdered in cold blood, though once again it was primarily innocent, unarmed civilians who were being killed by "our troops", i.e.the *contras*. Similarly, we see the same kind of cover-up and lying in the Iran-Contragate scandal as that which followed the MyLai incident. The Lie is used to justify another dirty war; anti-communist rhetoric becomes the instrument for deceiving the American people and sustaining the idolatry of the Empire.

How did we, the American people, who believe in truth, justice and God, arrive at this state of self-deception? Why do we continue to allow lying about "evil communists" to justify our own crimes against humanity? The answer is not to be found in either elaborate philosophical reasoning nor in any complicated ethical justification, but through two very simple psychological adjustments. We go along *because it is easy* and *because we refuse to look at the connections between cause and effect.*

The "good life" we enjoy in these United States becomes a subconscious rationalization for supporting U.S. foreign policy. For many Americans, unquestioned support of what the White House does overseas stems directly from their sense of gratitude for living well in a free country which has provided them a good life! For that reason alone, many citizens believe they should support the Empire's battles and oppose her enemies without asking questions. This linkage between patriotic gratitude and blind allegiance is a critically important aspect in selling U.S. foreign policy to the American people. Reagan's refusal to raise-taxes isn't only a conservative *economic policy*, it provides the psychological grease for winning mass support for his *foreign policy*. As long as life remains good and affluent for the majority here in the States, many people don't care what happens "south of the border!"

The other aspect of our affluent myopia is that *we don't want to admit that our "good life" here is directly related to impoverishment there*. This contradictory dialectic damages our self-image, yet the truth is that we are not a developed nation because of our "genius" nor are they poor because of their "laziness", but because we Americans representing 1/6 of the world's population consume more than 40% of the world's goods and resources. Furthermore, we control the financial mechanisms which perpetuate this imbalance between rich and poor. Through the International Monetary Fund (IMF) excessive debts and their repayments bring debtor nations under IMF rules which tax and exploit the poor to pay for the errors and greed of the rich. This "debt-servicing" from the Third World not only brings millions in hard currency (dollars) into the United States every month but requires increasing cutbacks in social services here, causing skyrocketing inflation for the poor, making their life extremely precarious.

> *In the world of the South, 500,000,000 persons presently suffer from hunger. This figure will climb to about 1.3 billion by the year 2000. By then, more than a billion will exist under conditions of extreme poverty...According to data from the Pan American Health Organization, 1,000,000 children die of hunger and malnutrition every year in Latin America.(12)*

How do we respond to this contradiction between the rich North and impoverished South? To be sure, many Americans are appalled when they first learn about this inter-connection between our Life and their Death. As a result, thousands of Americans have responded with great compassion to this unjust situation with aid but *they don't know what to do about the systemic nature of the problem.* How does one rid a world of structural evil? It is instructive that many highly-trained academicians and political scientists have known about these negative dialectics for decades, but seldom communicate such facts to their students.(13) But we are pressing for more than knowledge here. What concerns us in this relationship is that the American people understand that the Empire is on the side of Death and think through the implications this has for us as citizens of this society; our own complicity in this Sin against humanity.

Dr. Scott Peck helps us understand why we go along so easily with certain injustices in practice which, if pressed, we would certainly oppose in theory. He says that one of the main reasons for it is that we are lazy:

> *How could this have been? How could a whole people have gone to war (in Vietnam) not knowing why? The answer is simple.*

*As a people we were too lazy to learn and too arrogant to think
we needed to learn. We felt that whatever way we happened to
perceive things was the right way without any further study.
And that whatever we did was the right thing to do without
reflection. We were so wrong because we never seriously
considered that we might not be right. With our laziness and
narcissism feeding each other, we marched off to impose our
will on the Vietnamese People by bloodshed with practically no
idea of what was involved.(14)*

This is a telling reflection about a common human sin, but it is
frightening when we realize what a perfect opening it provides any
government in terms of being able to thoroughly implement its foreign
policy goals unimpeded. As President Johnson once told the U.S.
Congress at the time of the Bay of Tonkin resolution... "if you knew
what I know, you'd understand why we have to go to war."(15) On the
basis of our ignorance and acquiescence, Lyndon Johnson led us
deeper and deeper into a Vietnam nightmare of our own making, an
"*Apocalypse Now*".

Dr.Peck believes that out of the bitter experience of Vietnam we
are finally beginning to take the time to learn about and understand
what we have done. We respond: *as an event yes, but not as to its cause.*
Over the past five years, we have been watching the events of Vietnam,
through numerous movies and books on the subject, but the American
people have not looked into the causes: why we went there; the nature
of the *imperium*; the need for the Great Lie. This is why Central America
happened only five years later. As a result, people for the first time are
beginning to look into America's imperial history in terms of our
relationship to class injustices, the need to use surrogates and have our
puppets; why Reagan keeps the war going. While it is extremely
important to demand "No More Contra Aid", it is equally important to
understand the causes behind it. *Why does the Reagan administration
hate the Sandinistas so much? What is behind his obsession?*

Reflecting on where the rationalization of the Lie is taking us and
the theological implications of this phenomenon, an Argentine theologian formerly living in the States, Daniel Statello, struggled personally
— before his untimely death — to understand and describe this death/
life relationship between America and the rest of the hemisphere. To
focus his thoughts, Statello used Erich Fromm's distinctions between
necrophilia (love of death) and *biophilia* (love of life). In his PhD thesis,
Statello linked the necrophilous need of the individual to control those
around him with the role of the United States in its relationship to the

other countries in the Americas. He writes, both reflecting on and quoting from Fromm:

> *The necrophilous person relates to power not as the process in which he "is able" but rather as the ability to control. Power is understood primarily as a controlling force. "For him there are only two 'sexes': the powerful and the powerless."*
>
>> *The necrophilous person can relate to an object — a flower or a person — only if he possesses it; hence a threat to his possession is a threat to himself; if he loses possession he loses contact with the world. That is why we find the paradoxical reaction that he would rather lose life than possessions, even though by losing life he who possesses has ceased to exist. He loves control and in the act of controlling he kills life. He is deeply afraid of life, because it is disorderly and uncontrollable by its very nature...*
>
> *These characteristics paint us an accurate picture of the imperialist environment which surrounds us. A serious analysis of a personal and societal identification should consider these characteristics in order to make an evaluation of our contemporary reality.(16)*

So our necrophilous behavior is not only built on the structures of economic dependency and political domination but on our *psychological need to control others* leading to our fury towards any nation that tries to break out of this imperial captivity. Reagan's obsession with Nicaragua stems directly from this attitude: as President (personifying the United States as empire) he cannot tolerate the fact that Nicaragua which was once at our beck and call is no longer under our thumb nor acquiescent. Notwithstanding the creative possibilities opened up by the Sandinista revolution (*biophilia*) compared with the Somoza regime, the response of the Reagan administration is to either bring it back into subservience or destroy it (*necrophilia*). Reagan's phrase "until they cry uncle" was not a slip of the lip; it came from deep within his emotional psyche and reflects an underlying goal of the Empire: control; possession. This is why when referring to Nicaragua, Reagan analysts speak about "losing" Nicaragua, adding "to the communists" whereas what they really mean is "*from* our grasp."

As Dr. Scott Peck argues in his book, this drive to control others not only represents pathological tendencies but in some cases moves across the line of the abnormal into the realm of the demonic. He wrote about it in his book *People of the Lie*, as part of his attempt to better understand the phenomenon of evil. His observations forced him to conclude that *sometimes this pathology of possession is more than a psychological disturbance; it reflects a person possessed by an evil spirit.* His startling interjection of the MyLai incident into a book that deals primarily with individuals and couples attracted our attention because it strongly suggests that in certain cases, such as in Vietnam and now in Central America, the Empire has crossed this same line. Its pathology of possessing other nations has reached demonic proportions; in its killing in Vietnam and in the Isthmus today America as empire has become possessed.

Struggle Between Personal Morality & Imperial Patriotism
Constitutional distinctions about the separation of Church and State have long been a useful tool for guaranteeing freedom of religion and a government that is not dominated by any particular faith, but it has also produced a duality of loyalties between "my faith in God" and "my loyalty to country." For a long time, many Americans assumed that the two were basically compatible as long as one kept "politics out of religion." But since WW II, as the United States has stepped up its imperial campaigns, many Americans began questioning *whether their personal faith and mores were in fact in accord with this imperial patriotism.* During the Vietnam war, this issue exploded into the streets and across this nation into a struggle defined as one between the "hawks and the doves," the war-lovers versus the peaceniks. The question is: how far can this nation go as an empire before engaging in practices that are completely antithetical to our Judeo-Christian beliefs. The question of loyalty has thus resurfaced with a passion over the war in Central America. While some Americans have increasingly questioned their continued identification with such policies, others have become more vigorous in defending them... leading to a growing split in the American society between the *"critically conscious" and the "true believers."*

In the case of the critically conscious, since 1965 a growing number of CIA officers and career diplomats have broken from administration policies, disassociating themselves from that particular form of patriotism which they see as pro-imperialist — while still believing that they are loyal Americans. We see this transformation not only in a Padre Guadalupe in Honduras but in the case of Philip Agee, a CIA defector who left government service to write an expose of the agency. While stationed in Montevideo, Uruguay, during the U.S. invasion of the Dominican Republic, Agee wrote:

> *I still can't believe the reasons for the Dominican invasion that we're trying to promote... Why is it that the invasion seems so unjustifiable to me? It can't be that I'm against intervention as such, because everything I do is in one way or another intervention in the affairs of other countries... But what's really disturbing is that we've intervened on the wrong side. I just don't believe "fifty-eight trained communists" can take over a movement of thousands that includes experienced political leaders. That's a pretext. The real reason must be opposition to Bosch by US business with investments in the Dominican Republic.(17)*

Agee was absolutely correct in his assessment of the Dominican situation. The 1965 U.S. invasion not only stifled democracy and was led by a broad-based popular movement (the so-called "Constitution- alists" who were not Marxists) but it returned to power the reactionary military and elites who had supported the old dictator, Rafael Trujillo. Furthermore, the first law signed by the new president, Joaquin Balaguer, gave special privileges to the Gulf & Western Corporation in relation to its sugar estate in La Romana. Such policies openly clashed with Agee's personal convictions and his idealistic reasons for joining the CIA.

What we are observing in his case is an intelligent, religiously- dedicated Catholic civil servant who as a loyal American was forced to struggle with his conscience because of the horrendous events swirling around him. Like so many of us, it was inevitable that this shock- awareness should occur to Philip Agee while in Latin America, where the contradictions of this imperial policy surface in the form of gross human suffering. When Agee broke from the imperial mindset (which meant he had to leave the Agency), he did so as a loyal American struggling to be honest to his convictions and to speak the truth. When he began to write about this process of change in himself (in his book, *CIA Diary*), he became a real threat to the Company and anathema in the eyes of the Empire. As a result, he was threatened and had to flee for his life to Paris and even there threats were made against his life.(18)

On the other hand, in the case of *the true believers*, their commitment under pressure ceases to be "blind loyalty" and becomes more and more self-conscious and intentional on behalf of the Empire's goals. At a certain moment, a shift occurs in them also, from a generalized sense of patriotism (not so dissimilar from that of Philip Agee in the beginning) to a sense of mission, in which they move from conviction to crusade. This is what happened to Col. Oliver North. When that occurs, instead of the patriot questioning the obvious contradictions between his personal mores & religious beliefs and what the government was demanding of him, he goes along and becomes more and more "gung ho." His hatred of the "communist menace" then became a fetish, or more accurately, a fanaticism. Col. North had "to stop the commies" in Nicaragua, even if it meant committing illegal, immoral and even un-Constitutional acts. In the name of imperial patriotism, he was willing to "do anything." His anti-communist passion had become an idolatry, completely blinding him to the limits of the law.

Col. Ollie North's anti-communist ideology is based on a collection of political assumptions which are more precisely called *State Theology*. While this ideology contains concepts that have been in vogue for a long time in the Western world, especially since the days of Joseph McCarthy, they have become much more explicit and absolutist over the past 15 years. These popular assumptions have hardened into ideological positions on the right that are today considered sacrosanct. Three of the most common of these premises are: law & order, anti-communism and America as the political quintessence of a Republic.

Law & Order. It is obviously the right and duty of every State to maintain law & order within its territory, yet these words often become the justification for excesses under certain leaders and abuses by certain governments. In the case of Central American despots, for example, "law & order" is commonly used to rationalize a dictatorial system wherein obedience is forced and corruption justified, as in the case of Somoza in Nicaragua. We see the same abuses under pseudo-democracies, such as the white-male-minority-democracy in South Africa where the black majority is coerced into submission or marginalized from real power. Christians in South Africa have challenged the use of the phrase "law & order" by an Afrikaner government in the *Kairos Document*:

> *[The State does not have] divine mandate to maintain any kind of law and order. Something does not become moral and just simply because the State has declared it to be law, and the organization of a society is not a just and right order simply because it has been instituted by the State.(19)*

Most Americans assume that the term "law & order" as used by our government is based on real justice, but consider these examples to the contrary. Some of us in the religious community have visited and personally experienced the justice and openness of such societies as Chile under Salvador Allende, Grenada under Maurice Bishop and Nicaragua under the Sandinistas. Yet all three have been condemned by U.S. administrations as unjust and without any law & order... something that is quite false. On the other hand, many of us have witnessed or lived under right-wing regimes such as Indonesia (under the CIA-approved pogroms), Iran (under the Shah) and today in El Salvador (under Duarte) where the extent of human rights violations and lawlessness have been condemned by every human rights organization in the world. Therefore, we must reject the term "law & order" as meaning anything when it is mouthed by the White House or State Department, *unless and until* the people living under those systems confirm that such a slogan also means justice and freedom for them at a day by day level.

Anti - communism. While "law & order" is the positive slogan used to justify the actions of despotism and imperialism, its negative battle-cry is anti-communism. Under this banner, States use this term, employ it to create fear and obtain acquiescence since it requires no further elucidation or substantive facts. Communism becomes *ipso facto* the justification for murdering someone, destabilizing a government or even going to war. Its secondary utility is that it blocks any self-criticism, so that "loyal citizens" accept the charge at face value and focus on the enemy, not on their own injustice and untruths. Again, the *Kairos Document* condemns the arbitrary use of this term:

> *No account is taken of what communism really means. No thought is given to why some people have indeed opted for communism... even people who have not rejected capitalism are called "communists" when they reject "State Theology". The State uses the label "communist" in an uncritical and unexamined way as its symbol of evil.(20)*

We should be particularly careful, therefore, when the Reagan administration uses the phrase "Marxist-Leninist-Totalitarian State" to describe and condemn the Sandinista government in Managua; because it is a sign of ideological demagoguery. Yet, without question or challenge from the U.S. Congress, this slogan and label has been used over and over again by Reagan until — after seven years — it has filtered down into our very subconscious. As a result, today, any positive or moderate interpretations of the Sandinista revolution are greeted by catcalls or angry hoots of protest from those who assume that the advocate is either stupid or brainwashed. Many Americans now believe the LIE that the Sandinistas are nothing but a communist state controlled by Moscow, demonstrating how far U.S. propaganda has gone towards winning the war; how much the Lie is believed.

America as the Political Epitome of Excellence. The final premise of State theology is the assumption that America is the political "quintessence" of all other viable political systems in the world today. Whether compared to the hard-lined socialist bloc or the liberal socialism of the Scandinavian countries; whether measured by other operable democracies in England or Israel or compared to the non-aligned revolutionary experiments in the Third World... America is automatically assumed to be superior. If we measure our nation objectively, however, using data from the United Nations or the World Health Organization, in many categories we fall well below the social standards found in both Western European and Eastern-bloc countries. Some Americans would quickly counter these discrepancies by pointing out that the United States is the most open and permissive society in the world. The point may be true, but this only proves that such political judgement is based on those social values a people consider most important... but it does not prove that America is the "political epitome of excellence."

A better way of comparing different systems is to use the criteria of *power and powerlessness*. When we consider the behavior of the Big Powers — the United States, Soviet Union and China — towards smaller, poorer countries, especially those which are satellites or dependents of the Big Powers, we find considerable similarity in terms of domination, cultural imperialism, economic exploitation and propaganda manipulation. We also find considerable uniformity between the smaller, poorer countries in wanting to break out of this foreign influence; not towards seeking relations or control by some other "Big Brother." They want to be free to build their own societies without having to copy the models of either the East or West. Uniformly, Third World countries seek *non-alignment*, relations & trade without domination from Russia or the United States.

From the U.S. perspective — seeing itself as the political quintessence of all republics and as the dominant power in this hemisphere — such an alternative is both unthinkable and dangerous. If any country in this hemisphere doesn't want to be under the beneficent influence of the United States, many hard-liners would argue, it will necessarily fall under the domination of the Soviets. This simplistic

Manichaean view of the world — East/West in mortal combat — is deeply threatened by a *non-aligned policy*. Such American xenophobia is then turned into a self-fulfilling prophecy when the Empire does everything within its power to so damage and disrupt any experiment in alternatives as to make it appear to the world, as well as its own people, as untenable. This is what we did to Vietnam and it is what we are now doing to Nicaragua. We have systematically wrecked their economy in order to prove a political point... that the experiment is ideologically defective.

Prophetic Theology Challenges State Theology

In affirming prophetic theology for our time and circumstance as the faithful remnant living inside the United States who are deeply concerned about our Central American brothers and sisters, we make a distinction between prophetic theology and a theology of liberation. Like Jeremiah, we Americans find ourselves *on this side of judgement* (the fall of Jerusalem; of Babylon; of American imperialism), so our emphasis must be on a prophetic challenge of that imperial idolatry. For our Latin American and Caribbean compañeros who are already *on the other side of God's judgement* though still living in captivity, they correctly affirm a theology of liberation just as Ezekiel — after the fall — became a messenger of such hope.

State theology, on the other hand, uses the name of God and the holy Word to justify its beliefs and actions whereas prophetic theology places the State, the People and indeed, itself, under the Word of God, accepting God's judgement and open to the Word's command. The temptation of every State and Empire is to invert the authority of God, refusing to be its subject but always seeking the blessing of the Word upon its projects. This practice began in the time of Constantine (311 A.D.) when the Roman empire accepted its baptism into the Christian faith, but with the understanding that this Jesus-religion *should serve it and save it*. Since then, Western Christendom has used Christianity and the name of God to justify every war, act of exploitation, crusade, slavery and in our day neo-fascism in Central America.

Conservative biblical exegetes would challenge this interpretation of Church/State relations by claiming that St.Paul admonished the faithful to submit to the State as part of their Christian duty before a legitimate authority:

> *You must obey the governing authorities. Since all government comes from God, the civil authorities were appointed by God, and so anyone who resists authority is rebelling against God's*

decision, and such an act is bound to be punished.
—Roms.13:1-2

Subservience to the State is not, however, what Paul had in mind in these words. He was concerned about individual anarchy and that otherworldly tendency among first-century Christians which had little respect for authority because they were soon to be with Jesus in paradise. Paul's position, therefore, was that the State (and its **just** laws) should be respected while at the same time the State should serve the people...

> *The state is there to serve God for your benefit... The authorities are there to serve God; they carry out God's revenge by punishing wrongdoers.*
> *—Roms.13:4*

Thus while the apostle was challenging both anarchism (antinomianism) and otherworldliness (triumphalism) among the faithful, he also opposed imperial license and unjust power which murdered legitimate prophets like himself.

The great flaw in State theology is that it sees God and religion as a nationalistic prop intended to undergird the *status-quo*. When a given state is also an Empire, its well-being and way of life requires the exploitation of the products, people and resources of those outside the *imperium* which implies for them a "*logic of death*." But faithful Christians and Jews know that God is the God of life *for all people* and that the Word stands against all unjust, exploitative and domineering policies... and thus against imperialism. The very universalism of the biblical perspective and its prophetic plumb-line standing above all nations necessarily condemns State theology.

Those theologians defending the American state and the Capitalist system try to answer this contradiction by standing courageously against the evils of this world (communism and socialism). Fearing the collective and hating the undisciplined, they seek to conquer these evils through rugged individualism and courageous patriotism (as sophisticated Rambos). Thus the theologian Michael Novak in his book *Democratic Capitalism* challenges what he sees as a false vision of human solidarity and societal unity emerging in the Third World which he identifies as mass blind allegiance to a socialist dream which will (he believes) ultimately end in totalitarianism:

*By contrast, traditional and socialistic societies offer unitary
visions. They suffuse every activity with symbolic solidarity. The
human breast hungers for such nourishment. Atavistic memo-
ries haunt each free person. The "wasteland" at the heart of
democratic capitalism is like a field of battle on which individuals wander alone in some confusion amidst many casual-
ties. Nonetheless, like the dark night of the soul in the inner
journey of the mystics, this desert has an indispensable purpose.
It is maintained out of respect for the diversity of human
consciousness, perceptions and intentions. It is swept clean out
of reverence for the sphere of the transcendent to which the
individual has access through the self, beyond the mediation of
social institutions... But is finally centered in the silence of each
person. (21)*

Glorification of capitalist competitiveness and exaltation of courageous individualism is very Protestant and very American... but it also
reflects a loneliness and isolation found in many Western males and
certainly in the capitalist way of life with its constant pressure to
succeed and advance over others... "every man for himself!" What we
see in this courageous stand of the lonely hero (like Col. Oliver North)
is a philosophy which takes the "suffering of this emptiness" and
"presents it to God as a sacrifice," that is, as a noble commitment which
must be endured in order to be faithful to self and honest to God (one
can picture the solitary Dane, Soren Kierkegaard saying, "yes!"). By
contrast, a very Western man, a German theologian-economist who has
spent many years in Central America examining this phenomenon and
going through his own transformation, Franz Hinkelammert, believes
that Novak's thesis of God as emptiness is really a form of nihilism, as
was Nietzche's "God is dead" thesis:

*The real intention of these theologies is to destroy hope in the
Kingdom of God and its consequences of our life here on earth.
That there is no longer any hope becomes the hope of such
theologies. They preach a millennium as a situation in which
no one any longer dreams of a millennial kingdom. It is in fact
Dante's kingdom over the entrance to which are written the
words: "Abandon all hope, ye who enter here!(22)*

This view of the lonely man and empty God is completely
antithetical to the biblical call to community and to the personalities of
the Hebrew prophets and the liberator we call Jesus the Christ. In spite

of the world of sin in which we live, God offers us the promise of life
and indeed, abundant life... but in relationship with others wherein
community (religious and secular) become signs of the Kingdom. But
this loving community in the United States is often soft and indulgent
and refuses to take risks or make sacrifices — all things hated by
courageous patriots like Oliver North. However, those of us who have
experienced Central America, its exile and suffering, have found there
both community and courage; both collective love and personal sacrifice but dedicated to the liberation of their people.

The great danger and weakness of State theology is that in
defending the "truth" and being willing to die for its "beliefs", the
biblical virtue of love for our brothers and sisters is often lost... both in
the American and the Russian super-patriot. This is why we must
expose the idolatry of American imperialism just as we see Gorbachev
challenging the idolatry of Russian imperialism (vis-a-vis Afghanistan)... for both of these great nations *as empires are accursed.*

CHAPTER 13 — FOOTNOTES

1   William Appleman Williams, *Empire as a Way of Life*, op.cita, p.126.

2   *The Collected Poetry of W.H. Auden*, Random House, New York,
1945, "For the Time Being". "Just how, just when it succeeded we shall
never know. We can only say that now It is there and nothing We learnt
before It was there is now of any use...", p.410.

3   The film "*The Portrait of Dorian Grey*" tells of a deal he made with
the Devil whereby he would remain physically young, handsome and
presumably pure while his portrait would reflect his evil deeds and turn
into a hideous reflection of all he had done.

4   *Americas Watch* and many human rights groups who have tracked
Guatemalan history estimate this to be the conservative number of
political assassinations in Guatemala between 1954 and 1980.

5   Julia Esquivel, opus cita, p.81.

6   Peter Wyden, *Bay of Pigs*, Simon & Schuster, New York, 1979,
pp.7-8.

7   *Washington Post Magazine*, Sept. 27. 1987, J. Anthony Lukas, "The Spy & the Reporter," p.13.

8   Rear Admiral Rickoffer, retired, sent a scuba team to Havana in 1982 to carry out a diving expedition to examine the hull of the U.S.S. Maine. He discovered that the explosion had been set from inside and thus was not caused, as speculated, by a Spanish mine. Many stories circulate about William Randolph Hearst having sent a reporter to Havana, Cuba to cover a big story in the Summer 1898. Upon arrival in Havana and finding no hostilities, the reporter cabled Hearst to ask him what to do. Hearst replied by cable that he should stay there and he, Hearst, would provide the story. A few days later the Maine blew up, producing the slogan "Remember the Maine" which convinced the American public to support the Spanish-American War of 1898.

9   Two U.S. Senators, Sen. Wayne Morse of Oregon and Sen. Ernest Greuning of Alaska, opposed Pres. Johnson's message to Congress and his assurance that this was not "an escalation of the war" and that no further U.S. troops would be sent. Sen. Morse said, "a snow-job is being done on us by the Pentagon and the State Department... we are in effect giving the President...warmaking powers in the absence of a declaration of war." (Talk by Duane Shank at the People's Filibuster, Aug. 7, 1986.)

10   Foreign Minister Miguel D'Escoto carried out numerous missions to Tegucigalpa trying to find a formula for border peace between Honduras and Nicaragua but the Hondurans claimed the *contra* forces weren't located in Honduran territory.

11   M. Scott Peck, *People of the Lie*. Simon & Schuster, New York, 1983, pp. 213-214. The book is, surprisingly, about individual and small group examples of pathology in terms of "group" control and lying which makes his use of the MyLai incident all the more fascinating.

12   Victor Araya Guillen, *La Diakonia Samaritana*, EPICA, Wash., D.C. Summer 1987 p.7. Data from FAO, UNESCO and Informes of the Club of Rome; second citation from UNICEF "The World State of Infancy", New York, 1981-82, *El Pais*, Madrid, Dec. 18, 1981 p.30.

13   Andre Gunder Franks' thesis "The Development of Underdevelopment" has been widely studied since the mid-1960s.

14   M. Scott Peck, op. cita, pp.250.

15   Stephen E. Ambrose, *Rise to Globalism*, Penguin Books, 1971, p.328.

16   Estéban Daniel Statello, "Towards A Theology from Critical Consciousness," American Baptists Seminary of the West, Los Angeles California, June 1975, pp. 45-46.

17   These are all statements made by former CIA agents concerning the role of the U.S. government overseas: a) Philip Agee, *Inside The Company: CIA DIARY*, Penguin Books Ltd., Middlesex England, 1975, p. 425.; b) John Stockwell; and c) Philip C. Roettinger, both quoted in "Lifting the 'C' from Covert Action," *The Washington Post*, Washington, D. C., November 26, 1987.

18   Philip Agee, op. cita., *CIA Diary*, pp. 578-581,Cf.

> *"... on Friday Therese was arrested and taken to an interrogation centre at the Ministry of Interior (Paris). For several hours she was questioned about me and the book— they know of my CIA background and said the U.S. government considers me an enemy of the state,"* p. 581.

19   New York 1982, p. 53. The Kairos Theologians, "Challenge To The Church." *The Kairos Document*, Russell Press Ltd., Nottingham, England, Sept. 1985, 2.2., p. 8.

20   *The Kairos Document.* ibid., 2.3., p. 9- 7.

21   Michael Novak, *The Spirit of Democratic Capitalism*, American Enterprise Institute, New York, 1982, p.53.

22   Franz J. Hinkelammert, "The Politics of the Total Market, Its Theology and Our Response", *Pasos*, DEI, San Jose, Costa Rica, translated & republished by *North/South Dialogue*, Washington, D.C., Vol.I, Number i, Fall 1985, published by EPICA., p.7.

CHAPTER 14
RELIGIOUS AMERICA AS EMPIRE CANNOT
BE SAVED
IMPERIAL IDOLATRY DEMANDS A CHURCH
THEOLOGY

MAURA CLARK

DOROTEA KAZEL

JEAN DONAVAN

ITA FORD

Carlos Reyes/Andes Press

The fact that most Churches & Synagogues in America did not see in the murders of Oscar Romero & the four Maryknoll religious a modern crucifixion means that their spirituality lacks the prophetic vision needed to save imperial America.

Down with you, sit in the dust,
  virgin daughter of Babylon.
Down from your throne, sit on the ground
  daughter of the Chaldaeans;
never again shall men call you
  soft-skinned and delicate
strip-off your skirt, bare your thighs, wade through the
  rivers, so that your nakedness may be plain to see
  and your shame exposed.
I will take vengeance, I will treat with none of you,
  says the Holy One of Israel, our ransomer,
  whose name is the Lord of Hosts

—*Is.47:1-4*

This is the patent age of new inventions
  for killing bodies, and for saving souls,
All propagated with the best intentions.(1)

—*Lord Byron*

Isaiah's condemnation of Babylon coupled with the promise that the Lord of history will ransom the people of God from exile has only one logical parallel in our day: that imperial America shall be brought low and the suffering peoples of Central America shall be liberated from their captivity. This combination of judgement and promise represents the biblical definition of the work of the Spirit which openly challenges the truism about British imperialism reflected by Lord Byron. Thus when the American empire kills human beings while blessing evangelists who go into a region to save souls, we are witnessing not only a repetition of that 19th-century imperial practice but a demonic, anti-spiritual strategy. Whether religious leaders justify their mission as "only saving souls" or our political leaders as "only saving the region from communism", the result is the same: continued captivity and institutionalized violence, both utterly-repugnant to the Holy Spirit.

These are, then, spiritual as well as political matters in which the work of the Spirit — vengeance and ransom — challenge the superficial "spirituality" being preached in most American churches and synagogues today. Such pseudo-spirituality contradicts the prophetic and gospel understandings of the Word, its use — while making people feel good — in fact, facilitates avoidance of *our primary spiritual task: to save the soul of this nation from its collusion with American imperialism.*

Most religious Americans automatically assume that God is on our side and that America as a nation will always have God's blessing, regardless of its corrupt policies and sinful deeds. In this we suffer from the same naiveté and false hope that cursed the Jews in the ancient kingdoms of Israel and Judah and led to their downfall. As the Exilic prophets made clear, neither "belief" as formal commitment to the Covenant nor "religion" as mere religious rite and temple-attendance offer a guarantee for the future of any nation. Because the Jews abandoned their "high-calling" — their spiritual inheritance — religiosity could not prevent their decline and fall. Nor could the mere coming together of Israel physically in exile (Valley of the Dry Bones) as bones, sinews, flesh and skin produce life until the Spirit of God was breathed into their hearts. Thus, while the presence of "spirit" is obviously crucial to any nation's future, being "born again" with no relationship to societal justice means that only a politically-converted America can be spiritually saved.

The difference between form and substance in terms of the spiritual can be seen in the way the Empire uses moralistic cliches to dismiss gross immorality in contrast to the way Mons. Oscar Romero saw the spirit moving in El Salvador. When José Napoleón Duarte recently urged the Salvadoran people (in late 1987) "to forgive and forget" the slaughter of 63,000 persons and disappearance of 7,000 others since 1980, we are witnessing a U.S. puppet president mouthing words which in all probability were supplied by a U.S. ad-agency or the CIA! God is not mocked-and indeed the prophets tell us just the opposite about the workings of the Spirit of God: Yahweh will not forget and will take vengeance upon such evil-doings! On the other hand, Oscar Romero saw in that same sacrifice of 70,000 persons the seed giving birth to a liberated society of the future. In spiritual terms, if "saving a soul" requires individual change of heart and confession of sin, even more so the salvation of a nation or an empire. There is no societal salvation with only spiritual talk!

Spiritual Evils of Imperialism

As we reflect on this contradiction between the abundance of pseudo-spirituality and the absence of the truly spiritual in America today, we are reminded of the old adage "Hear no evil, See no evil, Speak no evil." In times past, this moralism was supposed to keep the faithful pure and unspotted from this evil world. Today, just the opposite has come around: this evil empire has become increasingly a part of our American way of life while the adage is now used to keep us from bringing the Word to bear on it. We have turned this saying inside-out, making it read: "Hear *not*of our evil, See *not* our evil, Speak *not* of our evil." If we refuse to look at our national sins or discuss our wrong-doings, we block our own spiritual ability to hear, see and speak the truth.

Dishonesty Among the Conservatives (Speak not of our Evil). The importance of the Iran-Contragate scandal and hearings is that they exposed the dishonesty of the Reagan administration on a national scale. Not by chance the title of Bob Woodward's book on this scandal "VEIL" (code-word for a disinformation program employed by the United States against Moammar Gadhafi of Libya) reflects a key methodology used by U.S. imperialists down through the years... to *veil* their imperial goals behind America's democratic system. As the majority report from the Iran-Contragate Hearings declare, this kind of deception was key to the whole Reagan strategy.

> *Reagan aides fabricated chronologies to disguise the facts of the shipments, and some White House officials withheld details from others... Reagan is described in the report as-being at the forefront of those who misled the nation last fall.(2)*

Whereas dishonesty is part and parcel of the Reagan strategy, just as it was for Hitler's propaganda minister Goebbels: to blatantly lie, to repeat the lie and to lie ever more loudly, if anything our present dishonesty is even more diabolical because of its subtleties and sophistication. For example, Reagan's greatest deception preceded his presidency though it was related to his becoming America's chief executive. During the 1980 presidential campaign Reagan secretly promised the Ayatollah Khomeini that if he would wait to release the American hostages until after the November elections, he would — upon entering the White House — give Iran those weapons which the Carter administration had refused the Shiite leaders. Khomeini agreed and in 1981, Reagan complied.(3) Is it any wonder that one of the most diabolically evil men of our times, the Ayatollah Khomeini of Iran — who is responsible for the political torture and murder of at least 60,000 Iranians to say nothing of the hundreds of thousands sacrificed to the Iran-Iraqi war — would call the United States "the Great Satan"?(4) Not because the American empire does evil things or even carries out "dirty wars" — for Khomeini does the same — but because our leaders prevaricate, deceiving the American people and indeed the whole world, pretending to be something we are not.

Prophetic voices are today challenging this deception. The efforts of the Christic Institute's broadly based public education campaign has gone a long way in exposing an important aspect of this deception... the role of the "Secret Team", which has been operating behind the scenes of U.S. foreign policy since the days of the Cuban revolution and especially since Vietnam. With meticulous historical detail, the Institute's spokespersons reveal how this Secret Team has made a mockery of the U.S. Constitution by using the White House, CIA, NSC and State Department as covers for its covert operations.(5) Similarly, Peter Kornbluh in his book The *Price of Intervention,* details the nefarious programs orchestrated by the White House under Reagan against the Sandinistas, including the use of false reporting, misappropriation of funds, murder and misinformation. The author correctly affirms that the goal of the Iran-Contragate hearings was itself a cover-up:

> *Yet, as the Iran-Contra imbroglio dramatically revealed the perils of the Reagan Doctrine, it remained unlikely that any lesson would be learned. Congressional investigations insured that evidence of wrong doing would be exposed but not that necessary solutions would be imposed. Restructuring the NSC, revamping congressional oversight laws, indicting Oliver North and his cohorts — all were probable responses that failed to address the underlying cause of the scandal: the historical assumption of foreign policy makers that* **the United States has the right and the might to impose its will on smaller nations around the globe** *.(6)*

Dishonesty Among Liberals. (Hear not of our Evil). A new danger is now facing the Central American people with the decline of the Reagan administration and the possibility of a Democratic victory in November, 1988: that the liberals may return U.S. policy to a period of "benign" imperialism. In the fall of 1987, during the "Days of Decision" at a rally on the steps of the U.S. Congress, Sen.Tom Harkin, a liberal from Iowa, said he believed we had stopped the Reagan administration's intent to destroy the Sandinistas and called us to return to the "Good Neighbor" policy of Franklin Delano Roosevelt!(7) Harkin's presumably good intention in that allusion to the 1930's reflects his naiveté or forgetfulness about the fact that the "Good Neighbor" strategy was, in fact, a cover for the beginning of the use of U.S. surrogate forces, such as the National Guard in Nicaragua led by Anastasio Somoza. The danger is that his off-hand remarks reflect a liberal foreign policy which while it would end illegal and immoral covert wars like that of the *contras,* would continue U.S. imperial domination in the region both militarily and economically.

Some readers may feel this is an unfair evaluation of Sen.Harkin's real intent, perhaps because he hadn't thought the issue through. Even though we have a great deal of admiration for the Senator because of his courageous stands on Nicaragua, we think not. Consider, for instance, that he is a strong supporter of José Napoleon Duarte in El Salvador, who has been clearly a puppet of U.S. foreign policy in the region since 1980... legitimizing a titular head of state and the thousands of assassinations which have occurred over the years of his powerless rule. What does Sen. Harkin make of Duarte's act of publicly kissing the American flag at the White House but a sign of his complete sell-out to U.S. policies and lack of patriotic integrity? More importantly, would the Senator from Iowa call for a halt in U.S. military aid to the Salvadoran military as Mons. Romero requested of Jimmy Carter? Would he oppose U.S. military aid to the Guatemalan military recognized around the world as a fascist operation guilty of the most horrendous human rights violations? We raise these questions not so much of the man Tom Harkin but of *the liberal philosophy espoused by many Democratic leaders in America which has taken us into some of the worst wars of U.S. imperial history.*

A decline in U.S. power arising out of the Vietnam war and the oil crisis of 1973 led to a public questioning of our geo-political policies in the Third World which in turn challenged the basic premise of traditional liberalism. By the mid-1970's, the United States no longer had the luxury of waging war overseas without it adversely affecting our domestic economy. As Joseph Holland noted in 1976:

> *In past periods of American history, the expansion of the American empire has relieved the pressure on the internal contradictions of the domestic capitalist system; thus, an imperialist foreign policy became the foundation for liberal policies at home. Now, however, the decline of the American empire pulls the rug out from under domestic imperialism. As a result, the nation faces a crisis not only in foreign policy but in domestic policy as well. Further,* **foreign policy now aggravates domestic social tensions** *.(8)*

This negative development between the domestic and overseas sides of liberal economic philosophy seems to be contradicted by the strong U.S. economy during the Reagan years, but that may only be because Reagan's propagandistic hand is faster than the American public's eye. Over the past seven years, the U.S. economy has been able to thrive by what some (including George Bush himself) have called "voodoo economics" in which the military budget has enormously expanded while the majority of Americans continue to live the good life without any increase in taxes. But the price of this magic has been incredible indebtedness, a serious negative balance of trade and a rising dependency on compounding interest from Third World nation debts. Reagan economists have been able to accomplish this sleight-of-hand (no increase in taxes) by putting off repayment of this expanding debt to future generations. The stock market crash of October 1987 was a reminder of the high price America may eventually have to pay for this folly... the possible economic decline of the United States as a world power! Even now, the poor in America are forced to pay for this pipe dream through greatly reduced social services. In other words, Holland was right and the fact that an aggressive foreign policy no longer guarantees domestic well-being means that the old liberal formula has been shattered.

This philosophical contradiction became apparent in relation to the *contra* war which revealed itself as a kind of litmus test on liberal priorities. Through Republican brashness, extreme patriotism and anti-communist rhetoric, the Democrats were forced to choose between the *contras* as imperial warriors defending the system and their concern over human rights violations of innocent civilians in Nicaragua. While Democratic "doves" detested covert war, Democratic "hawks" took the patriotic side in the name of anti-communism, siding with conservative Republicans sufficiently to shift the balance in favor of Reaganomics. The real weakness of the liberal position emerged, however, from their inability to challenge the Republicans ideologically because they *had exposed the imperial roots of the liberal position*. Held up to public scrutiny and media pressure, liberal Democrats could not name the evil — U.S. imperialism — and thus were forced to suffer defeat after defeat to a coalition of hawks in both parties. In effect, liberals faced by the possible exposure of that "evil they would not hear of", i.e. *imperial idolatry*, capitulated before right-wing patriotism. As a result, the Democrats can now only re-enter the White House by staying clear of this crucial issue and hoping they can win by Republican default.

Dishonesty Among The Religious Establishments. (See not our Evil). Despite such political covertness and ambivalence, a growing number of religious leaders and committed clergy along with their congregations are beginning to recognize this blindness and identify the idolatry. Increasingly, many in religious communities are beginning to take strong stands on U.S. foreign policy issues and especially in reaction to Central American suffering openly challenging Reagan's practices in the region as unacceptable from a biblical perspective. Yet, notwithstanding these bright lights, the majority of pastors and prelates in U.S. religious establishments — Christian, Jewish and Pentecostal — remain blind to America's imperialism or simply "do not want to see our evil."

In the case of the Protestant and Catholic establishments in America today, there is a strong tendency to evade such hard issues. They don't want confrontation with the government and its policies for that leads to conflict and upsets the institutional apple cart... the great religious sin of affluent America: *keep peace at all costs.* Take, for example, the recent Immigration Amnesty Bill (Simpson-Rodino) which would allow a small percentage of Central American political refugees to remain in the States while making the great majority "illegal" and prohibiting them from working.(9) This Bill gave the religious establishments an "out" from the moral tension raised by the Sanctuary movement, allowing them to both help out a refugee minority while also collaborating with the government. Many rushed to do so, even in some cases abandoning previous Sanctuary-related work in order to focus almost exclusively on amnesty. While such assistance was helpful to those affected, the Bill hides the main thrust of this new legislation which is designed to exclude, exploit, expel and deny justice to those who have fled to the United States from the war and repression with which the present administration is complicit. Supporting such amnesty while avoiding the primary evil of the ongoing holocaust in Central America is nothing less than *harloting with the Empire.*

In the case of the Jewish community, one must certainly give high marks to those synagogues that have declared themselves Sanctuaries, as well as to the thousands of Jews committed to Central American solidarity work, some of whom, like Ben Linder, have even given their lives. But when we look at the Jewish establishment in the United States, we find most rabbis blindly following the repressive policies of Israel against the Palestinians. We note this, not only because of what has been happening in Lebanon, Gaza and the West Bank, but in terms of Israel's role in the repression bleeding Central America. The Zionists have since 1977-78 become the primary arms dealer to the repressive dictatorships in the region, and more importantly, the counterinsurgency trainer, funder and military surrogate of the United States to the fascist military government of Guatemala.(10) It has done so in exchange for massive economic assistance from the United States for which it has been servicing Guatemalan fascism. In this process, the administrations of Carter and Reagan used Israel to by-pass Congressional restrictions on sending military aid to Guatemala because of its human rights violations. Such practices represent political hypocrisy on the part of the Israelis, especially in light of their condemnation of President Waldheim of Austria for a similar kind of collaboration with German fascism...and thus nothing less than *harloting with imperialism.*

In the case of the Pentecostals, exemplified by electronic evangelists like Pat Robertson and Jimmy Swaggart — the two pentecostal leaders most active in Central American affairs — we see an even closer identification with imperial politics, typifying the position of most "born-again" Christians. As we have already detailed, Pat Robertson was directly involved in the cover-up of the Indian massacre in Guatemala through the pseudo-presidency of "born-again" Efraim Rios Montt. In the case of Jimmy Swaggart, his evangelistic empire has invested millions in salaries, buildings and TV time in Central America where he has been preaching non-involvement in politics as his part in an overall strategy to pacify the poor into accepting their present captivity. However, if you ask these evangelists what they are doing in the Isthmus, they will tell you (as Lord Byron said) "just saving souls for Jesus" while the killing and starvation goes on. Thus, when Jimmy Swaggart confessed his personal sins with a prostitute weeping crocodile tears, his artificial and staged repentance sidestepped his real sin... *harloting with the Empire!*

In all three instances, the religious establishments in this country refuse to see the evil side of America and in the name of our modern shibboleths — "pseudo-democracy" and "anti-communism" — gloss over U.S. policies of death. The degree to which they remain blind and dishonest about what is happening to the poor and outcast in this hemisphere, just so this nation as Empire cannot be saved. If these religious bodies who supposedly understand the Word of God can't see that the Bible demands a disavowal of the Empire's immoral practices, then America's soul is surely lost.

Spiritual Decline of America

The fact that these spiritual evils of dishonesty, avoidance and often religious harloting with imperialism are being inculcated into the very psyche of the American people implies nothing less than the spiritual decline of our nation. We can see this decline at many levels of our functioning as a society, even though our military might is still great, our wealth awesome and our "external" body kept beautiful. We notice it in terms of the loss of America's financial leadership, the rising technological superiority of the Asians, the political innovation coming out of China and Russia and the emergence of the most creative theological insight coming from Latin America and other Third World countries. These changes represent a shift in creative energy away from the old European/North American metropolitan centers to the "outlands", a shift in motor force to those once considered outside the pale... reflected ironically in the fact that the Cubans have trounced mighty USA in fifteen boxing tournaments in a row! But more than a loss of "power creativity", America is losing its "soul power" as its moral integrity declines and its respect around the world wanes.

How do we account for this spiritual decline once thought to be the bedrock of our American dream? Perhaps one answer lies in the way we look at life; our perspective. For America wears different masks and we behave differently depending on which mask we are wearing. First of all, there is America's *domestic* face wherein one finds the "good life" within the affluency of the great city of Babylon; what is described so graphically in the book *Pilgrim's Progress* as Vanity Fair. Herein, one finds all kinds of goodies and temptations: elegant cars, comfortable houses, plenty of money, drugs, sex and the freedom to enjoy them all. In terms of things and convenience, there is no question that we are #1 and that the poor and less fortunate come flocking to our shores to partake in this great marketplace of abundance.

Second, America has her *international* face wherein she deals with foreign powers; with both allies and enemies with whom she must be careful and respectful. From this perspective (under this mask), the United States cannot afford to alienate such powerful foes as Russia and China or offend such friends as Great Britain and West Germany. So, in this realm, we are polite and proper, cautious and diplomatic... even respectful of the supposedly hated communist enemy whom we vilify at the propagandistic level.

Third, there is our hemispheric face wherein we are the dominant power and never permit any upstart nation (like Nicaragua) to free itself from our control, for that would appear to the American people and to the world as a sign that we are "getting soft". In this realm, we exploit, coerce, intervene, kill (with "low intensity" warfare) and treat our neighbors to-the South with disdain as children, dependents or rebels. Since our society is a mixture of all three of these personalities, the question is which is most reflective of our true nature? From the biblical perspective, the answer is clearly our *hemispheric* face, for this is where we deal with our poor neighbor, with the person fallen among thieves and left half-dead alongside the path of life. It is precisely concerning these persons that Jesus said, "inasmuch as you did not do it unto one of the least of these my brothers and sisters, that you did not do it unto me." (Lk.10:25-37; Mt.25:41-46). In the parable of the Good Samaritan, these are the ones we pass by "on the other side" because to stop and help them might, as one knows, damage our image, interrupt more important business, upset relations back home. So, while we are able to handle ourselves very efficiently in our domestic realm and very diplomatically in our international realm, the stench and suffering arising from Central America and the Caribbean are very disturbing and preferably to be avoided. It is this avoidance that has turned the Caribbean/Isthmian region into our great "trouble spot", reflecting our priorities.

This dialectic between the "North" and the "South", between affluent USA and impoverished Latin America represents a dialectic between life and death; a relationship of exploitation and control which results in life for us and death for them: *a relationship of necrophilia.* Since 1898, this dynamic has meant in effect that everything flows from the South to the North to our benefit: agricultural products, raw materials, oil, "cheap labor", Indian artifacts... everything. This has created severe economic and social problems for them, producing in turn rebellions and revolutions, which in turn have necessitated U.S. invasions, repression and war. In both the economic and political realms, this North/South dialectic has produced *a death-logic,* poignantly described by a Central American theologian, Victorio Araya:

> *We can express our basic thesis this way: the principle contradiction which presently polarizes human history (in the international context) is not East/West tensions but Life/Death contradictions.*
>
> *This North/South contradiction, that is, the contradiction which faces the countries of the "South", the poor and underdeveloped nations of the Third World, including those non-persons in the countries of the "North"— impoverished social classes, humiliated races and ethnic minorities, despised cultures, manipulated religions, women and children marginalized and discriminated against...(11)*

How can we break out of this syndrome of indifference, death and blame... this mad rationality for perpetuating oppression? The psychiatrist Erich Fromm examines this problem in his book *Anatomy of Human Destructiveness* in which he affirms something most Americans don't like to admit: that humankind is, in many ways, intrinsically a killer and an exploiter... and thus as much evil as good. Indeed, Fromm argues that it is far easier to document the human tendency for evil than to defend the virtues of the human race. However, he quickly adds that it would be unhelpful to emphasize this negative side of our human nature. Fromm's alternative is that we must impose a rationality over our phobias; we must conquer our "irrational fears" with wisdom and reject the use of "false Messiahs" as mechanisms of solace or escape.

> *The position we are defending in this work is that of a rational faith in the capacity of humankind to save itself from the seemingly fatal network of circumstances which it creates... in the capacity of the human species to avoid a final catastrophe. This humanistic radicalism directs itself to the roots and therefore to the causes; seeks to liberate humankind from the chains of illusion; declares that fundamental changes are necessary not only in our economic and political structures but also in our values, in our concept of human goals and our personal conduct.(12)*

Such rationality and human hope are precisely the elements which undergird the thinking of progressive Latin American leaders as well as today's liberation theologians, completely apart from any Marxist ideas they may or may not have.

On the other hand, our North American leaders — secular and religious — are increasingly dominated by irrational fears (communism as the destroyer) and false Messiahs (empire as the rescuer). These fears and idolatries have been exploited to the hilt by the Reagan administration to such an extent that during his two terms of office these values have been driven deeply into our subconscious as well as into our public thinking, so that our paranoia has been greatly exacerbated during the 1980's. In fact, *we are losing ground in our ability to rationally counteract our leaders' manipulation of our phobias.*(13) While Gorbachev's visit to the USA in 1987 and the possibility of a Democratic victory in 1988 might check this drift, we must recognize how much ground we have lost during the Reagan years.

Imperial Idolatry Requires a "Church" Theology

To undergird and reinforce its idolatry, the Empire has turned increasingly to "Church Theology" by which it hopes to "save itself" just as the Roman empire did in 311 A.D. One aspect of this lifeline approach involves attacking liberation theology as Marxist and more importantly undercutting the rising religious idealism, humanism and radicalism that has been growing over the past decade in the States. To a significant degree this new vision is due to a growing involvement in Third World problems, including those in Central America. The Empire hopes that by lifting up certain political ethical themes at the popular level, it can counter the prophetic voices that are beginning to re-emerge within the religious communities, albeit at the periphery not at the core of the Church and Synagogue. While the religious establishments would prefer to remain neutral in this ideological/theological conflict, the system uses moral and religious cliches in order to enhance and reinforce its idolatry.

We all know there is an armed struggle underway in Central America today between the forces of reaction and liberation, but we sometimes forget that the real battle is for the "hearts and minds" of the faithful (both in the religious and secular spheres) and through them for the soul of the Americas. Imperial idolatry needs a "Church theology" because the real struggle is not for or against Marxism (which few people in the region understand or espouse) but rather between a false spirituality manipulated to serve imperial goals and the Prophetic Word which rejects this idolatry in behalf of justice and liberation. What we see being played out in microcosm in Central America reflects that long-standing effort by imperial interests to confuse and capture American hearts and minds. The better we understand this imperial strategy the better able we are to do battle with the Powers here in the heartland of the Empire.

The primary theological issue revolves around the tension between dualism and incarnation, that is, between those who would divide reality into two distinct spheres called the "political" and the "spiritual" (earth/heaven, body/soul), versus the biblical position that these distinctions are only different aspects of a basic unity and that the Word must become incarnate in both. Prophetic theology doesn't tell us what particular political system or economic model to follow, but it does demand that we engage the forces of evil versus focusing on "a heavenly prize". When religious leaders urge the faithful to "stay out of politics" they are literally turning the world which God has given us over to the Powers. Three elements used by Church Theology are: reconciliation, otherworldliness and non-violence.

Reconciliation. One of the classical terms employed by Church theologians and Western Christendom down through the ages to overcome conflicts between the Word and the World has been the theme of "reconciliation". The purpose of this term and effort is to avoid conflict "out there" while sustaining a pleasant fellowship "in here" through eliminating tensions. This approach often produces superficial goodwill at the expense of real justice. The search by the Church for peace at any price has often been expressed in Latin America by the Catholic hierarchy projecting the ecclesial institution as a "mediator" of human conflicts, calling themselves "peacemakers". But such "reconciliation" falsely suggests that the Church is "above" politics and that in the name of God it can morally stand "in the middle" without taking sides.

A clue to the real purpose behind such neutrality through mediation can be seen in the fact that after such intervention by the Church, almost always the crisis is converted into a false peace with the despots, empires and system still in control! As the *Kairos Document* from South Africa states, the goal of such ecclesial mediation is to legislate in behalf of the Powers and their demand for the *status quo*:

> *Why does this theology not demand that the oppressed stand up for their rights and wage a struggle against their oppressors? Why does it not tell them that it is their duty to work for justice and to change unjust structures? Perhaps the answer to these questions is that it appeals to the "top" of the Church and tends very easily to be appeals to the "top" in society. An appeal to the conscience of those who perpetuate the system of injustice must be made. But real change and true justice can only come from below, from the people...(14)*

On the other hand, when certain prophetic leaders, like Desmond Tutu in South Africa or Mons.Oscar Romero in El Salvador try to mediate *for peace based on justice* they are either marginalized or murdered by the Powers.

Take, for example, the role of Cardenal Obando y Bravo in Nicaragua who is supposedly serving as a mediator between the Sandinistas and the *contras* whereas in fact he stands solidly on the side of the counter-revolutionaries and their reactionary view of that society. Or again, the role of the Catholic Archbishop in the Dominican Republic in mediating the conflict between the Dominican military-elites and the Dominican poor-middle class Constitutionalists in the rebellion of 1965. The Archbishop negotiated a peace at the pleasure of the Empire, supposedly reconciling the two opposing interests in the conflict. But that peace only brought Joaquin Balaguer to power, who thereafter headed up a twelve-year reign of terror (1966-1978) which represented a return to the "peace of Trujillo"... a false peace in which the U.S. government was totally complicit, advising, training and arming those repressive forces.(15) This is why the Exilic prophets attacked such false spirituality encompassed in the words, "They cry 'Peace, peace when there is no peace.'" Because what this kind of reconciliation really wants is calm, a cessation of hostilities and ultimately a return to the *status quo* , not a peace born of justice.

Otherworldliness. Different expressions of "otherworldliness" (self-enlightenment, eternal bliss, reincarnation, etc...) found in non-biblical religions all concur on the following: that history is irrelevant, the world only vanity and change merely the "eternal return of all things," i.e., an unending repetition of what always was. Holy Scripture counters these heresies at every point: through God's act of liberating the Hebrews from Egyptian captivity (divine involvement in history); God's destruction of Jerusalem and the Babylonian captivity (ending old orders and bringing the new into being); and, Jesus of Nazareth condemning religious legalism and challenging the Pax Romana (giving us hope in the midst of systemic despair). In other words, the truly spiritual can only be discovered through our struggles with evil and oppression in this world, never by fleeing from them.

We are reminded by José Miranda that this otherworldly tendency is not found, however, only in religious evasion of historical reality nor in secular rejection of a moral imperative but in that deep philosophical cynicism that runs all through our Western tradition:

> *Aristotelian deduction is a disguised affirmation of Socratic-Platonic recollection:* ***There is nothing new****; what seems new was always known by us, even though we were not aware of it; everything is deductible from the self; neither time, history nor any event is able to constitute a break from the continuity of my recollection.(16)*

Existentialists like Soren Kierkegaard and Karl Marx were not struggling primarily against Christianity's sell-out to a particular State or System (religion as the opiate of the people) but with the more subtle and dangerous notion imbedded in all of us who come out of the Western tradition: *that history is unredeemable, life unchangeable.* The idea that "we cannot change ourselves nor remake our world" is the ultimate idolatry because it represents historical hopelessness. From such cynicism (and behind it despair) flows much of the crime against humanity, that is, repression in the name of maintaining *the status quo,* whether in the form of "do not trespass for this is my private property" or "we must control the hemisphere for its own good." In so saying, those in power and with possessions are arguing for no change in the system because everyone knows "this is the best there can be." These phrases represent what the philosophers call "the eternal return of all things", expressed in today's TV ads as "the more things change the more they remain the same." The American empire cannot allow the Sandinistas to build a new society in Nicaragua for that would suggest such change is possible in every country in the hemisphere and that would directly threaten U.S. hegemony.

This resignation (despair) has been traditionally justified by the Church through its concept of *the two kingdoms* (of God & of this World), as found in Lutheran theology of the Reformation and in the dualism of the "born again" theology of many Pentecostals today. By contrast, at those few moments in history when the Spirit has broken in upon this static cynicism, challenging oligarchic domination, hope was reborn among the people and especially among the poor. This happened in the 1870's, when the new Protestant missionaries joined hands with Liberals to challenge feudalism in Central America.(17) It happened in the late 1960's when Catholic pastoral groups made a "preferential option for the poor" challenging the oligarchs and capitalists on behalf of justice for the poor majorities. When those moments of truth arrive, such prophetic hope is condemned as subversive and Marxist because it threatens the Powers, whether those of the State, the Church or the Empire. For the people, however, these breakthroughs are signs of life and hope, symbolic of the biblical promise that God's will "be done on earth as it is in heaven."

Non-Violence. For many North American pacifists, "non-violence" is an absolute ethical criteria in the sense that anyone who doesn't ascribe to it is suspect by them as advocating violent change. We submit that a more fundamental principle underlay the motivations behind our heroes Mahatma Gandhi and Martin Luther King: a radical commitment to their suffering people in the face of an oppressive system... and their determination to liberate their people from that captivity. Our quarrel is not, then, with their witness which we hold in the highest regard, but with the way the term non-violence is used by many Americans to avoid conflict, commitment to people and challenge of the Powers. Consider some ways in which non-violent advocates divert our focus away from the situational ethics of suffering people to the absolutization of a principle.

First, non-violence is not a biblical term but a Western ideal which has evolved in large measure because of the misuse of Christianity by Western powers to justify imperial wars, class injustice and racial prejudice. Biblical ethics are based on the positive terms justice and love, which represent *pro-people involvement not conceptual abstention*. More importantly, the base-word "violence" is used in the Bible to describe what the oppressor does, so that without proscribing precisely what someone defending himself should or shouldn't do, there is a clear indication that the people of God have a right and duty to resist. Consider the words of Christians from South Africa in their attempt to deal with apartheid as expressed in the *Kairos Document*:

> *Throughout the Bible the word violence is used to describe everything that is done by a wicked oppressor (e.g., Ps. 72:12-14; Is.59:1-8; Jer.22:13-17; Amos 3:9-10; 6:3; Mic.2:2; E:1-3; 6:12). It is never used to describe the activities of Israel's armies in attempting to liberate themselves or to resist aggression. When Jesus says that we should turn the other cheek he is telling us that we must not take revenge; he is not saying that we should never defend ourselves or others... There is a long and consistent Christian tradition about the use of physical force to defend oneself against aggressors and tyrants. In other words, there are circumstances where physical force may be used...(18)*

Second, the examples of non-violent resistance employed by Gandhi and King must be assessed within the parameters of the societal ethics and historical circumstances operative in their respective times. It is precisely because non-violence has been elevated to the level of an absolute principle that such situational considerations are viewed as a compromise if not a sell-out on this principle. But they are not at all. Gandhi succeeded against the violence of colonial Britain in India in 1945ff and King succeeded against the violence of racist American in 1956ff because there were limits beyond which those systems and their societies would not let them go. By contrast, what happens to the principle of non-violence in the context of Hitler's fascism (6 million Jews, 20 million Russians), Somoza's dictatorship (45 years of oppression) and institutionalized violence (since the 1950's in Guatemala and El Salvador)? Non-violence cannot be employed then "without regard for who is using it, which side they are on or what purpose you have in mind." Notwithstanding societal moral ambiguities and the fact that "good guys" often sin, there are times when in defense of life armed struggle against extreme oppression is morally valid and certainly biblically acceptable. More important for this discussion is the fact that Jesus upon encountering truly demonic evil used both force and absoluteness. He drove the money-changers out of the Temple with a lash and he ordered the devil out of the Garasene demoniac adamantly. We cannot hedge on such examples by saying, "well, but he was the Christ." No, what he was and is represents an example for us to follow, applying that spirit as the faithful against the Powers of evil in our day.

Third, what is ultimately important in the Gospels and Epistles is the motivation of love not the adherence to a principle, not even the so-called "highest" ideal. When Paul says, "If I give my body to be burned and have not love, I am nothing" (1 Cor.13), he really means "if I make even the ultimate sacrifice based on a *principle* of love, justice or non-violence but do not have *real love* for the people... it is not done in the spirit of God." Blind obedience to any principle however lofty can lead to disaster, hypocrisy and sterility if it is not tempered or motivated by love. This is evident in Pol Pot's "revolutionary justice", in the Pope's refusal to bless the mothers of *contra* victims, and in North American advocates of non-violence when they seek to avoid conflict at all cost. On the other hand, those involved in the *good fight* in spite of all their personal sins and moral ambiguities, those who give their lives in love to the poor and oppressed are precious in God's sight though their methods may be quite different. Whether it be a Camilo Torres (Colombian priest & guerrilla), Guadalupe Carney (Honduran revolutionary chaplain), Ben Linder (Jewish solidarity worker in Nicaragua who carried a rifle in self-defense) or a Mitch Snyder (North American homeless advocate who affirms non-violence). In all of them, the logic of life superceded the logic of death *because they gave themselves to their people with a passionate love.*

Prophetic Theology Challenges Church Theology

Prophetic theology challenges Church theology at the level of the Spirit, charging the latter with false spirituality, in-house piety and personal religious salvation all reflecting a non-biblical faith. To the degree that Church theology avoids the political and moral battles related to this life and our present-day history, it reveals its spiritual hollowness. We are observing here a very subtle but important temptation — for the devil is very cunning — to sell-out on the promise of the Word to the people in the name of protecting the Church and advancing the spread of the Gospel *as personal faith concept not historical good news!* Prophetic theology counters these sins of avoidance, other-worldliness and collusion with the Powers, not in the name of some political agenda but because they represent sin against the Holy Spirit.

By the Spirit of God, the Bible means all that struggles against sin, injustice, revenge and oppression. True spirituality is, therefore, a perspective from which we engage this world not escape from it. It is a commitment to the vision of the Spirit as life-force and historical possibility; to those goals and efforts that are set on life not death, which respect all people and use not love things. The best known description of the spiritual is, not by chance, a definition common to both Hebrew and Christian scriptures:

> *The spirit of the Lord Yahweh has been given to me,*
> *for Yahweh has anointed me,*
> *He has sent me to bring good news to the poor,*
> *to bind up the hearts that are broken;*
> *to proclaim liberty to captives,*
> *freedom to those in prison;*
> *to proclaim a year of favour from Yahweh,*
> *a day of vengeance for our God...*
>
> *For I, Yahweh, love justice*
> *I hate robbery and all that is wrong*
> *I reward them faithfully*
> *and make an everlasting covenant with them.*
>
> —*Is.61:1-2;8*
> *(emphasis added)*

This understanding of the spiritual implies three emphases having to do with truth, justice and hope. First, Prophetic theology challenges the basic dishonesty of Church theology *in its refusal to deal with the truth* about what is going on in Central America today... its attempt to avoid the connections between our life and their death. Over the past eight years in debates with representatives of the State Department or right-wing organizations, they consistently tried to avoid past U.S. history in the region. They only wanted to deal with the present or project into the future but without any historical framework or systemic context. They would say, "let's not talk about Guatemala in 1954 nor about the class structure in El Salvador in 1980!" Why this avoidance? Because it is there, in that past history where the truth of the Empire can be clearly seen. *One cannot build a new and better future without examining the sins of the past.* "Those who forget the past will live to repeat their errors." Because Ray Bonner of *The New York Times* told the truth about U.S. policy in El Salvador (*Weakness & Deceit*), he was fired because neither the imperial system nor its media collaborators could tolerate the truth. Without knowing what Ray Bonner's theological orientation is, his attempt to tell the historical and political truth about that crucified country of El Salvador represents, in our view, a prophetic word, a genuine spirituality.

Second, when Prophetic theology challenges the death-logic of the Empire, it is always accused of being communist by imperial ideologues

like the IRD. In fact, true prophesy lifts up the Word of God — such
as the plumb-line of Amos — above both-systems, capitalism and
communism. *This prophetic priority of the Word over all systems and all
states* never naively assumes that the Soviet Union isn't without its
serious sins nor believes that the Bolshevik state under Stalin didn't
commit horrendous crimes against humanity. But neither will it allow
one superpower (the United States) justify its own crimes against
humanity (in Central America) by pointing the finger of guilt at the
Soviets. This is why we find in the prophets that consistent habit of
accusing one nation after another for their sins... but then, always,
returning to judge and condemn Israel and Judah on the same grounds.
The more one scrutinizes these two empires — Russia and America —
what emerges is the striking similarities, especially with respect to the
"holy innocents" who live in those lands under their captivity, whether
in Afghanistan or El Salvador. To that degree, then, the Word of God
becomes "a curse on both your houses."

Thirdly, the message of *Prophetic theology is a promise of hope in
history,* never some pious "pie-in-the-sky" promises, reflecting a loss of
hope in this world and in the historical process. Prophetic theology
rejects the cynical despair of the West and firmly believes that out of
the ashes of the present systems of death and exploitation new societies
are being created and will be created in Central America. There is, of
course, a price to pay, a price too heavy for the worldly, who only
believe in power, money, war and lying: *their very existence.* Yahweh
promises the poor people that they can live again but only after
kingdoms fall. So too with us: the American people will only find new
life after the imperial idolatry has been rejected.

The primary goal and sin of the institutions of this world — whether
State, Corporate or Ecclesial — is *their own preservation,* which they
will lose, for as our Gospel goal states: "whoever loses his life for my
sake and the Gospel will have it unto eternity." Either the Catholic
Church in Latin America is reborn from the base communities or it will
become a Western relic; either the American people discard their
foolish dream of being #1 through the Empire or the imperial idolatry
will destroy them.

Life doesn't come to an end with the fall of a single mighty nation,
not even the United States... time and history march on. The Word of
God, the Holy Spirit, lives on ever-unfolding, ever-bringing down, ever-
lifting up... peoples and nations and new possibilities! At each stage in
history where the once New has become corrupted and follows after
the Idols, the God of history has judged it unworthy in order to redeem
the People. This dialectic of life into death, and then out of that death

into a new life, is not only the spiritual and theological truth of how God works, but is spelled out in the political, social and cultural aspects of our lives as well. Nor is this promise of new life for those in a dismal situation as a far-away dream, a vision never to be realized "in our time". Even now, we see the emergence of the new in Central America just when everything seems hopeless and unending. For seven years the Reagan administration has tried to destroy the Sandinista revolution, but Gog from Magog has been turned back. The powers of darkness have done their worst. Even at the very last moment, Reagan may send down his crack troops from the north to try and undo the fragile peace in the region.

But then, a new possibility suddenly opened up, totally unexpected by everyone. The Sandinistas and the *contras* sat down together and agreed to stop fighting for 60 days... perhaps the first days of the beginning of an unending peace in that country! Reactionary politicians, liberal Congresspersons, churches, synagogues, even the solidarity community... all shook their heads in amazement, asking "How is this possible? The lion and the lamb laying down next to each other." "Behold we see new heavens and a new earth." In God's strange work in history, once again, the strategy of the demonic has failed and the Word has prevailed over the Empire.

FOOTNOTES - CHAPTER 14

1   Graham Greene, *The Quiet American*, Viking Press, New York, 1956, Preface.

2   *The Washington Post*, Nov.19, 1987.

3   Barbara Honegger & Jim Naureckas, "Did Reagan Steal the 1980 Elections?, *In These Times*, June 27-July 7, 1987. Apparently, some of the same men involved in the Iran-Contragate scandal first contacted Khomeini in 1980 promising him a large quantity of weapons if he would hold off on releasing the U.S. Embassy hostages until after the Nov. 2, 1980 elections. Shortly after Reagan took office in late January, 1981, the weapons promised began to flow to Iran.

4   The term "the Great Satan" comes from Rev.12:9: "The great dragon, known as the devil or Satan, who has deceived the whole world." The People's Mojahedin Organization detailed in 1985 the names and particulars of 12,028 victims of Khomeini's executioners. The totals who have died under his regime, as presented with documentation to the International Red Cross on Sept.3, 1985, included: 60,000 murdered; over 100,000 political prisoners; over 1 million dead in the war.

5   The members of the "Secret Team" are listed in the Christic Institute's La Penca lawsuit filed on May 29, 1986 and in Sen. Kerry's staff report of Oct.14, 1986.

6   Peter Kornbluh, *Nicaragua: The Price of Intervention*, IPS, Washington,D.C., 1987, p.220, emphasis added.

7   The withdrawal of U.S. Marines from the Gran Caribe in 1934 was accompanied by their replacement by National Guard (Guardia Nacional) forces in various countries of the region which in turn led to the evolution of dictatorial regimes which Washington tacitly approved, such as those in the Dominican Republic under Trujillo and in Nicaragua under Somoza.

8   Joseph Holland, *The American Journey*, IDOC/North America, New York & The Center of Concern, Washington, D. C., 1976,p.67.

9   Immigration Reform & Control Act of 1986 went into effect May 5, 1987, and on June 6, sanctions went into effect.

10   Frank & Wheaton, *Indian Guatemala*, opus cita, pp.72-74.

11   Victorio Araya Guillen, "Samaritan Servanthood: An Option for Life", translated from the Spanish (PASOS, DEI, San Jose, Costa Rica), *North/South Dialogue*, EPICA, Washington, D.C., Vol II, No.1, Summer, 1987, pp.3-4.

12   Erich Fromm, *Anatomia de la Destructividad Humana*, Siglo Veintiuno, Mexico, 1975, p.430.

13 Retreat of United Church of Christ trainers for the Mid-Atlantic region held in Frederick, Maryland in May, 1987. The subject matter was liberation theology and base Christian communities. These very warm and committed Christians often found it difficult to deal with some of the analysis and theology because their historical knowledge of the region was so limited.

14 *The Kairos Document* from South African Christians, opus cita., 3.2,"Justice", p.14.

15 The United States Government, Pentagon, CIA and labor leaders from AIFLD entered the Dominican Republic after the peace had been signed and reorganized the Dominican police, military, security forces and set up sophisticated labor unions to challenge the existing indigenous labor organizations.

16 Jose Miranda, *Being and the Messiah*, opus cita, p.24.

17 From a presentation to a *North/South Dialogue* group visiting Nicaragua in April, 1987 by Benjamin Cortez of CIEETS, Managua.

18 *The Kairos Document*, opus cita, 3.3, "Non-Violence", p.15.

CHAPTER 15
AMERICA'S FAITHFUL REMNANT IS BEING REDEEMED
THROUGH THE INCARNATE WORD IN CENTRAL AMERICA

A project as big and complex as the redemption of America is beyond the scope of this reflection, whereas that of the faithful remnant is already a sign of our times. About this nation as empire we already sense decline and judgement in the air whereas for those faithful North Americans who already serve their Central American sisters and brothers, redemption is no longer just a promise but an experience. Through this dialectic from death unto life — this strange work of God in today's history — the faithful have already been forgiven and invited to share in their *compañeros'* vision of a new heaven and a new earth. The future of this country will be decided finally on a decisive principle of the exilic prophets: what this mighty nation does about its captives. Can they be saved?

> *Can the prey be taken from the mighty, or the captives of*
> *the tyrant be rescued?*
> *Surely, thus says Yahweh:*
> *Even the captives of the mighty shall be taken, and the prey*
> *of the tyrant escape*
> *I myself will contend with those who contend with you, and I*
> *will save your children*
> *I will make the oppressors eat their own flesh, and they*
> *shall be drunk on their own blood as with wine.*
> *Then all humankind shall know that I am your saviour and*
> *that your redeemer is the Mighty One of Jacob.*
> *—Is.49:24-26*

Yahweh's assertion "I will save the children" is not a saying but something we see happening in the Guatemalan highlands, in Babylonian exile in the States and in the process of "going home" to El Salvador.(1) Here, as in all biblical revelation, the promise is integrally linked to judgement, whether in the Warning of Jeremiah or the Magnificat of Mary. Furthermore, however it comes about — and usually it is a mystery to us — God is clearly working in the process: "I will contend with those who contend with you." The answer which is coming to us as part of the faithful remnant is not ours because we are better or different but because we are finally asking the right questions, seeking it in the right places and are open to being both chastised and converted. In the strange dialectics of God, the captives are being rescued and we, through their incarnate Word, are being redeemed unworthy though we are.

People vs. the State: Parallels Between Central America & the USA

There is abundant good in the American people despite all the efforts of the imperial system to frustrate this creativity, highlighting the contrast between these two opposing ways of life, one imperial the other popular. One of the clearest examples of this contrast here in America can be seen in the practice of *voluntarism*. Early in his presidency, Ronald Reagan called on the American people to respond to the social needs of the poor at the local level — soup kitchens and food distribution centers, daycare facilities and hospices for street people, free clinics and job referral offices — and the American people answered the call. Indeed, they became committed to voluntary service for the poor to a degree seldom seen before in American history except during moments of natural disaster. Yet throughout his administration, President Reagan systematically cut back on almost all social programs for the poor and slashed governmental support for social services underway for many years. Reflecting this policy, the White House has literally emasculated Health & Human Services (HHS) and its programs for the poor, needy and elderly, while aggrandizing the Pentagon's budget in order to make war and expanding the Voice of America (VOA) in order to make propaganda. In 1980, HHS occupied 4/5 of its building facilities in Washington, D.C., while sharing a small portion of its space with VOA, whereas by 1987 VOA dominated 3/5 of the floor space!(2) As if to make this shift towards an anti-social philosophy abundantly clear, the *New York Times* reported:

> *The Reagan administration has adopted (Oct.15, 1987) a new policy that will reduce welfare benefits for many elderly, blind and disabled people who receive free food, shelter, firewood or winter clothing from churches and charitable organizations... Administration officials are continually urging the private sector to do more to help the poor people, but now they are throwing up roadblocks to such voluntary efforts.(3)*

The original call of the administration to voluntarism now appears to have been motivated by cynicism and even "revenge" against the underprivileged sectors of our society. The government's refusal to do its part in helping the poor after seeking the voluntary help of good-willed Americans suggests an attempt to diminish excessive public outcry against its own cutbacks. The Reagan philosophy seems to be based on the principle that the poor "must fend for themselves" or if not, be abandoned. Yet an important insight has emerged from this imperial indifference: it has enabled the American people to see in *domestic America* the kind of anti-social policies which have devastated Central America for decades: elitist indifference to the plight of the poor leading to suffering and impoverishment.

Many liberal volunteers working in Central America during the 1960's saw the same thing on the part of the oligarchs who opposed the reformist projects of the Alliance for Progress. Others saw it when the military took advantage of humanitarian aid sent from many countries during the earthquakes in Nicaragua (1972), Guatemala (1976) and El Salvador (1986), siphoning off much of such aid for personal elitist gain. Similarly, during the 1970's, humanitarian and ecclesial efforts to build schools, open clinics, dig wells and install electricity were consistently opposed by reactionary governments because they saw such reform and improvements as giving "power to the people" and that as being a "communist threat." In all these examples, it is clear that the primary contradiction is between the rich and the poor, between *The State and the People*.

What does this imply for us as the faithful remnant living within the American empire? What is the biblical message for us as we watch in dismay at America's dirty wars in Central America? Two basic messages emerge from Scripture which have their roots in the exilic experience: *to prophesy against the old order* and *to wait on the Word in anticipation of the new day*. The first of these admonitions is very hard for most religious folk in the United States to deal with. Most of us would rather do almost anything than prophesy against the *Imperium* (something quite different from using prophetic-sounding words from the pulpit directed against an evil world). We are ready and willing to give, serve, write, vote, visit, read or pray... but not to prophesy. In our hearts, the timid voice of our conscience warns us: "Don't take on the Empire," "Don't challenge the idolatry openly," "Don't expose the LIE!" One can get into big trouble that way. As those working in liberal circles in Washington to change U.S. foreign policy often counsel: "You don't want to hurt your credibility!"

Yet such liberal timidity may not be marching to the drumbeat of the majority of Americans today. When Martin Luther King, Jr. raised his prophetic voice to challenge racism the spirit of all America was revived. When Jesse Jackson speaks out boldly for a new vision, thousands of whites follow and vote for him. When the Christic Institute prophesies against the Secret Team, the people "eat it up" and public response has been overwhelming because many in America want to hear the truth. To be sure Danny Sheehan, Billy Davis and Sara Nelson have gotten into some trouble as a result and they have received some threats, but more importantly, they have been faithful to the prophetic mandate:

> *If, however, the sentry has seen the sword coming but has not blown his horn, and so the people are not alerted and the sword overtakes them and destroys one of them... I will hold the sentry responsible for his death.*
>
> *—Ez. 33:6*

We are the faithful remnant; we are the sentries. Who else will speak out? This is our responsibility if we are to be true to our brothers and sisters suffering in Central America. Their voices cannot be heard in Babylon. We must speak for them.

But how do we recover our prophetic voice? *By waiting on the Word!* It is not just a matter of talking nor even acting but of seeing the contradictions develop; of perceiving the "signs of our times." This seems like just the opposite of those courageous and aggressive stances exemplified in the prophets... but is it? Repeatedly, the prophets had to wait, bide their time, watch in awe and respect at the mystery unfolding before their eyes, analyzing what history was telling them about God's workings. This meant waiting, however, for an active, involved Holy Spirit... as described in Isaiah: "'I will contend with those who contend with you,' says Yahweh, 'I will save your children.'" We are called to observe the drama of God's mighty arm at work in history; at the strange work of Yahweh in our own time... *the dialectics of redemption through role reversal!*

Even today, we are watching the arrogance and power of the Empire undo itself; the meek and oppressed rise up through the very repression under which they suffer. Surely, you recall the famous Pauline text in which this thesis of biblical dialectics is laid out:

> *No, it was to shame the wise that God chose what is foolish by human reckoning, and to shame what is strong that he chose what is weak by human reckoning; those whom the world thinks common and contemptible are the ones that God has chosen—those who are nothing at all to show up those who are everything...*
>
> *—1 Cor. 1:27-28*

We the citizens of Babylon — great activists that we are — are sometimes called to be silent and perceive how we are being quietly judged and hiddenly redeemed through the suffering of our little brothers and sisters south of the border, the anguish of the incarnate Word.

These apparently contradictory tasks — prophesying and waiting — have one thing in common: they force us out of our traditional religious lifestyles, for they are either too aggressive or too passive for our typical behavior. Notwithstanding our timidity and over-activism, we have been given — as the Catholics would say — a holy dispensation. In spite of our sin, we have been invited to play an important role on behalf of our *compañeros* in the continent: we have been called to accept a critical role by *accompanying them in this strange work of God* which is gradually freeing Central Americans from its imperial captivity.

On Recovering the Prophetic Word in America

As new and intriguing terms like "*liberation theology*", "*pedagogy of the oppressed*" and "*comunidades de base*" began to emerge from Latin America during the 1970's, challenging the sterility of neo-orthodoxy, many faithful Americans yearned to appropriate these ideas, this new wisdom from the underside of history. Typically, they attempted to learn these new secrets as "formulas" which then could be applied in the States. The first serious experiment of this kind involved the pedagogy of Paolo Freire and the largely unsuccessful attempts to transliterate his methodology into our North American ethos, notwithstanding the advice that our society would first have to change.(4) The effort reflected a typical Western approach to change: taking a model and inserting it into a foreign environment without analyzing the sociological context out of which the insight flowed. In most cases, wherever the conceptual assumptions of Freire were put into practice, they lacked power and avoided the prophetic content they had in Latin America. The attempt thus serves as a basis for our asking today how we are to recover the prophetic Word in America. Is it even possible to prophesy in an imperialist environment?

The failure of these truths to "take hold" or "have power" in the States resulted not only from our individualistic, non-collective and competitive ways of life in America, but from the fact that Freirean advocates had no intention of changing this society in any fundamental way at that time. Their goal was to raise *individual consciousness* while leaving the imperialist environment unchallenged for the most part, whereas the pedagogy is based on the transformation of society and the liberation of people from unjust structures and limiting situations. To be sure, these Freirean advocates fought hard for the rights of the poor and opposed the injustices under which they suffered in the United States. But during the 1970's, the goal was not to assume a prophetic role nor to "upset the apple cart." This is not a critique of their efforts but a description of where they were at that moment in our history in terms of political development. The question of our "empowerment" as a faithful remnant was yet to come.

Since 1980, however, as more and more North Americans travelled south and as more and more Central American refugees were forced northward into exile, we had first hand experience with the poverty and suffering that produced Freire's pedagogy so that liberation became an experience, not just an idea. The faithful began to appropriate these same insights not as ideological novelties or fascinating concepts but as life-and-death matters. They began to see this new wisdom through the eyes of a peasant of El Salvador, a Nicaraguan worker or an Indian in Guatemala... and how it had empowered them. The longer the encounter lasted, the more North Americans realized three rather shocking truths to which they were unaccustomed: a) these poor people are agents of their own change; b) they don't want to "escape" to the States but to build new societies back home; c) that U.S. policies are often and increasingly behind their suffering! This necessarily upset our notion of these poor people from Central America as objects of our charity instead of being as they are, victims of our system and creative agents of their own change. As we realized this and sided with them, we North Americans began to recover our own prophetic voice!

The most surprising side-effect of this recovery of our prophetic potential was realizing the striking similarities between these struggles for liberation and justice in Central America and those found in the Bible, especially during the pre- and post-Exilic times. We began to see the parallels between the corrupt Jewish kingdoms and today's corrupt dictatorial regimes. We saw the parallels between ancient and modern exiles into imperial captivity. We began to recognize that just as Babylon took over Palestine and ruled through puppets, so today imperial USA rules the Isthmus through puppet presidents. Even more surprising was the fact that we weren't learning these biblical-and theological lessons from pastors and intellectuals but from poor peasants, workers, "non-believers", indeed, sometimes even from Marxists. In this spirit, we listen to Tomás Borge tell us:

> *The Nicaraguan revolution has demonstrated that Christians and non-Christians can work together for a common objective, and has demonstrated there can be an integration between Christian moral principles and revolutionary moral principles.*

*That is why the theologians of death are fighting, as open peons
of U.S. imperialism, against the Nicaraguan revolution, so
much does it signify by way of example for the Christians of
Latin America.(5)*

The discovery of such "common objectives" between revolutionary
goals and biblical principles is extremely threatening to Western
ideology just as liberation theology has become a serious challenge to
the traditional elitism of the Catholic hierarchy in Latin America. Such
common morality shifts the discussion from the ideological to the
sociological; from the pious and abstract to the political and concrete.
As Che Guevara once said, whenever the Christians and the revolutionaries get together, the Empire is finished in Latin America.

Thus, for many of us in the States, the recovery of our prophetic
voice is coming from our relationships with the wretched of the earth
in Central America (as elsewhere in the Third World). *They* have
provided us the contextualization for understanding the prophetic
power of the Word of God in our own society. Refugees present in our
midst, especially in the Sanctuary movement, keep putting the question
to us about our biblical stance and commitment in human terms, saying:
"*héme aquí*," here I am, what are you going to do about my suffering
and our tragedy? With all the messiness and differences of opinion
about what the Sanctuary movement is, our common touchstone, the
common focus of our commitment *is the refugee as victim of the Empire*.
It is in them and in that recognition that we have begun to recover our
prophetic voice. It is in our relationship with them as human beings that
the ideas of the pedagogy of the oppressed and liberation theology
have become incarnate and the Word filled with power.

So, how do we apply such a prophetic voice and perception to our
imperialist environment in the States? Consider, for example, the new
Immigration Act which has further complicated, indeed, endangered
the lives of tens of thousands of refugees from Central America who are
already victims of imperialist policies. This Act is blatantly unjust for at
least four reasons: a) it legitimizes the on-going exploitation of poor
workers from Mexico and Central America through allowing them to
work in our "harvest of shame"; to remain in the States, *but only
them*(6); b) it rejects most of the "strangers in our midst" by arbitrarily
setting a date — Jan.1, 1982 — as the cut-off after which the vast
majority cannot even apply for amnesty; c) it makes no distinction
between "economic" immigrants and political refugees who have fled
here because of persecution and war and who under the 1980 Refugee

Act have the right to remain here until the danger to lives ends; and d) by laying down heavy employer sanctions against those who would employ undocumented persons, in effect creating a penalty of death because they cannot find work either here or in Central America.(7) Thus this Act stands diametrically opposed to the biblical mandate that we are "to love the stranger in our midst and treat them justly" (Lev.19:33-34). It is a law of Death.

While this Act is *THE LAW* and has been passed *BY CONGRESS*, its main goal is to maintain our way of life while condemning these aliens to death. Furthermore, it isn't working because the refugees from Central America, desperate and dying, keep pouring into our country in ever-increasing numbers, notwithstanding the new technologies of the INS.(8) So what are we, as good citizens and also faithful remnant to do? Many out of genuine love and concern for the refugees coupled with their sense of duty have been trying to help the refugees comply with the new Law. Yet they know that this Immigration Act is unjust; that it will not serve most; and, in fact, errs on the side of exclusion rather than acceptance in its rigorous interpretation of each case and its demand for more and more documentation. Therefore, this Immigration Act demands more of us than mere charitable service... it requires *a prophetic voice and witness*. It means we have to challenge the Law as unjust and assist the refugee; we have to challenge the Congress, explaining why it has sinned. No longer is the Law or the Congress sacrosanct as such; both must be measured by whether or not they serve the people... and especially the poor and outcasts among us.

What does this new Immigration Act really reflect about our nation and our role as citizens who are trying to be faithful? What are the systemic and theological implications of a Law which reinforces our self-interest, fear and prejudice, rather than alleviating the tragedy and suffering in Central America? The purpose of this Law is to expel and exclude those who come to America looking for escape from their tragedy and death... we turn them away in order to protect our "good life"! In response to the outcries of Sanctuary folk, Witnesses for Peace and solidarity workers, the INS and State Department say: "Sorry, that's the Law." But this Law, like our Imperial strategy is a being of our own creation; reflecting what we think and want and thus who we really are... or have become.

We are dealing here with a profound philosophical question... not just whether or not the Immigration Act is just or unjust, but rather, that it is *a reflection of who we are*. The Mexican theologian José Miranda analyzes what this means:

*Being, which seemed demonstrably independent of us, turns
out to be unavoidably conditioned by our thought processes. It
is constituted as it is because of our plans, our desires, our
longings. In other words, far from being independent of the self,
being is an extension of the self. It can be manipulated. I am
referring to being as it is understood by metaphysics and
realism of whatever stripe, not figments of fantasy.(9)*

The "self", in this case represents all of those imperial advocates who
down through the years have created this "being" we call U.S.
imperialism. Those in Latin America and the Caribbean who suffer
under its policies do not consider this *being* a "figment of fantasy" but
a highly developed and intentional structure of power and control. The
purpose of this being is to profit off of and maintain its dominance over
those who are held captive by its system and who perish under it.

Challenging this imperial Being is the voice of the people who
suffer under it but who cannot be silenced... "cannot" not because they
can't be killed or imprisoned but because they are dying and their
protest is the only hope they have; "cannot" because their voice is a sign
of life against this system of death and thus a reflection of the presence
of God among us. Again, José Miranda reminds us that...

*...the outcry of the neighbor in need — the only true content of
the voice of conscience — absolutely cannot be manipulated.
In it there is indeed otherness. It is not a branch office of the self
and its world and projections (Being)... This outcry is imperative. Its demand, insofar as I heed it, increases my responsibility. I am no longer alone. In a word, it is otherness, and
manipulation of otherness is impossible.(10)*

This prophetic word which challenges the Being of Empire has many
expressions in Central America today. Perhaps the most succinct of
them is the Sandinista cry: "*Ni se vende ni se rinde*" (We won't sell out
nor give up). This is essentially the same cry of the Hebrew slaves
before the cruelty of ancient Egypt to whom the Word of God
responded with a mighty act of liberation. It is the same Word that came
from the Exilic prophets who rejected the old orders of Israel and Judah
just as today's prophets in Central America reject the old orders in
Guatemala and El Salvador. Their prophetic voices are gradually
enabling us to recover our own prophetic voice here in the States.

Such a prophetic challenge voiced inside Babylon will not be easy
to maintain given the sophistication of our Western propaganda, the

rationalization of our experts, the casuistic explanation of our clergy, and the cynicism of our politicians. It is even possible for us to use words like "Being" and "Pedagogy of the Oppressed" to play philosophical and ethical games with ourselves without changing anything. Even an intellectual genius like Soren Kierkegaard while he could say that "existent man cannot be assimilated by a system of ideas"(11) was also guilty of turning his protest into a philosophical discussion and his moral premises into a matter of individual honor. It is common for even the best "theology to abandon real people to their wretched luck" because while "I" may personally oppose injustice in the Americas, I then refuse to lift a finger to challenge it!

On the other hand, we the faithful remnant must not forget that God *is the defender of the poor and the liberator of the oppressed.* This means that in our strong moments and weak, we have out there before us our example in the prophets and in Jesus of Nazareth constantly challenging our ambivalence and encouraging our determination. But God's goal is them — the oppressed — and the call is to serve them not to worry about ourselves. Ultimately, the task of the prophetic Word is not "to enunciate truths but to proclaim the gospel."(12) The recovery of this Word in America means taking the side of the victim or otherwise all this is mere talk.

Waiting on the Word: Return to the Land in the Fullness of Time

The spiritual opposite of prophesying involves that mysterious aspect of grace called "waiting on God" and the fullness of time. It involves our humble recognition that in this world of sin and insidious power there is often nothing that we can do but wait. Over the past seven years of the Reagan administration, many of us have had our moments of "despair" when it seemed to us that there was nothing we could to stop its madness; nothing we could do to convince the members of Congress that they were being lied to, taken in, conned... manipulated by a cheap form of patriotism. Nothing we tried seemed to work. The powers were just too great; the lying too insidious; the deception "bought" by too many naive Americans. We felt powerless. Even though we kept on working, doggedly pursuing our tasks, we often secretly wondered if we were ever going to "win". Then came the Iran-Contragate scandal, and suddenly, without us doing anything, the whole fabric of Reagan's lies seemed to unravel before our eyes and there was nothing he could do to stop it. Without knowing it, we had been taught a lesson in the graceful art of "waiting on the Word". And with that disintegration of the Empire's monolithic control over things, new dynamics began opening up whereby — as one of the signs of our times — the people of El Salvador began the process of returning to their promised lands... in the fullness of time.

> When I bring them home from (foreign) peoples, when I bring them back from the countries of their enemies, when I reveal my holiness in them for many nations to see, they will know that I am Yahweh their God, when I rescue the captives from the pagans and reunite them in their own land.
>
> —Ez.39:27-28

During this same period of time, another group of people waited and watched. Over 10,000 Salvadoran refugees from the scorched-earth tactics and the collective massacres of 1980 and 1981 at the Sumpul River and the Lempa River crossings... waited at a site some forty-five miles from the Salvadoran border; at a place without trees, water or land to till, at Mesa Grande, a mesa of desolation. There they existed, barely surviving, some of the children dying because of bad water, some adults taken by force and disappeared forever... there they waited and waited, these poor peasants from the land of The Saviour. They waited without resources or protection, they waited through the constant searches and harassment by the Honduran military. They waited without any chance of return because conditions inside their own land were worse than this "impossible" situation in Honduras. The waiting seemed interminable because they couldn't "do anything" in their powerless situation. So they waited without relief as hours turned into days, days into weeks, weeks into months, and months into years... 1981, 1982, 1983, 1984, 1985, 1986, 1987.

Yet while they waited, they also organized themselves into a single, united community of interdependence. As they waited, they planned for their return, they forged themselves into a collective community whose single, focused goal was to return to their homelands. They were not waiting for some miracle or divine intervention, nor for some reprieve from the Honduran government, nor a change in the policies of the Empire, but for the right moment, for the fullness of time. Instinctively, religiously (though not being a self-consciously pious community), their prayers came not out of rote words but out of deep passion. On the other hand, those internationalists and religious volunteers who accompanied them didn't understand this "fullness of time." To be sure, these foreigners understood the suffering, injustice, kidnappings, unjust searches, lack of food, infant mortality and the bureaucratic foot-dragging of the UNHCR. They were sensitive to all that but not, as the refugees were, to the "fullness of time." That is why when the time came, in the Spring of 1987, and the refugees knew that the time had come, the internationalists were aghast at even the thought of return.

What concerned the internationalists — who thought this was a crazy plan — were the *powers* and the *dangers*. They were convinced that the refugees couldn't make it; that the plan was fraught with too much danger; that the military simply wouldn't allow them to leave, or worse, would harass or kill them along the way. These observations were very realistic; the threats very real. Indeed, what could these powerless and penniless peasants do against the power of the Honduran and Salvadoran militaries? Didn't these campesinos realize the forces they were up against, including the UNHCR and the U.S. Empire which didn't want them to return, as repeatedly expressed by their own puppet President Duarte in San Salvador? One could almost hear Pilate screaming at the powerless carpenter from Nazareth: "Don't you realize that I have the power to release you or have you killed?" This was the repeated warning of their friendly counselors from abroad: "they won't let you go!" "they will kill you!"

But the refugees who had been patiently waiting on the Word all these years knew two things which their well-intentioned friends could not know: they knew all about d*eath* and they knew about the *fullness of time.*

First, these peasants knew the power of death... and they had conquered it! They had seen death so many times in the face of their friends and family members. They had had to look death head-on so many times that they were no longer afraid. Their advisors only knew "about death" but they had not conquered their fear of that threat.

> *I am no longer afraid of death,*
> *I know well*
> *its dark and cold corridors*
> *leading to life.*
>
> *I am afraid rather of that life*
> *which does not come out of death*
> *which cramps our hands*
> *and retards our march.*
>
> *I am afraid of my fear*
> *and even more the fear of others*
> *who do not know where they are going,*
> *who continue clinging*
> *to what they consider to be life*
> *which we know to be death!(13)*

And not only these refugees from Mesa Grande but throughout the whole Salvadoran society, familiarity with death and daily choices between one form of death and another, are commonplace. These choices have steeled them not only to choose life in spite of death, but having passed through death they are now, like the Guatemalans say, "threatened with resurrection", meaning that they have already died and new life is their only option. This is why, in the larger, longer view of the present conflict, they have already won and the Salvadoran military-U.S. imperial strategy has lost. When people are no longer afraid of death and that is the only "power" you have over them, then its "sting" has been taken away, its power is gone.

The other thing these refugees in exile knew which their "wise" friends from the North did not understand was the meaning of *kairos* and that it had arrived. For most of us Americans, time is all the same — it is just calendar time, —— chronological time which goes on and on — just like America as an empire presumably just goes on and on. This is why we assert that historical progress in America has reached a dead-end because the imperial idolaters don't want any fundamental change; they want to maintain the *status quo*. For the refugees from El Salvador, however, everything has already come to an end, and therefore they could sense when the new was breaking in upon history, when the fullness of time had arrived, when an eschatological moment was upon them. Perceiving the time, they press on to receive it, to embrace it, to prepare for it. "The time is coming, *and now is*."

> We wish to return to our homes. We are Salvadorans and have a right to live in our country. We long to cultivate our lands and to provide for our families. We are peasant farmers and we are not used to living off charity... We long for our country, El Salvador, to be at peace. As Salvadorans we must help bring peace. We are peasants and the way that we struggle for peace is by planting our crops in our lands and demanding that our lives be respected. If we go back to our lands in large groups, we will be able to provide for one another, pool our resources, and share our gifts and skills.(14)

And so believing, they organized to return home. When their unbelieving friends from abroad saw that the refugees were actually going to do it, despite all the dangers, they began to accompany them, to organize others in the North to assist in the preparations... but doubting all the time. Indeed, final permission to leave was not given until 4 A.M. on the day of departure, so opposed were the authorities to the move. Nonetheless, on October 10, 1987, the first mass contingent of 4,312 refugees left Mesa Grande and despite all the odds and warnings, returned home without incident. Unlike their harassed, detoured, delayed and uncertain wanderings from El Salvador into Honduras (just as in the wanderings of the Hebrews from Egypt to Zion), this "new exodus" was direct and straight. It was, as Ezekiel speaks of it, a *procession back to Zion*, not to conquer but to rebuild, with a new heart and a new spirit... to create a new El Salvador today. As a sign of this new life, a baby was born along the way, so that they arrived *with a powerful witness of God's blessing in spite of all the powers of death around them.*

How did this "miracle" happen; this return of a totally powerless people against the wishes of the Powers? In our world of *real politique*, let us play prophetic detective for a moment and ask ourselves,"How in God's name were these peasants of El Salvador able to challenge the principalities and "powers"? And how do we, as a people of faith, understand the dialectics of *Dios?*

Is it not true that the refusal of the Honduran government until the last moment proves that all the reactionary powers opposed it... for they are all collaborators in this project of death together?

Did not Duarte finally allow the refugees to enter because of the awkward space created by the Central American presidents at Esquipulas II?

Didn't the Reagan administration decide it had better "play it cool" for the moment because its international image might otherwise have been damaged in light of the Peace accords and with the Russian Summit coming up?

Wasn't this caution the result of White House ambivalence due to the Iran-Contragate scandal weakening its resolve?

Didn't that scandal become exposed because of the downing of the Hasenfus plane by a Sandinista soldier?

Wasn't there a great deal of "luck" in that soldier's shot reaching the target, whose bullets had to pass through the airwaves of God's creation?

Wasn't that lucky shot a divine response to the years of prayers from Nicaragua in light of all the blood shed by the forces of evil?

God works in mysterious ways her wonders to perform!

If we are honest about this whole matter, is it not true that it was the will and vision of these humble peasants who challenged the powers and carried the day? Notwithstanding all the important financial and logistical and political assistance which North Americans provided which was sorely needed and much appreciated, isn't it still true that it was these refugees who made this thing happen because they knew that their time had come? Can any of us doubt that Yahweh was accompanying them on this journey of "going home"? Let those who have eyes to see and ears to hear, repent and believe in the good news!

> *The Lord Yahweh will wipe away*
> *the tears from every cheek;*
> *he will take away his people's shame*
> *everywhere on earth,*
> *for Yahweh has said so.*
> *That day, it will be said: See, this is our God*
> *on whom we waited for salvation.*
> *   —Is.25:8-9*

Towards a Revolution in Values: South vs.North

No society on earth is ever the kingdom of God, neither the United States nor the Soviet Union; not Japan nor Nicaragua. But the possibilities for breakthrough into the new are far greater in Nicaragua today than in the United States *in terms of values*. With all their faults, the Sandinistas are closer to breakthroughs because they are engaged in the struggle against an old order while the United States is trying to preserve one. In America today, every creative popular effort to create something new is co-opted by the system in order to take advantage of novelties as a way of reinforcing the old order. By contrast, in Nicaragua — where the society is externally a mess (mainly due, as we have repeatedly said, to the *contra* war), popular creativity is encouraged because they are forging a new society, an open future in which all experimentation is welcome. As Tomás Borge says:

> *There is in each of us an ongoing struggle between the values*
> *of the society we wish to destroy and the values of the society we*
> *wish to build: a ceaseless struggle between selfishness and*

generosity, between individualism and solidarity, between extravagance and austerity, between hate and love.(15)

In the West, by contrast, we are obsessed by values that reinforce the *status quo*: *anti-communism,* which labels any serious prophetic challenge as evil or absurd; *being # 1,* which is intent on winning so much that it dismisses value for expediency; and *consumerism,* which concentrates on indulgence rather than on sacrifice and challenge. At the outset of every revolutionary struggle, radical values were at the forefront of the new vision of society: generosity, solidarity, austerity... all so necessary for the creation of a new and more open society. This vision and breakthrough was similarly true in the Exilic experience, in Christianity and in the Bolshevik revolution at the outset. Can such high values and unselfish behavior be lost or corrupted? Of course. The point is that though we, too, once had these values in America, they have been gradually undercut by the greed, power, ambition and egotism of the system.

When a foreigner first goes to Nicaragua today, these new values are not immediately apparent because the economic environment is so harshly impoverished. One has to get down inside the society to the large percentage of committed supporters of the revolution in order to realize that these values are not built on Marxism or authoritarianism. Rather, they have been inculcated into the "new Man" and "new Woman" who have had to struggle with their own reversal of values; have had to resist egotistical attitudes; have stopped thinking about self and work for the common good. This is no small thing, for it often means self-deprivation for the good of one's *compañeros.* However cynically some Americans may react to this ideal, remember it is a biblical norm as well as a revolutionary value. It did not come from Marx (though he also held it) but from Sandino and from many Sandinista examples today, such as that found in the writings of one Sandinista leader, Omar Cabezas:

> *... the new man was being born with the freshness of the mountains. A man — this might seem incredible — but an open, unegotistical man, no longer petty — a tender man who sacrifices himself for others, a man who gives everything for others, who suffers when others suffer and who also laughs when others laugh. The new man began to be born and to acquire a whole series of values, discovering these values, and cherishing them and cultivating them in his inner self.(16)*

In the Nicaraguan revolution, this kind of personal transformation is equally evident in the role of women of which there are hundreds of examples, from the Sandinista leadership to rank-and-file enthusiasts. Not only have women played decisive roles in the process of the struggle against Somoza but in power sharing and offering creative new ideas since the revolution came to power. *Machismo* is far from eliminated in Nicaragua, yet the primary thrust of this feminist involvement has not been "women-first" but female equality within a larger revolutionary process aimed at transforming the whole society in progressive directions. This holistic feminist philosophy is well represented in a woman named Zela Diaz de Porras who is a founding member of the women's organization AMNLAE, an advisor to small farmers, a leader in the Apostolic Institute for the Family, and a lawyer and President of the Second Regional Court of Appeals in Leon. As a Christian and revolutionary, she shares with us how her faith commitment and revolutionary ideology intertwine:

> *The fact that we call ourselves "Christians in the Revolution" is just a way of putting a public name on a presence and a commitment we need to make explicit, as I said, so people will know that, without ceasing to be members of the church — indeed, because of it, because we are Christians, followers of Christ — we are within the revolutionary process, along with the people, propelled by our faith. In order to better carry out the gospel option for the poor, to build up the kingdom of God, which is of the poor and primarily with them.(17)*

What does this say to us in America about the recovery of such values in an imperialist environment? There have been some noble attempts in the last three decades to find answers, by those seriously committed at either the revolutionary or religious levels in this society. One aspect of this search has involved *relinquishment — or self-denial*... both secular and religious. But this personal willingness to sacrifice self in the form of personal austerity has often led to the loss of personal integrity or isolation from society. Abandonment of material things or comforts has tended in the United States towards crusade or puritanism which has led to self-righteousness or the condemnation of others. As a result, those attempts at a sacrificial lifestyle in the 1960's and 1970's tended to produce cynicism about such efforts, leading to capitulation or even comfort-seeking. The failure of this American vision was not, we think, due to the extremism of "zealots" nor the lack of resolve on the part of liberals, but to our individualism which runs very deep and finds it hard to take anything collective seriously.

Now, however, out of the South (i.e. Central America) where such values are taken very seriously, we have a witness to a societal collectivity that works and from it a call for us to join them in what they call *accompaniment*. Whether this sharing is expressed as Sanctuary, Witness, "Going Home", Underground Railroad, Sister Cities or whatever, it has produced a tremendous out-pouring of love-response on the part of North Americans, indeed, a form of sacrifice and relinquishing which clearly goes beyond traditional missionary work or Peace Corps voluntarism. What is behind this new vision of a *accompaniment*? Why is it different from previous forms and moments of incarnating a vision? In the first place, Americans from the States are not running the show, despite the fact that participants have been very active. Even if we take, for example, the massive activist response of "Quest for Peace" run by the Quixote Center, they are at the service of the Nicaraguan people and what they do is based not only on w*hat* the Nicas need but on *how they want* this help sent.

Second, *accompaniment* necessarily involves becoming part of a community, a society, a whole people... all of whom participate in a collective process of transformation. Thus personal sacrifice is lifted up beyond itself to the body politic where self-denial is no longer (as so often in the States) something weird but rather something very natural, a necessary ingredient of the liberation process.

Both by their example to us as new men and new women, as well as in their generosity in inviting us (citizens of the evil Empire) into their struggle, our Central American brothers and sisters have called us "back home" to those very values which are fundamental to our biblical heritage though almost lost through the distortion of Western cynicism. Their call holds up before us a form of ministry which we have taken for granted in the formal sense, but which had to be demonstrated to us anew in everyday life for us to recognize it in its true sense... *diaconia*, service to others. In a number of Western religious traditions — like the Episcopal Church — the role of deacon is perceived to be a secondary ministry from which one moves upward to get to the "higher" office of priesthood and the episcopacy. In so doing, the more elevated tasks of intercessor, spokesperson, man of the "cloth" and honored priest became the concern, rather than service.

But by Jesus' own example and the prophets' own ministry, the deaconate or servant role is held up as the fundamental ministry to which we are called. In the exilic prophets they speak over and over again of the "Son of Man" and the "Suffering Servant". These are precisely the examples we find in Oscar Romero, Guadalupe Carney, Nora Astorga, Rutilio Grande, Don Vicente Menchu, Julia Esquivel, Padre Hermogenes and the four Maryknoll sisters who gave their lives in El Salvador. Nor is it surprising that the fourth order of apostolic ministry which has almost disappeared in the West, the *prophet*, re-emerges at precisely the same moment the Church is rediscovering its ministry and mission in radical *diaconia*.

This revolution of values and rediscovery of ministry which the faithful in this country are so desperately seeking, emerges out of the poor from the South to those of us proud ones in the North. Most humbling of all in this process is that they don't think they have any corner on these virtues and values, but in their generosity invite us, as citizens of the Empire who have caused them so many problems, to come and accompany them along this new path of suffering servanthood.

Steps Towards Entering the Kingdom of God

All through our lives we deal with doors and keys: how to unlock the entrances to where we want to go; how to get "inside" and not be shut out... whether we are talking about a house, a job, a position in society or recognition. In our routine lives, dealing with worldly pursuits, we generally know the answers to these questions or we know someone who can open the more difficult doors to life for us. But when it comes to things of the spirit, to dealing with the standards of the poor or living up to revolutionary criteria, we Americans are less sure how to make it; less sure that we can qualify. When it comes to unlocking the door to the Kingdom of God, we are more guarded and uncertain. We may know the technical biblical words and the theological language about being "saved" but we also recall Jesus' warning about the "straight and narrow" or his more ominous words: "It is harder for the rich to enter the Kingdom than for a camel to pass through the eye of a needle." To be worthy in this spiritual realm, — according to the prophets and the gospel — it is quite clear that entrance into the Kingdom of God will be *inversely* related to those entrees which usually work for us in this worldly life, where values of money, power and status dominate.

In this struggle between the siren songs of the Empire and the tough call of the Poor, we are watching a drama unfold that has life and death implications for hundreds of thousands of people, and quite possibly for the very destiny of this hemisphere. On the one hand, there is a real possibility that the exploitative, repressive hells in El Salvador and Guatemala could continue for another decade, or, as in the recent peace accords between the Sandinistas and the *contras*, peace could come about suddenly and the rebuilding of society begin immediately. We are watching unfold a titanic struggle in which we can see the alternatives between "heaven" and "hell" reveal themselves before our very eyes. This is why our experience with Central America today like the Exilic experience centuries ago cannot be viewed with detachment. The suffering in the Isthmus is a mirror of our own future.

Just when we think we have a certain grasp on this spiritual mystery, we are thrown a surprise pitch, as they say in baseball a "left hook", a complete change of pace: to enter into the Kingdom of God *you have to go out!* The ancient Jews in Jerusalem opposed the Jeremidic solution because they were convinced they were already on the "inside", within the Holy City where God was on their side; that they were spiritually speaking "in." To the contrary, Jeremiah made it clear that in order to be redeemed, they would have to "go out" into exile. It would be there in Babylon as strangers and outcasts they would find their way back home. Similarly, in the gospels whereas the disciples longed to sit in the chief seats in the Kingdom, they would learn the hard way that what they sought would not be found in the Temple inside the great city of David but outside the walls of Jerusalem at the foot of an ignominious cross. This is just as true today in relation to Central America: we the faithful must leave the comforts of Babylon and share with the exiles and the street people if we are to be saved.

One of the common images used by theologians and story-tellers in describing what one must do to enter the Kingdom is that of having to pass by the "guardians of the gate", often depicted as fierce lions jealously guarding the entrance to the holy of holies. Today, this can only be interpreted as meaning our willingness to stand up to the terror of the praetorian guards of the Empire and the fear and shame that implies. As international solidarity workers, what has repeatedly impressed itself upon us is the extent to which the Central Americans have passed this test and are no longer afraid to die. Normally in the States, we don't have to worry about such things, but in the Isthmus it is a constant threat, a real possibility. Nor are we talking about the courage to die, but the spirit of self-sacrifice for a greater good. Many American soldiers in Vietnam were willing to die "for their country" or more accurately to help save a buddy in danger, but in most cases it was a hollow and empty sacrifice because they weren't sure why they had been called to give their "last full measure of devotion." In their hearts, they were willing to die... but in their minds and souls they had deep doubts about dying... for the Empire. Not so for Central Americans today who know exactly why they are dying... for their People and the recovery of their Land.

The difference points to another more critical aspect of the motivation behind self-giving "unto death"... what we call "*the scandal of the Cross*", the scandal of shame versus the pride of honor. Like Jesus' twelve disciples, the issue wasn't whether they were willing to die for him or take up the sword against the Roman soldiers (as Peter did), but how they felt about him when he became an "outlaw", an "alien", an "illegal" in the eyes of the authorities who denounced him, arrested him, mocked and killed him. That is when they denied him and fled. Some exegetes say that Jesus' final cry from the cross — "lama, lama, sabachthani" (*My God, my God why have you forsaken me?*) was motivated not by his physical pain nor his doubts about God, but at his betrayal by his faithful disciples. Some of us have had to face the same scandal in relation to Central America — our stands on behalf of the victims and exiles — from our families and our leaders. Quite a number of us have been shamed: mocked, criticized, called "communists", arrested, ejected from foreign countries by our own embassies, run over by trains (as Brian Willson was), and killed (like Ben Linder in Nicaragua). As American citizens, so accustomed to having *carte-blanche* and "easy access", it is hard sometimes to now find ourselves *outside the door*, dismissed as crazy or irrelevant, as trouble-makers or potential terrorists by those in authority. This is a small taste of what our brothers and sisters in Central America must endure every day.

What we must try to understand, both theologically and politically, is why the Cross isn't a scandal in the West and for us as citizens of the Empire? In the United States the Cross isn't a scandal... just the opposite. We take it for granted and we're not ashamed by its "implications" but, rather, boldly claim we are followers of the Cross. Ah, because it remains a theological symbol and a political abstraction. *What is still scandalous is actual crucifixion*, whether that one on Calvary Hill in 33 A.D. or those in Morazán, El Salvador, in 1980 A.D. When they put someone "up against the wall" in Latin America today, with all the blood and pain, all the suffering and shame that it implies... then crucifixion is just as scandalous today as it was in that classic assassination of the carpenter from Nazareth. We can thus live with the symbol of the Cross because we have rationalized its significance and idealized its meaning, but we can't do that about real life and real murders. As Jon Sobrino reminds us:

> *Gradually the scandal of the cross was reduced to little more than a cognitive mystery. Jesus died in accordance with some*

mysterious divine plan that can be discovered in the Scriptures.
When we interpret the Scripture correctly, we will find no
reason to be scandalized by the cross... By focusing all consid-
eration on this positive redemptive value of the cross, people
could forget the scandalous fact that the cross affected God
himself...(18)

Thus if our empty crosses do not remind us of the real crucifixions of today, then our symbolic crosses in the West can't save us! By contrast, the real crosses in Central America today, like that real dying on Calvary can... save both souls and societies. Indeed, it is only in this real sacrifice of love in the face of the shame and death that the old orders are judged and the resurrection becomes real. In other words, a symbolic death by Jesus in which he wasn't really crucified, wouldn't have saved us. The power of a real Easter comes out of a real Good Friday. The crucifixions of Oscar Romero and the four Maryknoll sisters recovered for us the reality of Jesus' crucifixion and resurrection. And yet like Jesus, what took them to their deaths was not mere courage and the willingness to self-sacrifice but their standing by the "wretched of the earth", their willingness to be called "communists" and accept the shame. Only so can we too pass the guardians of the gate which lead to the Kingdom of God.

This is also why so much of the "preaching" in Central America and the United States today is false gospel and not good news for the poor and the exiles. Indeed, many preachers today flee from the shame and the scandal of the cross about which they talk all the time because they are men-pleasers and system-accommodators: they want the good life without any risk-taking. Many of our so-called evangelists today preach the Empire Glorified rather than Christ Crucified. If they see any threat, to themselves, they assiduously avoid any confrontation with the Beast. Their kingdom is "in heaven" not on this earth. They have no intention of building the Kingdom of God on earth but are, in fact, ready to chuck the whole experiment of historical incarnation and dialectics waiting instead "on the rapture." They prefer to "get out of it" rather than "facing up to it."

Not surprisingly, the evangelists and apostles faced the same temptation for historical avoidance in the early Church, the tendency of many Christians who wanted to escape from this earthly travail and thus their willingness to go into the Roman arena with the lions, singing. Often, their theology was *triumphalistic* as they sought to escape from this evil world in order to be with Jesus in paradise. Their willingness to die for the cause, as they say, for the "faith" is however anathema to the Gospel. A Spanish theologian Xavier Alegre reflects on how the evangelist Mark dealt with this tendency towards otherworldliness in his gospel:

> *According to Mark it is not enough to know intellectually who Jesus is — not enough to have an "orthodox" faith, if you allow me this formula which would have been anachronistic for Mark, but what is essential, to understand who Jesus is, is orthopraxis, that is, of being willing to follow him in his path, nothing glorious in the eyes of the world, of the cross. The lack of understanding by the disciples after every announcement of the passion tries to lift up the fact that if the disciples did not understand the willingness of Jesus to die on the cross out of fidelity to God's project, understood until the very end, as the good, as the life of humankind, it was due to the fact that they had an excessively triumphalistic attitude about his person... For Mark, a triumphalistic Church would have been, clearly, a scandal.(19)*

From our Central American experience, we are learning two fundamental biblical truths having to do with faith and life. First, *we are not to seek a noble death on behalf of a faith principle but a sacrificial life in behalf of our people.* This means *orthopraxis* instead of *orthodoxy.* If our commitment to the poor and outcast leads to the cross, so be it, but if in the name of the faith we avoid the cross, then we have missed the whole point. As the exilic prophets reminded the Jews time and time again, the end-point is not the Promised Land, just as the evangelists reminded the early Christians time and time again, the end-time of a heavenly Kingdom is not the point. This is why geography (North or South) is not the point but community and why our theology ultimately depends on our sociology and how we treat our neighbor, not on adherence to a creed or a willingness to "be saved." In the mystery of the Word which is unfolding before us in this dialectic between North and South, the imperial goals of control and self-image are idolatrous whereas the Call to the faithful is not to believe in Babylon and to put behind us our concern for creature comforts.

And yet, that Call is not to Loss but to Life. As we tell our story time and time again, we are gradually being liberated of this imperial albatross that is hanging around our necks; we are being loved back into new possibilities for life by those who have nothing and have lost everything. It is from those who have sacrificed everything and passed the shame that we find Hope and see Life emerging. As that Marxist ideologue of the Sandinista revolution, Tomás Borge, has reminded us Jews and Christians about our own biblical Word often forgotten...

> We do not renounce, we will never renounce, our commitment to life, to a society of human fellowship, where the moral principles of the revolution and the moral principles of Christianity come together so as to enter into a synthesis that goes beyond orthodoxy and formalized logic. In spite of everything, it is still possible to reject involution, to come together beyond dogmas, and finally to discover that human beings are vulnerable to love.(20)

FOOTNOTES — CHAPTER 15

1   These "children" are often the poor peasants in Central America whose childlike trust, joy and openness is that of which Jesus said, they are the essence of the kingdom.

2   On the first floor of the HHS building is a sign which reads "This is the Voice of America" (no such comparable HHS sign appears), while the restaurant serving all the employees there is now called the "Voice of America Restaurant" suggesting the administration's intent towards a total takeover of HHS by VOA.

3   *New York Times*, Oct.16, 1987.

4   Philip Wheaton, "Towards the Societal Transformation of America's Imperialist Environment," EPICA, Washington, D. C., Dec., 1975. This paper analyzes not only the insights of Paulo Freire but questions under what conditions they can be applied in the United States. Freire himself found it was only partially possible among minorities and the poor. He carried out his testing among Hispanics and Indians in the Southwest.

5   Andrew Reading, *Christianity and Revolution*, Orbis Books, Maryknoll, 1987, p.105.

6   A CBS Documentary during the 1960's about migrant laborers and the horrible conditions under which they lived was called "Harvest of Shame". Their conditions have not changed.

7   The preponderance of the INS education about the new Immigration Act was not aimed at informing the refugees about their rights but of warning the employers of the penalties they face if they continue to hire illegals. That is, in practice the emphasis has been on the vindictive and exclusionary side.

8   According to the Border Patrol of the INS in the Lower Rio Grande Valley of Texas, the total apprehensions of undocumented Central Americans were: 1984-7, 333; 1985-11,420; 1986-13,956; and 1987-18,152 (extrapolated from figures from Jan-June). This represents about 1/3 the total numbers estimated by INS which cross the border every year. These figures from four Texas counties must be applied then to the whole vast border area.

9   Jose Porfirio Miranda, *Being and the Messiah*, op. cita, p.55.

10   Ibid.

11   Ibid, p.48.

12   Ibid, p.79.

13   Julia Esquivel, *Threatened with Resurrection*, ibid., p.65.

14   *Going Home*, Report "Update on Salvadoran Repatriates from Mesa Grande, Honduras", Interfaith Office on Accompaniment, Washington, D. C., December, 1987, p.3. See also, Ralph Klein, *Israel in Exile*, op.cit, pp.81-83; and Ezekiel 20:40-42.

15   Andrew Reading, op.cit., p.56.

16   Omar Cabezas, *Fire from the Mountain*, Crown Publishers, New York, 1985, p.87.

17   Teofilo Cabestrero, *Revolutionaries for the Gospel*, Orbis Books, Maryknoll, N.Y., 1986, p.119.

18   Jon Sobrino, *Christology at the Crossroads*, Orbis, Maryknoll, N.Y., 1978, p.372.

19 Xavier Alegre, "Marcos o la correcion de una ideologia triunfalista," *Revista Latinoamericana de Teologia,* Centro de Reflexion Teologica, San Salvador, p.241.

20 Andrew Reading, <u>op.cita</u>, p.131.

ABBREVIATIONS & ACRONYMS

AF of L	American Federation of Labor
al norte	Spanish phrase meaning to "go north" as fleeing Salvadoran & Guatemalan refugees.
CACM	Central American Common Market
campesino/a	peasant farmer, person from the rural area
CEBs	Base Christian Communities
CFS	Christians for Socialism
CIA	Central Intelligence Agency
compañero/a	companion, friend, mate, co-struggler in a common cause
CONDECA	Central American Defense Council, created by the United States in 1963 with its headquarters in Washington, D.C. As a limited inter-nation military force it functioned in Nicaragua under Somoza's direction.
contras	Counterrevolutionary forces fighting the Sandinista revolution from their base in Honduras. Led by and mainly consisting of former Somoza National Guardsmen who were funded and directed by the CIA.
coyotes	Spanish for paid guides who were contracted for a price to lead Salvadoran refugees to the U.S.-Mexican border, often preying on their clients.
diaconia	servanthood; to serve
Dios	Spanish for God.
ecclesia	Greek word for church, coming together
el dorado	Golden treasure sought by the Spanish conquistadores.
GNP	Gross National Product
Gran Caribe	Caribbean Sea, its archipelago and the nations bordering it, including the Atlantic coast of Central America.
gringo	Mexican expression for Anglos, U.S. soldiers or citizens; used in a deprecatory tone.
IMF	International Monetary Fund
INS	Immigration & Naturalization Service, of the U.S. government.

Isthmus	Interconnecting land mass between Mexico and Colombia, South America.
kairos	Greek word meaning crisis; moment of judgement and promise; time of decision.
kaibiles	Highly-trained patrols of the Guatemalan military who often carried out the most sadistic murders of Mayan Indians.
La Prensa	Nicaraguan newspaper, formerly edited by Pedro Joaquín Chamorro; a daily news organ critical of the Somoza regime before 1979.
Mammon	god of money or its idolatry; the golden calf
necrophilia	love of death
NSC	National Security Council, of the U.S. government
ORDEN	Salvadoran peasant spy organization created by the Alliance for Progress in 1961, led by "Chele" Medrano; Spanish for "order".
orthopraxis	true practice
Pacification	Term given to the U.S. counterinsurgency strategy used in Vietnam to physically remove or kill Vietnamese peasants suspected of having progressive or communist tendencies; a practice of scorching the earth and replacing former peasants with sympathetic ones.
patria	fatherland
Popul Vuh	"Bible" of Mayan Indians, written shortly after Spanish conquest as a critique of it; based on much earlier Cakchiquel sayings.
Powers	Biblical term referring to the demonic forces in life or temporarily controlling it; as in "principalities & powers" in Paul's writings.
quetzal	National bird of Guatemala which cannot survive in captivity; symbol of the people's need to be free to live.
Sanctuary	Age-old practice mentioned in earliest Hebrew scriptures (i.e., "cities of sanctuary") revived by religious movement in the United States in 1982 to provide refuge and protection for Central American refugees fleeing military killings and death-squad torture.

traje	Indian blouse or dress used by the Mayan women.
UFCo	United Fruit Company, now called United Brands
UNHCR	United Nations High Commissioner for Refugees
va y ven	coming and going; back and forth
WWII	Second World War

—"We defend life"

BIBLIOGRAPHY

Agee, Philip, *Inside the Company: CIA Diary*, Penguin Books Ltd., Middlesex, 1975

Alegre, Xavier, "Marcos o la corrección de una teología triumfalista," *Revista* Latinoamericana de Teología, Centro de Reflección Teológica, San Salvador

Amanecer, Centro Valdivieso, Managua, Fall, 1985

Ambrose, Stephen, *Rise to Globalism*, Penguin Books, Baltimore, 1971

Araya Guillen, Victorio, La Diakonía Samaritana, DEI, San José, 1987, translated into English & reproduced by *North/South Dialogue*, EPICA, Washington, D.C., Vol. 2, #1, Summer/'87

Armstrong & Shenk, *El Salvador: The Face of Revolution*, South End Press, Boston, 1982

Auden, W.H., *The Collected Poetry of W.H. Auden*, Random House, New York, 1945

Bailey, A.E. & C.F. Kent, *History of the Hebrew Commonwealth*, Charles Scribner, N.Y., 1935

Berryman, Phillip, *The Religious Roots of Rebellion*, Orbis, Maryknoll, 1984

Boff, Leonardo, *Teología Desde el Cautiverio*, Indo-American Press Services, Bogota, 1975

Boff Leonardo, *Jesucristo el Liberador*, Ed. Sal Terrae, Santander, Spain, 1983

Bonner, Ray, *Weakness & Deceit*, Times Books, New York, 1984

Brockman, James, *The Word Remains: A Life of Oscar Romero*, Orbis, Maryknoll, 1982

Brueggemann, Walter, *Hopeful Imagination*, Fortress Press, Philadelphia, 1986

Cabestrero, Teófilo, *Revolutionaries for the Gospel*, Orbis, Maryknoll, 1986

Cabezas, Omar, *Fire From the Mountain*, Crown Publishers, New York, 1985

Cardenal, Ernesto, *Zero Hour and Other Documentary Poems*, New Directions, N.Y., 1980

Carney, Padre Guadeloupe, *To Be A Revolutionary*, Harper & Row, New York, 1985

Chamorro, Pedro Joaquín, *Estirpe Sangrienta: Los Somoza*, Ediciones El Pez y La Serpiente, Mexico, 1978

Christic Institute, "Secret Team," La Penca lawsuit, Sen. John Kerry, staff report, Washington, D.C., Oct. 14, 1986

Complin, José, *The Church and the National Security State*, Orbis, Maryknoll, 1979

Dilling, Ivonne, *In Search of Refuge,* Herald Press, Mennonite Publishing House, Scottdale, PA., 1984.

Esquivel, Julia, *Threatened with Resurrection*, The Brethren Press, Elgin, Il., 1982

Frank & Wheaton, *Indian Guatemala: Path to Liberation*, EPICA, Washington, D.C., 1984

Fromm, Erich, *Anatomia de la destructividad humana*, Siglo Veintiuno, Mexico, 1975

Greene, Graham, *The Quiet American*, Viking Press, New York, 1965

Gutierrez, Gustavo, *Theology of Liberation*, Orbis, Maryknoll, 1968

Harch, Earnest, "Behind Anti-Government Protests in Panama," *The Militant,* July 17, 1987

Herrmann, Siegfried, *A History of Israel in Old Testament Times*, Fortress Press, Philadelphia, 1975

Hinkelammert, Franz, "The Politics of the Total Market, Its Theology & Our Response," PASOS, DEI, San José, Costa Rica, reproduced in English by EPICA, *North/South Dialogue*, Washington, D.C., Fall, 1985

Holland, Joseph, *The American Journey*, IDOC/North America, New York & The Center of Concern, Washington, D.C., 1976

Honegger and Naureckas, "Did Reagan Steal the 1980 Elections?," *In These Times*, June 27 and July 27, 1987

Interfaith Office on Accompaniment, "Update on Salvadoran Repatriates from Mesa Grande, Honduras," ("Going Home" campaign), Washington, D.C., December, 1987

Jewett, Robert, "Zeal Without Understanding," *The Christian Century*, September 9-16, 1987

Kairos Theologians, "Challenge to the Church," *The Kairos Document*, South Africa, Russell Press, Nottingham, England, 1985

Kierkegaard, Soren, *Either/Or*, Princeton University Press, Princeton, 1946, "Ancient Tragical Motive As Reflected In The Modern"

King, Martin Luther, Jr., *A Testimony of Hope: The Essential Writings of Martin Luther King, Jr.*, Harper & Row, San Francisco, 1986, "A Time To Break Silence"

Klein, Ralph W., *Israel in Exile*, Fortress Press, Philadelphia, 1979

Kornbluh, Peter, *Nicaragua: The Price of Intervention*, IPS, Washington, D.C., 1987

Kuenning, Larry, *Exiles in Babylon*, Publishers of the Truth, Cambridge, 1978

La Feber, Walter, *Inevitable Revolutions*, W.W. Norton, New York, 1984

Lukas, J. Anthony, "The Spy & the Reporter," *Washington Post Magazine*, September 27, 1987

Mahan, Alfred T., "The U.S. Looking Outward," *Atlantic Monthly*, LXVI, 1890

MacEoin, Gary, *Sanctuary*, Harper & Row, San Francisco, 1985

May, Robert, *The Southern Dream of a Caribbean Empire*, Louisiana State University Press, Baton Rouge, 1973

Mecham, J. Lloyd, *United States-Latin American Relations*, H. Mifflin Co., New York, 1965

Millett, Richard, *Guardians of the Dynasty*, Orbis, Maryknoll, 1979

Miranda, José, *Being And the Messiah*, Orbis, Maryknoll, 1977

Miranda, José, *Marx and the Bible*, Orbis, Maryknoll, 1974

Mondragon, Rafael, *De Indios y Cristianos en Guatemala*, COPEC-CECOPE, Mexico, 1983

Nicaraguac, *Los Cristianos y La Revolucion*, Ministerio de Cultura, Managua, April-June, 1981

Nicaragua in Revolution: The Poets Speak, Marxist Educational Press, Minneapolis, 1980

Noth, Martin, *The History of Israel*, Harper & Row, New York, 1958

Novak, Michael, *The Spirit of Democratic Capitalism*, American Enterprise Institute, New York, 1982

O'Conner, Elizabeth, *Cry Pain, Cry Hope,* Word Books, Waco, Texas 1987.

Peck, M. Scott, *People of the Lie*, Simon & Shuster, New York, 1983

Reading, Andrew, *Christianity and Revolution*, Orbis Books, Maryknoll, 1987

Robertson, William, "Growing Anti-Contra Movement in Honduras," ANN, Central American Information Bulletin, Managua, March 25, 1987

Rockefeller Report On The Americas, Quadrangle Books, Chicago, 1969

Russell, Philip, *Mexico in Transition*, Colorado River Press, Austin, 1977

Rossett and Vandermeer, *The Nicaragua Reader*, Grove Press, New York, 1983

Statello, Estéban Daniel, "Towards A Theology From Critical Consciousness," a doctoral thesis, American Baptist Seminary of the West, Los Angeles, June, 1975

Selser, Gregorio, *Sandino*, Monthly Review Press, New York, 1981

Sobrino, Jon, *Christology At The Crossroads*, Orbis, Maryknoll, 1978

Sunshine, Catherine, *The Caribbean: Survival, Struggle & Sovereignty*, EPICA, Washington, D.C., 1985

Sunshine & Wheaton, *Grenada: The Peaceful Revolution*, EPICA, Washington, D.C., 1982

Videla, Gabriela, *Sergio Méndez Arcéo: Un Señor Obispo*, Correo del Sur, Cuernavaca, 1968

Volk, Steven, "Honduras: On The Border Of War," *Report on The Americas*, NACLA, New York, November-December, 1981

Westminster Study Edition of *The Holy Bible*, Westminster Press, Philadelphia, 1948

Wheaton, Philip, "The Honduras/Salvadoran Soccer War," EPICA REPORTS, Washington, D.C., September, 1969

Wheaton, Philip, "Agrarian Reform in El Salvador," EPICA, Washington, D.C., 1980

Wheaton, Philip, *Panama: Sovereignty For A Land Divided*, EPICA, Washington, D.C., 1976

Wheaton, Philip, "Inside Honduras: U.S. Regional Counterinsurgency Base," EPICA, Washington, D.C., 1982

Wheaton & Dilling, *Nicaragua: The People's Revolution*, EPICA, Washington, D.C., 1980

Wheaton, Philip, "Towards a Societal Transformation Of America's Imperialist Environment," A Study Of Paulo Freire in the USA, Inter-American Foundation Report, Washington, D.C., 1975

Williams, William Appleman, *Empire As A Way Of Life*, Oxford University Press, New York, 1980

Wyden, Peter, *Bay of Pigs*, Simon & Shuster, New York, 1979

EPILOGUE
A PARABLE

All this fascinated us so much that we decided to take a trip to Central America to see for ourselves. There were just the three of us on the journey: a Christian, a Jew and a humanitarian atheist. At least, he said he didn't believe in *the gods*. We laughed and said we didn't either. What we did have in common was enjoying different kinds of people and seeing new places. But mainly we had decided to go down because we were searching for a new "way of life", a new vision for the future because we had become pretty cynical and jaded by too much money and too many comforts. That's why we decided to go down on our own and not as part of a delegation, so we could get to know people personally along the way.

We started our journey in Nicaragua because of all we had heard about the revolution. The conditions of life were really terrible there because of the war but we met some fantastic people who welcomed us, both Sandinistas and some uncommitted peasants. A number of them were poets and singers who shared their vision with us through verse and song which spoke of being liberated from tyranny and going to "The Promised Land." Then we went on to El Salvador up in the North where we stayed with peasants and exiles in one of the resettlement communities. They showed us the vision through their collective work together and the way in which they shared burdens and respected the women and children. Finally, we went up into the highlands of Guatemala and it was in the Quiche where we had our most interesting experience. Strange, too, because it had to do mainly with death and our having to come to terms with all the suffering in Central America.(1)

As we were walking along through the mountains one day, heading up a very steep and dusty road, we came to a little hill with a few trees on it. As we got closer, we were startled to see three bodies hanging there with nails driven into their hands and feet. Though they had lost a lot of blood they weren't dead yet. We were aghast and didn't know what to do. We couldn't take our eyes off of them for they were looking straight at us, saying nothing. Then we noticed that their eyes were staring down at our hands and as we shifted our gaze downward, we were horrified to see hammers and nails and blood all over us! Though we didn't understand how, we realized that we had nailed them to those trees. We said to ourselves, "My God, my God, what have we done?"

Realizing we couldn't just stand there staring or leave them, we climbed up the trees, pulled the nails out of their hands and feet and helped those poor, miserable creatures down. To our surprise, they seemed to revive right away and soon were strong enough to stand. After a little of our food and drink, they suggested that we walk along with them to their home in a nearby village. So we did, having nothing better to do. As we walked along, we were amazed at how well they knew their Bible and how they related their own experiences to things like the exodus, the exile and the life they had and the death they had experienced, everything that had happened to them since the time of the Panzos massacre in 1979.

We asked them who they were and what organization they belonged to (wondering why they had been so badly mistreated). They told us they were Indians from the Mam grouping and that they belonged to GAM, a human rights group for mutual assistance.(2) "We help each other, and report on all the crimes of the military," they said, rather matter-of-factly. Then we asked them how they came to be nailed to those trees and they said it was the *kaibiles* (3) with money we Americans had sent to them. We felt terrible but asked why these soldiers took such extreme measures. They replied, "well, they're into their thing called "Death" and they don't like us because we keep pushing our thing called "Life." Then they told us about all the thousands and thousands who had been murdered by the military since 1954 when our CIA folks came down. We were aghast at the enormity of this crime against such a gentle people and began to cry. They said it was all right now and for us not to worry anymore because:

They came out of great tribulation and have washed their robes and made them white in the blood of the Lamb.

Finally, we arrived at their little house about nightfall and we made as if to go on. But they urged us to stay and invited us to have supper with them, though they could only offer us some corn tortillas and little sour wine. After we "broke bread" together and drank we felt much better and suddenly like we knew them quite well, indeed, well enough to share with them our secret mission. We asked them if they had ever heard of a guy called the "Son of Man". They laughed and said "sure, he visits us all the time, and if you stay with us awhile, you can meet him". Then they asked us where we came from and we were a little embarrassed. We told them that we had come from Babylon but we assured them that we didn't worship the Beast. They were relieved to hear that. Then they said that we must be some of those good North

Americans they had heard so much about. We said, yes, that we belonged to the faithful remnant. They hooted at that because they did too... so we drank a little toast to the "good fight".

By then it was getting pretty late and we were all very tired given what had transpired that day, so we were about to leave. Just then, a shy little girl about 12 came forward from the shadows where she had been standing with the other children watching and listening. When she came into the light, we saw that she was very beautiful and dressed in her Indian *traje*, she looked like a princess. She asked us if she could recite a short verse which she had learned from her grandmother who had disappeared when the evil ones came and burnt down everything. We said, "sure" and were amazed at how adult her voice sounded when she started to speak with a wisdom beyond her years. She read the following from a tattered piece of paper:

While I was still dreaming
they, the same ones,
ripped out my heart
and took off with it like booty.

They left behind
only that which they thought useless.
They took away everything
except the Spirit
which they were incapable of seeing.
From it life was reborn
A new path opened up
and the darkness
became Light for me.

So I have experienced all of it
from the scandal of the Cross
to the joyous surprise of Mary Magdalene.
Sometimes weeping,
sometimes singing.

With the heart of my people
burning in my breast.
I have regained Life,
and with it the Future.
Like you, Guatemala! (3)

FOOTNOTES — EPILOGUE

1   It's ironic that this theme of death which is so central to the Judeo-Christian revelation is what the Empire visits upon the hemisphere and that which the faithful in churches and synagogues want to avoid at all costs. Ironic, for it is precisely those who have been forced to deal with death as victims that are struggling to understand it theologically and who therefore are filled with so much hope for the future.

2   GAM — "Grupo de Apoyo Mutuo",

3   Julia Esquivel, opus cita, "Parable", pp.117 and 119.